SPIRITUAL FOLK-SONGS OF EARLY AMERICA

TYPICAL OF THE COUNTRY SINGERS OF EARLY AMERICAN SPIRITUAL FOLK-SONGS is this group of their leaders in Winston County, Alabama. For over fifty years their Fourth of July singings have gone on uninterruptedly at Helicon, where this picture was taken in 1927.

THE "BIG SINGINGS" TAKE PLACE AT COUNTY SEATS AND IN EVEN LARGER CENTERS. Here the country folk join in song with those who, though they live in the cities, have grown up in the same rural musical tradition. The Alabama State Sacred Harp Singing Association was pictured (above) in its 1929 summer session in the court house in Birmingham, Alabama.

Spiritual Folk-Songs of Early America

Two Hundred and Fifty Tunes and Texts
With an Introduction and Notes

Collected and Edited
by
GEORGE PULLEN JACKSON

DOVER PUBLICATIONS, INC.
NEW YORK

M
1629
J147
S85

Published simultaneously in Canada by General Publishing Co., Ltd., 222 Adelaide St. W., Toronto, Canada.

Published in the United Kingdom by Constable and Company, Limited, 10 Orange Street, London W. C. 2.

This Dover edition, first published in 1964, is an unabridged and unaltered republication of the work first published by J. J. Augustin, Publisher, New York City, in 1937.

The publisher is grateful to the University of Virginia Library for furnishing a copy of the book for purposes of reproduction.

Library of Congress Catalog Card Number: 64-8268

49233

Manufactured in the United States of America

Dover Publications, Inc.
180 Varick Street
New York 14, N.Y.

DK/NN

TO THE MEMORY

OF MY WIFE

INEZ EMELINE WRIGHT JACKSON

Preface

The ancestors of the bearers of the Southern tradition of folk-music began in very ancient times the practice of singing religious songs to folk-tunes. Nor must one think that this custom showed a lack of respect for religion. On the contrary, it rather emphasized the respect and love of the folk for their traditional music. As their most loved and treasured possession, they brought this noble musical heritage and laid it on the altar of their worship. There is a strong probability that this practice has continued unbroken for at least thirteen centuries. William of Malmsbury, writing in the twelfth century, gives an anecdote of St. Aldhelm, the Anglo-Saxon abbot of Malmsbury during the seventh century, which he took from the notebook of King Alfred the Great, which was extant at that time. According to this story, the Saint would station himself on a bridge in the guise of a gleeman and would collect an audience by singing popular songs. He would then gradually insert into his entertainment the words of the holy scriptures and so lead his hearers to salvation. The chronicler also states that one of the popular songs made by St. Aldhelm and mentioned by King Alfred was still being sung by the folk at the time of his writing, altmost five hundred years later.

Chappell, in his *Popular Music of the Olden Time*, says: "We may date the custom of singing hymns to secular tunes from this time [The Norman Conquest] if, indeed, it may not be carried back to the time of St. Aldhelm. William of Malmesbury records of Thomas, Archbishop of York (created in 1070), that 'whenever he heard any new secular song or ballad sung by the minstrels, he immediately composed parodies on the words to be sung to the same tune.'

"In a contribution to *Notes and Queries*, Mr. James Graves gives a curious list of eight songs similarly parodied in *The Red Book of Ossory*, a manuscript of the fourteenth century, which is preserved in the archives of that see. Six of the songs are English (there are two parodies on one of them), and the remaining two are Anglo-Norman. The Latin hymns seem to have been written by Richard de Ledrede, Bishop of Ossory from 1318 to 1360. The names of the six English songs are as follows:

1. Alas! how should I sing, yloren is my playinge.
   How should I with that olde man,
   Sweetest of all, singe,
   Leven and let my leman.
   Sweetest of all, singe.
2. Have mercy on me, frere, barefoot that I go.
3. Do, do, nightingale, syng ful mery
   Shall I never for thine love longer kary.

4. Have good day, my leman *etc.*
5. Gaveth me no garland of greene,
But it ben of wythones (withies—wyllowes?) yrought.
6. Hey, how the chevaldoures woke all night."

In the sixteenth century, the early Presbyterians continued this usage, as is evidenced by Wedderburn's hymnal published in Edinburgh in 1560, quaintly entitled: *Ane Compendius Booke of Godly and Spirituall Songs, Collected out of Sundrie Parts of the Scriptures, with Sundrie of Other Ballates Changed out of Prophaine Songs, for Avoiding of Sin and Harlotrey.* Among these latter was a parody of 'John, Come Kiss Me,' the wide and enduring popularity of which is attested by its inclusion in Queen Elizabeth's *Virginal Book*, Playford's *Introduction*, *Apollo's Banquet for the Treble Violin*, Walsh's *Division Violin*, Playford's *Division Violin* and *Pills to Purge Melancholy.* There are also references to it in Thomas Heywood's *A Woman Killed with Kindness*, *Westminster Drollery*, Burton's *Anatomy of Melancholy*, *The Scourge of Folly*, Braithwaite's *Shepherd's Tales*, *Tom Tiler and his Wife*, and Henry Bold's *Songs and Poems.* Allan Cunningham quotes the parody in *The Songs of Scotland, Ancient and Modern*, as follows:

John, come kiss me now,
John, come kiss me now,
John, come kiss me by and by,
And make nae mair ado.

The Lord thy God I am,
That John does thee call:
John represents man
By grace celestial.

For John Goddis grace it is,
Who list till expone the same:
O John, thou did amiss
When that thou lost this name.

My prophets call, my preachers cry
John, come kiss me now
John, come kiss me by and by
And make nae mair ado.

A similar book appeared in 1642, called: *Psalms, or Songs of Zion, turned into the language and set to the tunes of a strange land, by William Slatyer, intended for Christmas Carols and fitted to divers of the most noted and common but solemn tunes, everywhere in this land familiarly used and known.* That the Puritans of that century did not invariably confine themselves to "solemn tunes" is indicated by Shakespeare when the Clown in *The Winter's Tale*, in praising the vocal prowess of the shearers, assembled for the sheep-shearing feast, says: "Three-man song-men, all, and very good ones........; but one Puritan amongst them, and he sings Psalms to hornepipes." In the *New Variorium Shakespeare*, H. H. Furness, in commenting on the passage, says: "He sings Psalms to the lively tunes to which horn-pipes were danced, — a practice which, we know was extremely popular in France, and from allusions like the present we can infer that it was not unknown in England."

In the seventeenth and eighteenth centuries the Puritan congregations of New England are said to have had music committees one of the chief duties of which was to go among the folk and gather attractive melodies to be used as hymns. And this was also the custom of the Primitive Methodists, both in Great Britain and in America. In writing of this usage at a later date, Chappell says: "The Primitive Methodists... acting upon the principle of 'Why should the devil have all the pretty tunes?' collect the airs which are sung at pot and public houses, and write their hymns to them... in this sect we have living examples of the 'puritans who sing psalms to horn-pipes.' They do not mince the matter by turning them into slow tunes,... but sing them in their original lively time."

This brings us to the nineteenth century, in which appeared the "shape-note hymnals" from which the material in this volume is chiefly drawn. The existence of these books was scarcely known to musicans and music-lovers until recently, when they were vividly brought to the attention of the musical world by Dr. George Pullen Jackson in his book, *White Spirituals in the Southern Uplands.* Music lovers were astonished to learn of the existence of these old books, containing a wealth of uniquely beautiful hymn-tunes, largely folk-tunes and others composed in the same idiom. A majority of these are in the old modes and among them are the tunes of folk-songs, ballads, country-dances and even morris-dances. But musicians were even more surprised to learn that there are literally hundreds of thousands of devotees, in homes, in little gatherings and big singing conventions covering a broad region which stretches from the Valley of Virginia to the plains of Texas, who enthusiastically preserve and practise this tradition. That this usage should have lived on from pioneer times into our present day, when not only what we buy but what we are, is stereotyped by the processes of mass production, seems little short of miraculous. But it is explained by the innate vigour of the tradition itself, by the great love of the tradition-bearers for the old tunes and, not least, by the fact that the books embodying the material used shape notes.

Shape notes, as is explained in *White Spirituals*, indicate their pitch by their shapes, independently of the lines and spaces of the staff. They were invented to simplify the reading of music. There are two principal systems, the Four Shape and the Seven Shape. In the Four Shape, the first and fourth degrees of the scale are called *fa* and are represented by a right triangle; the second and fifth are called *sol*, represented by a round shape; the third and sixth, *la*, by a square head and the seventh, *mi*, by a diamond. The Seven Shape system has a different form of note for each degree of the scale and the nomenclature accords with our general practice. The nomenclature of the Four Shape system is of especial interest because it was known and practised by Shakespeare. Numerous references to it occur in his plays. In *King Lear* this system is employed in an almost Wagnerian manner to characterize the archvillain, Edmund, who in soliloquy says: "My cue is villanous melancholy" and then sings: "Fa, sol, la, mi." These four tones measure the extent of a tritone, the forbidden interval called the *diabolus* or the devil and supposed to be filled with sinister, ominous and evil potency.

As shape notes increased in popularity, bitter controversy arose between their supporters and those of the ordinary staff notes. This was most fortunate, for it gave the fa-sol-la folk a coherence and a sturdier determination to abide by their principles and practices, which enabled them to resist the erosion of modern life and so preserve their beautiful heritage.

Many folk-tunes associated with sacred words have been passed down also solely by the process of oral tradition. Mr. Ernest La Prade, author of *Alice in Orchestralia*, recently learned of two groups of Primitive Baptists, one in New Jersey and the other in Philadelphia, which still use in their worship only tunes preserved by this process. He was fortunate enough to record several of the hymns from a member of the New Jersey congregation, some of which were modal and all of which were of the type contained in the shape-note books.

The value of these books to students and lovers of our folk-music is incalculable. For although many of the tunes are still extant in the oral tradition, a large portion of them, of indubitable folk origin, have vanished from the oral tradition and, but for these books, would be entirely lost. All who are familiar with the folk-dance revival in England realize the importance of Playford's *English Dancing Master* in preserving a large number of tunes and dances that were no longer traditionally extant. The folk material embodied in the shape-note books is no less important and far more varied; it is, in fact, indispensible to all who desire a comprehensive knowledge of British and American folk-music.

Gratitude is due Dr. Jackson for making this material accessible to the public. and admiration, for the painstaking and scholarly way in which he presents his fascinating subject. The tunes are historically important in showing approximately the state of the oral tradition at the time they were written down in the past century. It would be difficult to overestimate their esthetic value. In metrical and rhythmic structure, especially in balance and contrast in phrase lengths; in beauty and eloquence of melodic line, many are unsurpassed by even the best of our traditional tunes. It is not too much to hope that a revival of interest in this music may result in a general use of it in our churches, where its native vigour, unaffected straightforwardness and lyric beauty could go far in freeing us from the insipid banalities of much present-day church music.

John Powell

Table of Contents

Illustrations

"DINNER ON THE GROUNDS" is one of the traditional features of all country singings.

Introduction

Since the sort of folk-song indicated by the title of this book is in all probability unfamiliar to many, I shall assume that my chief task in this Introduction is to make its nature clear. The first step in this explanation will be to distinguish the present material from some other better known sorts of folk-song.

"Is it mountain songs you are collecting? Is it those old ballads?" "Is it the negro spirituals?" These questions were put to me again and again by interested persons while the present collection was in the making.

No, these are not mountain songs and still they are. What do we mean by mountain songs? The very first mountain song I ever recorded was sung to me on the treeless flats of North Dakota. It had arrived there from Kentucky by way of Saint Louis and Los Angeles and had been carried over this circuitous route to its northwestern place of recording by the singers in three generations of one family. The first sailor's shanty I ever heard was in the mountains of Virginia. It had come from a logging camp in Michigan by way of Chicago. Every folk-song hunter can tell similar tales; and all such experiences convince us that the naming of a type of song after a restricted region or a particular environment, while furnishing a convenient designation, may lead also to much misunderstanding.

The mountain songs designation is one of the least appropriate. Its only justification lies in the fact that some types of traditional song, the secular ballads among them, have persisted perhaps in larger numbers in mountainous regions like those of the southern Appalachians and the Ozarks and are more widely sung there than elsewhere. These songs were Irish, Scotch, and English across the water. They came from highlands and lowlands. They were the common possession of early Americans of those ethnic stocks, — those people who never left the tidewater parts, those who came into the highlands and settled there, and those greater numbers who trekked through the mountain gaps, down the western slopes and spread into the rolling country and plains. The present collection is of songs sung by all these people in all of these parts in early and more recent times and now. Hence, to call them "mountain songs" would be quite inadequate and misleading.[1]

Those who asked if the present collection were to be of the "old ballads" manifested by their question some acquaintance with one variety, an important one withal, of traditional secular folk-song in America. My answer to them was negative, as it is to my present readers. This collection is made up neither of the secular

[1] John Powell's article "In the Lowlands Low", in the *Southern Folklore Quarterly*, Vol. i., No. 1, provides a corrective for those who think loosely of our American music tradition as one observable in the highlands only.

ballads nor of their close relatives, the secular folk-*songs*, as far at least as their *texts* are concerned. Nor is it a collection of negro spirituals or negro songs of any kind. And yet it is one of folk-songs, and spiritual ones, as its title truthfully indicates. I shall now attempt to explain this; for it must seem to some an anomaly. The explanation will necessitate my making a brief survey first of recent trends in the activities of those interested in folk-songs.

Recent Trends in Song Search

Until recent years practically all the folk-songs published in America have been those with secular texts. The existence of traditional spiritual folk-songs in this land seems not to have been recognized by folklorists. Negro songs were, to be sure, largely spiritual and they have been regarded as folksongs; but that was an entirely different matter, one in which the students of the white man's culture were not primarily interested. Early curiosity as to the "slave songs" was not academic. It was rather a popular interest allied with one which was of a missionary-religious nature. The songs themselves, as they became known in northern and eastern centers during the post-Civil War period through the activities of traveling concert groups from southern negro schools, were popularly believed in those parts to be the negroes' own creations and to be rooted in Africa. They were regarded thus as lying essentially outside the sphere of the white man's cultural traditions. These attitudes of mind tended to hold apart the two groups, those concerned with the white man's song traditions and those interested in the religious songs of the black folk. It was a negro-song apologist, Henry E. Krehbiel, who signed, as he thought, the decree of complete separation of the two song bodies with his book *Afro-American Folk Songs* in 1914; and for most people that was definitive. Even as late as the end of the 1920's Krehbiel's word stood practically unchallenged. I shall adduce evidence presently however of the error of his assumption.

In the mean time knowledge of our own American folk-songs deepened and broadened. The earlier interest, one which grew out of the soil tilled by Francis J. Child and was confined to the ballads alone, shorn of their tunes, expanded in the latter part of the second decade of the present century into one which included also folk-*songs* and the tunes of both ballads and songs. Notable among folklorists with this more comprehensive outlook was the late Cecil J. Sharp who, after long experience in the English folk-song field, took up the hunt in the southern Appalachians. Even the first collection of a part of his findings, published in 1917, provided a revelation as to the wealth of the existing material and was recognized as a model in the matter of musical recording. From then on, the gathering of folk-songs was carried on with renewed enthusiasm and with greater stress laid on the melodies.

One phase of song hunting began in the middle of the 1920's outside the circle of the folklorists and in complete ignorance of the facts that what was sought was genuine folk material. I refer to the study in the field of the southern religious "country singings". I make this charge of ignorance the more unhesitatingly since it was my own, and since I worked alone in that field for some years. A report of the early stages of my work appeared in 1933 in a volume entitled *White Spirituals in the Southern Uplands*. Readers of that book have probably recognized that, while I may have told the story of the country singing institution quite thoroughly, I realized then only dimly that the songs under observation were folk-traditional. This realization has come since then gradually, first by reason of a series of accidental findings and more recently as the result of rather extended study.

Why the folklorists never came upon this material before it fell into my hands is not hard to explain. One reason is that the strongest link binding the songs in question to the traditional secular folk-songs is their *tunes*, and all musical considerations were generally neglected, especially by the earlier folklorists in this land. Another reason was probably that folklorists never thought, any more than I did, of singing *groups* which used *song books*, as likely environment for their search. A third reason was that the country songs were *religious*, a sort which was and is still generally thought of as *church music* and thus as being far removed from the folk. And finally, collectors have as a rule sought folk-songs in the mountains and other *remote* places; whereas the country singings are found in the less sparsely populated parts of the lower uplands.

Cecil Sharp should have escaped much of this prejudice and misconception; for his own British Isles are full of religious folk-songs, as he well knew; even though they do not appear there to any extent in a group-singing environment. But that he did not escape it is indicated clearly by his experience in the southern mountains, as he tells of it in the Introduction to his *English Folk Songs from the Southern Appalachians*. When he came to a home in the mountains and made known his desire to hear songs, he was generally misunderstood. The mountain people thought he wanted to hear them sing "hymns". But he did not; and though he does not tell us why, he indicates that it was because he was convinced that the "hymns" were not folk-songs. At any rate, he soon learned to ask for "love songs". And as a result there appeared but two songs of a religious nature, the 'Cherry Tree Carol' and 'Hicks' Farewell', among the 122 in his first publication. In the subsequent two-volume collection of his American findings, edited by Maud Karpeles and published in 1932, we find a group of but half a dozen religious songs under the heading "Hymns". There are also a few biblical ballads in the collection.

Some years after Sharp missed all but completely his opportunity to become the discoverer, or uncoverer, of American religious folk-songs, one of his English co-workers, Anne G. Gilchrist, found some remarkable analogies between the secular folk-songs of England on the one hand and the spiritual songs of the early Primitive Methodists of that land and the early American revivalists on the other;

and she published a report of her research in the *Journal of the [English] Folk-Song Society*, viii (1927—1931), pp. 61—95, in an article entitled "The Folk Element in Early Revival Hymns and Tunes." This was a real though brief contribution to the very subject which engages us here; for it demonstrated the linking of the nineteenth century religious songs with the older and principally secular folk tradition of her land.

At about the same time, two Americans made smaller contributions. Ethel Park Richardson recorded eleven of the white man's "spirituals" from oral tradition, as it seems, and included them in her *American Mountain Songs;* and Samuel E. Asbury furnished the Texas Folk-Lore Society with a group of camp-meeting songs which he had heard in the 1880's in western North Carolina. The Society published them in 1932.

On Miss Gilchrist's pages and even more often on the pages of American collectors in the late 1920's appeared indications of a growing belief that the old white spirituals were the progenitors of the negro spirituals and that, therefore, Krehbiel's assumption as to negro authorship of the slave songs was in a measure erroneous. Among those who shared constructively in this belief were Newman I. White and Guy B. Johnson. Mr. White consulted a number of the old country-song manuals to good advantage in the preparation of his *American Negro Folk-Songs*. His use of them was to find merely *textual* antecedents of negro spiritual borrowings. Mr. Johnson used some of the same manuals happily in the preparation of his *Folk Culture on St. Helena Island.* His purpose, like that of Mr. White, was to show negro song sources; but his work had the added merit of calling attention to some *musical* analogies between the spiritual songs of the white and the black Americans. My own contributions to the solution of the problem of negro song sources are mentioned on page 9 of this Introduction. All this evidence assumes considerable weight in proof of the thesis that the negro spirituals, instead of lying outside the white people's song tradition, represent a selective adoption and carrying-on of that tradition.

If the preceding paragraphs have in a measure made clear the nature of the songs to be presented here, they have done so by the method of elimination and by a review of some of the directions taken recently by students of song, trends which seem to have led inevitably to the uncovering of the body of song found in the old manuals of the country singers and to the establishing of its status as folk-song. It is the revealing of this material and the establishing of its identity which are the chief reasons for the existence of the present volume.

Varieties of Religious Songs

The old song books spoken of above contain various sorts of religious pieces. Among these are the early psalm tunes, evangelical hymns, spiritual songs, religious ballads, "fuguing" songs, and anthems. Each ot these varieties represents loosely a phase of, or a period in, religious, musical, or poetic development. Some are folk-songs and many are not. The psalm tunes with their Old-Testament texts — the sober song fare of the early Protestants in Europe, in the British Isles, and in the American Colonies — are probably to some extent of folk origin; but since psalm singing in early America can not be looked on as a free expression of the folk, and since the psalm tunes themselves gave way easily to other far more folky types of religious song, I have chosen to exclude them from the present discussion and collection. The fuguing songs are examples of an early American art development in composing and in group singing in New England during the latter part of the eighteenth century. Despite their enduring popularity in southern rural folk-singing circles and despite the fact that many of them are found to be constructed on the basis of folk-melodic themes, I have decided that they would be inappropriate to this collection. The same objection, that they are of an essentially *composed* nature, holds also for the anthems and has demanded their elimination.

After making these exclusions I centered attention on three mutually rather distinct types of song all of which seemed to be in varying degrees folk products — the *religious ballads*, *hymns*, and *spiritual songs*.

Religious Ballads

The religious ballads by and large are folk-produced beyond any reasonable doubt. They are uniformly songs for individual singing, not for groups. The sung *story* was the thing. In one ballad it would be the story of some bad woman, Wicked Polly for example, "who died in sin and deep despair" and went to hell; in another, of some good woman, the Romish Lady for instance, who was burned at the stake for espousing the Protestant cause. Much ballad material was furnished also by the Bible. Scriptural events like the curing of the man sick with the palsy, the restoring of sight to blind Bartimeus, Daniel's experience in the lions' den, the raising of Lazarus, the baby Moses in the rushes, the Prodigal Son parable, the birth of Christ, His crucifixion and death, — all are retold in the ballads.

A younger variety of song which I include under the heading of *religious ballads* is that in which the singer tells his story in the first person. Such stories are those of the poor wayfaring stranger just a-going over Jordan, the departing preacher or missionary, a dying boy or girl, and even a pious gold hunter dying on his way to California. The story may be also the plaint of the religious "mourner", the backslider, and the criminal sinner, or the exultant tale of the saved. Still another group of ballads is aimed more directly at the conversion of the "young, the gay, and proud." They usually begin by telling the religious experience of the singer and close with a warning as to the tragic results of worldliness and an exhortation to turn from "this vain world of sin." These songs are quite similar to the worldly ballads in form, and their tunes are, as will be pointed out presently, of the common folk stock.

Folk-Hymns

The ballads (excepting the *experience* variety) probably did not originate in any particular organized religious movement. The folk-hymns were, on the other hand, bound up genetically with the protestant evangelical activity which followed John Wesley's lead in England and then in America. The Wesleyan Revival began as an ordered small-group affair and spread and developed ultimately into a movement whose aspects and practices were completely free-affairs of the uninhibited masses. In the same way the song of that movement, beginning with merely the taste of textual freedom offered by Watts and the Wesleys, and of musical freedom offered by those who furnished the melodies, spread ultimately far beyond the "allowed" tunes and hymn texts of the authorities until religious gatherings were musically completely liberated.

When John Wesley picked up a popular melody here and there on his travels through England and set it to a good hymn text, he little realized that he was setting an example and starting a movement which was to bring into existence hundreds of folk-hymns; that is, songs with old folk-tunes which everybody could sing and with words that spoke from the heart of the devout in the language of the common man.

With the spread of this movement to America a fertile soil for its further development seems to have been found. Here it became known as the Great Southern and Western Revival. Here its store of songs, made after the pattern used in England, was greatly enlarged. In fact the masses took the matter of what they were to sing so completely into their own hands that the denominational authorities, especially the Methodists, though they tried to control it, became helpless.[1]

In looking through the folk-hymns in the second part of this collection one will see scores of tunes which are clearly recognizable as those still sung to 'Barbara Allen', 'Lord Lovel' and other ancient ballads. This is adequate evidence, I assume, as to where the folk sought and found its hymn tunes. The extent of this tune borrowing process is indicated on page 18f of this Introduction. The texts, on the other hand, may be from the pen of Watts or other eighteenth century English religious poets, or they may be the humbler creations of rural American religious verse makers, like John Adam Granade, or John Leland.

It is impossible to date the beginning of folk-hymn making and singing in America definitely. But on the assumption that they were a part of the Wesleyan movement, we cannot place the beginning of their general use in America before the 1770's. The part of the land where they first attained popularity — again judging by their Wesleyan affinities — was the upland and inland South; for during the last two decades of the eighteenth century (the time of the first spread

[1] The churchman's frown on the early intrusion of the folk into hymn making may be seen in *The English Hymn* by Louis F. Benson, pp. 291ff.

of the Methodist movement) four-fifths of the adherents to this sect were to be found in that section.[1]

Revival Spiritual Songs

The revival spiritual songs represent a further advance of the song movement which brought forth the folk-hymns, toward the folk level. As the eighteenth century expired the post-Wesleyan religious tide was high and the camp meeting, the significant institution which became the cradle of the revival spiritual songs, was born. One may therefore get a clearer insight into this new song development if one recalls the character of its early environment. One might well remember, for example, that the camp meetings began and remained in nature surroundings, in the wilderness; that they were immense holiday gatherings;[2] that they thus took on the free-and-easy aspects of the pioneers as a whole rather than of any particular class; and that they were completely free from denominational and all other authoritarian control.

Bearing all this in mind it is perhaps easier to understand how the folk-hymns — grown up in a less boistrous environment — failed to satisfy the new conditions. At the camp meetings it was not a question of inducing every one to sing, but of letting every one sing, of letting them sing songs which were so simple that they became not a hindrance to general participation but an irresistible temptation to join in. The tunes of the folk-hymns were adequate. But the texts (Watts, Wesley and their schools) still demanded a certain exercise of learning and remembering which excluded many from the singing. The corrective lay in the progressive simplification of the texts; and it was in the main this text simplification which brought about and characterised the type of camp-meeting song which was called, in contradistinction to all other types, the spiritual song.

The methods of song-text reducing are familiar. When the American youth sings

Found a horse-shoe, found a horse-shoe,
Found a horse-shoe, just now;
Just now found a horse-shoe,
Found a horse-shoe just now

he is not only following a practice of the early spiritual song makers and singers — his horse-shoe song itself is a parody of a spiritual in this collection — but he is singing in the infinitely older manner of his race. He is singing an organically constructed tune and refusing to let words interfere with it, a tendency which may be observed from 'Sumer is icumen in' to the nineteenth century songs of sailors and to other work-songs and children's songs, like that of 'The Big Bad Wolf', today.

[1] See Warren A. Chandler, *Great Revivals and the Great Republic*, pp. 109ff. and 138f.

[2] Samuel E. Asbury tells me that the camp meetings at Rock Springs, Lincoln County, North Carolina, which he attended in his youth in the 1880's had been the "mating grounds" for that state for fifty years.

The text simplification in religious folk-songs began modestly. The variety of spiritual song which is closest to the folk-hymn is that in which each short stanza of text (four short lines usually) is followed by a chorus of the same length, as for example:

On Jordan's stormy banks I stand
And cast a wishful eye,
To Canaan's fair and happy land
Where my possessions lie.
Chorus
I'm bound for the promised land,
I'm bound for the promised land;
O who will come and go with me?
I'm bound for the promised land.

The verse was mastered probably by comparatively few singers, even though it may have been "lined out" by the song leader. But the whole assemblage had its chance to join lustily in singing the chorus.

A simpler form of spiritual song went directly into a refrain after the first text couplet:

O when shall I see Jesus
And dwell with him above,
And shall hear the trumpet sound
In that morning.
And from the flowing fountain
Drink everlasting love,
And shall hear the trumpet sound
In that morning.

Then came the chorus:

Shout O glory
For I shall meet above the skies
And shall hear the trumpet sound
In that morning.

An offspring of this same 'Morning Trumpet' song may serve to illustrate the next step in simplification, one in which the singers, instead of using new poetic lines in subsequent stanzas, were satisfied with slight variations of those already sung:

Oh, brother, in that day
We'll take wings and fly away,
And we'll hear the trumpet sound
In that morning.
Oh, sister, in that day
We'll take *etc.*

Oh, preachers, in that day,

and so on, with "leaders," "converts," etc. without end.

The next step is seen in those songs where one short phrase is sung three times and then followed by a one-phrase refrain:

Where are the Hebrew Children,
Where are the Hebrew Children,
Where are the Hebrew Children?
Safe in the promised land.

These songs were sometimes called "choruses," for they are often really nothing else, — detached choruses, the text varied a bit from verse to verse, functioning as complete songs.

The last word in brevity of text is where simply one short phrase or sentence, sung over and over, is made to fill out the whole tune frame as a stanza. 'Death, Ain't You Got No Shame,' in this collection is one example among many. Such songs as this were too meager to be welcomed warmly into the old song books. They survive therefore chiefly in oral tradition. But meagerness of text is not, we must remember, any criterion of the worth of a religious folk-song. 'Hebrew Children,' for example, the song from which I have just cited a stanza, is at once extremely chary of words and rich in tonal beauty. This becomes evident when one sees Annabal Morris Buchanan's arrangement of it for modern chorus.

It was the *spiritual songs*, rather than the *hymns* or the *ballads*, which appealed subsequently most deeply to the negroes and have reappeared most often among the religious songs of that race. In *White Spirituals* I presented twenty different negro songs and traced them, both tunes and texts, directly to as many early religious songs of the white people. In the present collection upwards of 60 songs have been found to be the legitimate tune-and-words forebears of the same number of negro spirituals. (Incidentally, all of the songs just used here to illustrate the steps in text simplification have been borrowed by the black man and made over.) These negro offspring songs are mentioned by title, and information as to where I found them is given in the notes under each of the songs concerned.[1]

The *tunes* of the secular folk-songs came into the religious environment — into the folk-hymns and spiritual songs — with little change. What *one* could sing by himself to secular words *all* could sing in a gathering to religious words. The new surroundings made only one added demand, — that the singers indulge in fewer vocal liberties than they might have enjoyed when singing the same tunes in their homes and alone. I refer to those liberties in personal interpretation, a quaint characteristic of individual folk singing which has given the collectors their numerous variants of one and the same song. Group singers had now to agree on one version of a tune and stick fairly closely to it. I say fairly closely, for the religious singers allowed but few of their tunes to become completely standardized. This will become clear when one studies the variants of certain folk-hymn and spiritual-song tunes in this compilation.

[1] Compare my article on this subject *in The American Mercury* of June, 1932.

Folk-Song Collectors of Yore

In the earlier years of the camp-meeting movement, few if any of the songs produced in and for that environment appeared in print. The whole body of revival song was therefore generally known as "unwritten music." The first recordings were of the texts only. They appeared in the form of booklets and bore some such title as "Hymns and Spiritual Songs / for the Pious of all Denominations / as Sung in Camp Meetings." They were prepared first by itinerant preachers or song leaders who saw in the Great Revival a chance to serve the cause, and perhaps to make money. That these books filled a great need is attested by their ubiquity during the period which may be designated roughly as from 1800 to 1840.

The musical notation of the tunes they sang was the least concern of the revival folk. It is quite probable that the camp-meeting crowds of those times never saw their tunes in musical notation. It is evident that the first recordings of this unwritten music were not made by the revivalists themselves, and that the first book collections of such recordings were not made primarily for use in revivals. The books in which these tunes first appeared were the country singing manuals of which I have spoken above. The singing masters were quick to recognize the value of the rousing revival songs and saw to it that their own institution benefitted from their vogue. *The Christian Harmony*, published in New Hampshire in 1805 was perhaps the first book to record the revival tunes. *The Olive Leaf*, a Georgia book of 1878 was the last.[1]

We sometimes have the compiler's own story of his sources. In the preface to William Caldwell's *Union Harmony* for example, the compiler tells us that "many of the airs which the author has reduced to system [notated] and harmonized have been selected from the unwritten music in general use" among Baptists, Methodists and Presbyterians. William Walker says, in the preface to his *Southern Harmony*, "I have composed parts to a great many good airs, which I could not find in any publication or in manuscript, and assigned my name as the author." William Hauser's preface to his compendious *Hesperian Harp* is lacking in my copy of his work (the only copy in existence, I believe); but the compiler's method of finding songs becomes clear when we peruse his pages of song. On the page with 'Patton', for example, he notes that he first heard the Rev. William Patton, of Missouri, sing the song which bears his name "at a camp-meeting, North Cove, Burk Country, North Carolina, in 1831 or 1832." The song entitled 'Houston' was an "air I learned from my mother when a small child." As to 'Land of Rest' he states that the "inspiration of this tune [was] caught from a female voice at a distance, at Barbee's Hotel, High Point, N. C., June 9th, 1868." Under the song

[1] Anne G. Gilchrist, in her article cited above, assumes this song-book recognition of the revival tunes to have *begun* in 1842. The *height* of this activity was, to be sure, around that date, that is, from a decade earlier to a decade later. See JFSS, viii., 63f.; and compare p. 11 of this work.

entitled 'Rev. James Axley's Song,' in the same compiler's *Olive Leaf*, he tells who the Rev. Axley was and how he, Hauser, came to record the preacher's favorite tune. John G. McCurry gives a song called 'Good-By' in his *Social Harp* and tells that he put it down "as played on the accordion by Mrs. Martha Hodges of Hartwell," Georgia.

Instances like these cited above are numerous. They all go to convince us of the great service rendered by the rural singing masters of yore in the preservation of a body of song, in the collecting and publishing of which no one else seems to have been interested.

The country singing books on which I have drawn for most of the songs of this collection, are in the main those which were at my disposal while I was preparing *White Spirituals in the Southern Uplands*. From the Georgia-Carolina section were *The Southern Harmony* in its 1835 and 1854 editions; *The Southern and Western Pocket Harmonist* (1845); *The Sacred Harp* which first appeared in 1844 but whose oldest edition at my disposal has been that of 1859; its three descendants, *The Union Harp* (1909), *The Sacred Harp* (Cooper edition, 1902 and four subsequent printings; I consulted the fifth reprint), and *The Original Sacred Harp* (1911);[1] *The Hesperian Harp* (1848); *The Social Harp* (1855); *The Christian Harmony* (1866); and *The Olive Leaf* (1878). Among the books originating in the eastern half of Tennessee I searched *The Western Harmony* (1824); *The Columbian Harmony* (1825); *The Union Harmony* (1837); *The Knoxville Harmony* (1838); *The Harp of Columbia* (1848); and *The Western Psalmodist* (1853). From the Valley of Virginia I used *The Kentucky Harmony* (1814); the German *Choral-Music* (1816); *The Supplement to the Kentucky Harmony* (1820); *The Virginia Harmony* (1831); *Genuine Church Music* (1832); and *The Union Harmony* (1848). From Saint Louis I had *The Missouri Harmony* (1820). I found also some material in two publications which are still in use among the Primitive Baptists, *The Primitive Baptist Hymn and Tune Book* (1902) and *Good Old Songs* (1913).[2] Two books, invaluable compendiums of the very sort of songs I was seeking, came to my hand too late for consideration in *White Spirituals*. They were *The Revivalist*, published in Troy, New York, in 1868; and Jeremiah Ingalls' *Christian Harmony*, published in New Hampshire in 1805. The latter contains scores of religious folk-songs — among them many *spiritual songs* — which duplicate, though in variant forms, the songs which are found in abundance in the southern country-song manuals. The *Revivalist*, more than 60 years younger, is a veritable treasure trove of the same sorts of song. Together the two books open new vistas as to the spread and active life period of the song movement under observation. The New Hampshire book,

[1] The new edition of *The Original Sacred Harp*, 1936, was not used in making the present collection.

[2] All these books use the country people's own shape notation, described at length in *White Spirituals*. See also my article "Buckwheat Notes," in the *Musical Quarterly*, xix., No. 4, and the Preface of this book.

made by a Vermont compiler, proves beyond doubt that the movement did not remain in the South — the section of its first prevalence presumably and of its present persistence — but spread early also into New England. The New York book points definitely to the persistence of the tradition in the northeastern section far longer than we would, without this evidence, have been warranted in assuming.

I went song hunting also among the authorized hymn-and-tune-books of the big denominations, but I found little, and that little was already familiar to me from its appearance in the country-singing books.[1]

Further information as to the identity of the books mentioned above may be found in the Bibliography at the end of this volume. The abbreviations which will be used in the body of this song collection when referring to the source song books are explained in the List of Abbreviations of Titles.

Features of American Folk-Tunes

Even after recognizing the three types of religious folk-song as they are described above, it was not always easy in particular instances, to decide on acceptance into this collection or on rejection as non-folk material.

There are literally thousands of songs in the books searched. In the *Original Sacred Harp* alone there are 609, and the *Hesperian Harp* holds 677. And while other books are slimmer and duplications from book to book are numerous, it must still be quite evident that it was no easy task to identify just the songs I was after. At times I had to apply a number of criteria. Often the folky nature of the text pointed to an equally folky tune. There was another hint sometimes in the name given as that of the composer of the song. When I met with the names Moore, Walker, Chapin, Breedlove, White, Carrell, Davisson, Hauser, McCurry and a number of others, in the upper right corner of the song page, then I was practically certain that the song on that page was usable. For the men in question were, in reality, not composers. They were recorders and arrangers of unwritten music.[2]

[1] In Chapter xxi of *White Spirituals* is the story of how the city-controlled denominations have shown uniformly and increasingly an aversion to the old revival type of song.

[2] The following is a comment made in this connection by John Powell.

"It may be well to remember here that only in comparatively recent times has any distinction been made between the use of already existing material (melodic and thematic) and the use of material created by the composer. The Contrapuntists relied very largely on folk-music for their basic material. Bach followed this example to a great extent; Händel not only did this but took material composed by others at his own sweet will with no thought of deception and with no contemporary reproach of plagiarism. Haydn, Beethoven, Schumann and Brahms followed frequently the same practice. In the literary field in Elizabethan times it would be difficult to find a play the fundamental material of which was not drawn from already existing sources. The word *composer* literally means the one who puts together a piece. The material of this piece may, or may not, be invented by such composer. These reflections would seem to explain and to justify the modest claims of the American singing-school book compilers to authorship of songs, and such thoughts should make us approach their labors, not with caviling, but with gratefulness for their invaluable service to American traditional song."

When an example of the old unwritten music made its way into the authorized church hymnals — as happened to a restricted degree from fifty to seventy-five years ago — it was called a "Western Melody" or a "Southern Melody." Such designations became another reliable token of folk source.

More important than any external indications in determining whether I was dealing in a particular instance with a folk-tune, was the character of the tune itself. The ability to recognize a folk-tune comes to the student of such music gradually, somewhat as does the recognition of a strange language or dialect. It came to me that way; but after assembling my tunes I felt that their general folk character might to some degree be reduced to a set of definite traits. I therefore reexamined not only my own melodies but also those far more numerous tunes in the secular collections of Sharp and others, for such characteristics as tonal trend, rhythmic trend, tonality (modal character), and musical form. Since there is no available definition of a folk-tune and since probably no succinct one can be made, I am hoping that my deductions in the following paragraphs as to some earmarks of American folk-tunes may be helpful to others who are interested in our traditional melodism, as they have been helpful to me.

Tonal Trend, Tune Families

The very beginning of a folk-tune has charcteristic marks. The first accented note is usually the tonic of its scale. In almost all cases this first-accent note is preceded by an up-beat note which also is usually a tonic. The upbeat note coming second in frequency is the lower 5 of the scale, with the higher 3 even less often thus employed. The interval, if any, between the up-beat and the first accented note is thus either an ascending fourth, an ascending third (in those cases where these first two notes are 1 and 3) or descending third. And these intervals, though small, are often broken or bridged by an unaccented intervening note. Tunes beginning with an interval of a fifth (ascending 1 to 5 or descending 5 to 1) are quite rare. Common folk-tune beginnings are thus:

As to melodic trend within the body of the tune, I shall speak only briefly. It is a broad subject, too broad to be discussed adequately in this connection. A survey of my tune-thematic card catalog reveals, however, a few characteristics of this melodic trend. The first is that the tunes assume usually an initial upward trend. Another is that the steps or intervals employed are small, predominantly seconds, thirds, fourths, and fifths. Greater intervals are found however at the juncture of two phrases. From these observations we may assume that the American folk-singer does not like big intervals.[1] This assumption, based on recorded tunes, is strengthened when one listens to folk singing and notices their anticipatory slides or scoops in approaching a tone that is only a little higher or lower than the one just sung, a practice which may be interpreted as an anticipation of, and an attempt to master, that which is vocally difficult. But while the individual jumps from note to note are not as a rule great, the pitch compass of the entire tune is often surprisingly wide. The melodies usually end in a descending cadence to the tonic.

Along with the great variety in form which we meet among American folk-tunes, there are certain melodic formulas which seem to be favorites and reappear with unimportant variations as the tonal vestment of many different songs, so many indeed that they might well be looked on as wandering tunes (reminding one of the familiar wandering stanzas in folk texts) or, since they are not identical from song to song, tune families.

In the present collection I have come upon six tune families of different sizes and have named them in each instance after the song which seems to be the most representative member of the family. They are the 'Lord Lovel' family, cast in the ionian mode; 'I Will Arise', aeolian and ionian; 'Hallelujah', mixolydian; 'Kedron', aeolian; 'Babe of Bethlehem', dorian; and 'Roll Jordan', ionian. The tunes in this collection and elsewhere belonging to the 'Lord Lovel' family are listed under the song 'Dulcimer'. Those belonging to the other families are listed under the songs for which the family is named.

Metrical Patterns

In the matter of metrical patterns we find also a variety, and favorites. We have noted the almost universal use of the up-beat. The up-beat initiates two different rhythmic trends, one of which is the iambic, the prevalent one in American folk-tunes: $\frac{2}{4}$ ♩ | ♩́. This two-part type of accent unit (of notes or syllables, whichever way we approach the matter), while occurring in series of four and three, as we have seen, may be found occasionally also in twos, fives, and sixes. Indeed the folk-tunes not infrequently show a refreshing independence of the demands of perfect quadraticality. The other rhythmic trend initiated by the up-beat is the less often used one made up of three-part units, which appear either in three-four time, $\frac{3}{4}$ ♩ | ♩́ ♩ or slow six-eight time, $\frac{6}{8}$ ♪ | ♪́ ♪. With more notes (syllables) in this single amphibrachic unit, the series of such units grows naturally in syllabic

[1] On examining the first 50 tunes of the Folk-Hymns in this collection, I find *within* their melodic phrases a total of only 17 jumps of a fifth and 10 of a sixth. Sevenths and octaves — I found but two each — appeared only as the intervals between the end note of one phrase and the beginning note of the following one.

length. It often outgrows thus its function as a mere melodic phrase and tends to assume that of the melodic sentence. A fine example of this is in Sharp's recording of the 'Cherry-Tree Carol'.

But while the vast majority of folk-tunes follow one or the other of the above described patterns, we must remember that metrical precision or mechanical adherence to any formula is the least of the folk's concerns. Indeed, we should be justified in assuming such exactness, as seen in text lines of carefully measured lengths and in perfection of rhyme, to be sure signs of individual creative participation; whereas greater freedom and variability in tune and text aspects are obviously characteristic of the folk's vocalism.

Scales, Modes

The folk-tunes of America are not, in the main, built up on scales of the diatonic major and minor systems which, as is well known, have assumed their present form under the demands of *harmony;* but on a modal system which grew out of *melodic* exigences long before harmony made its conquest of the music of western civilisation. Nor do the folk-tunes of this country make use of all the tones of even these modal scales. They often employ but five or six of the seven available tones, leaving characteristic gaps in such scales.

American folk-tune collectors have had their troubles in the interpretation of modal melodies. I have had mine. Even such a life-long student of these things as Cecil Sharp met many a knotty problem in classifying his Appalachian tunes. In view of this difficulty I called on Hilton Rufty, a thorough musician and a reliable authority in the folk-music field, to lend a hand in the modal classification of these tunes. He generously acceded to my request; and by the time my requests had ceased and before his generosity had been exhausted he had checked or corrected all my modal classifications of the tunes in this collection. In making clear Mr. Rufty's effective and practical method of identifying the character of tunes I shall reproduce his Classification Chart and quote here his explanation of it.

> In identifying the modal character of the "gapped" tunes I have deemed it advisable to proceed by an entirely arbitrary method, free from any sort of theoretical connotation. Should a missing tone be presupposed to make either a major or minor, perfect or imperfect, interval with the tonic, there arise at once ambiguities of modality. For purposes of harmonic treatment it is quite necessary to decide upon which particular mode a gapped tune suggests, but in studying the purely melodic aspects it is reasonable to accept the tune as an entity, considering it in its actual tonal structure and not with regard to its possible modal permutations. To accomplish this purpose I have evolved a chart, based on methods used by Cecil J. Sharp in his *English Folksongs from the Southern Appalachians*,

which for the great majority of the tunes in this collection is an adequate system of classification. The arrangement of the chart is very simple: there are five columns, each beginning with one of the five pentatonic scales. Immediately below each pentatonic scale are four hexatonic scales which are formed by the addition of the missing tones, singly and in their variable positions. The system permits these variables to be read in terms of natural and flatted tones. Lastly in each column are three regular heptatonic modes which are the outgrowth of supplying both missing tones simultaneously and in variable combination. The gaps in the pentatonic and hexatonic scales are indicated by slurs and the numerical positions from the tonic of the missing tones. The supplied missing tones are indicated by black notes, and in fitting any given tune to any scale on the chart I have endeavored where possible to let these black notes indicate the weak tones. Since it was possible, so far as the *actual tonal structure* of the tunes was concerned, to have a choice in the placing of them, the device of indicating weak tones was a happy solution to a more careful classification. Above each tune in this book I have indicated the modal and, following this and in parentheses, the tonal pattern of the tune with the heptatonic scale as a norm, that is, treating gapped tunes arbitrarily as broken-down heptatonic tunes. A Roman numeral indicates a major or perfect interval with the tonic; an Arabic numeral a minor interval. In event of augmented or diminished fourths or fifths I have used conventional signs. A gap is indicated by a dash.

As a practical example of classification let us take at random, say, 'Weeping Savior', a song of the present collection. Counting the tones of the melody we find six with the sixth degree missing. We observe that the tune has a major second, minor third, perfect fourth and fifth, no sixth, and a minor seventh. By transposition we see that from a standpoint of the tonal pattern alone the tune can be listed either as Hexatonic, Mode 2, A or Mode 4, b. But the examination of structural detail shows clearly that 3 being a strong tone and 2 being decidely weak gives preference to the first classification under Mode 2.

While pentachordal and hexachordal tunes (which do not conform to this system of classification) may be perfect entities, I have, nevertheless, for purposes of uniformity classified them on a heptatonic basis, that is, as heptatonic tunes with the sixth and seventh, or seventh alone, missing respectively. Similarly, while it is somewhat tautological to say, for instance, a tune is heptatonic ionian, I have prefixed the term heptatonic to facilitate identification and to balance the constantly recurrent pentatonic and hexatonic.

An examination of these spiritual folk-tunes reveals a great predominance of gapped scales. Only 23 per cent of them use the full seven-tone series; 44 per cent

CLASSIFICATION CHART OF TUNES

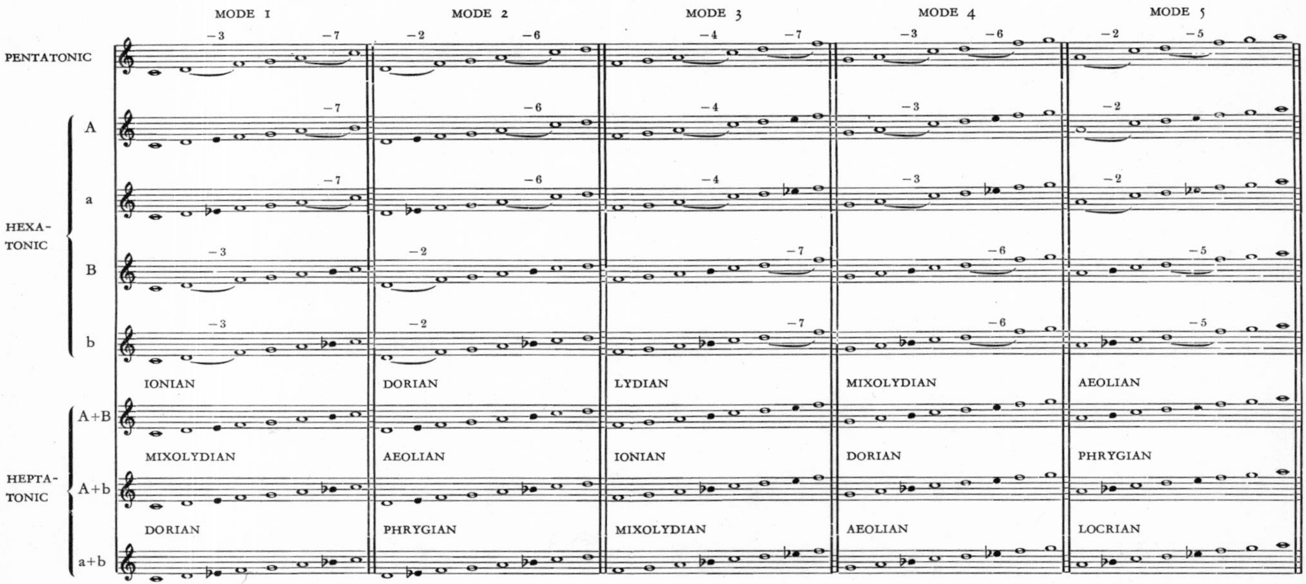

A, B = NATURAL POSITIONS OF VARIABLES

a, b = FLATTED POSITIONS OF VARIABLES

A, a = VARIABLE *E*

B, b = VARIABLE *B*

are hexatonic; 23 per cent are pentatonic; and seven tunes use only from 1 to 5 of their scale.

The incidence of the different modes has been impossible to ascertain. We are sure of a mode, as Mr. Rufty has noted, only when the scale tones are all represented in the melody. Proceeding however in questionable instances according to the more or less clear modal *implication*, I have found that about 52 per cent of these tunes may be interpreted as ionian (major), about 30 per cent as aeolian, 7.5 per cent each as dorian[1] and mixolydian, and three tunes as phrygian.

I leave the interpretation of the significance of these figures to others. I venture to suggest however that they will be found to indicate a survival of gapped and modal tunes that is unique in the folk-music of today among peoples of European stock.[2]

A modally constructed tune is, as I have indicated, almost sure to be a folk-tune. And if a melody shows the characteristic gaps, its folk nature is quite assured. Indeed, the complete filling-in of the gaps, creating two half steps, is a sign, though not always a sure one, of art influence.[3]

The above paragraphs show in a general way a few of the more important and evident *features by which American folk-tunes may be recognized.*[4] Their presence or absence in specific cases has helped me to decide as to the fitness of a tune for acceptance into this collection.

Tunes of Religious and Worldly Folk-Songs Compared

I have indicated above (page 6) that many of the present tunes were borrowed outright from secular folk-songs. The tune-to-tune relationships were discovered to some degree, as I have indicated, by accident. A spiritual tune would remind me of a secular one. I would look it up in Sharp or elsewhere, verify the relationship,

[1] My own hearing of these tunes at the southern country singings has convinced me that the dorian mode is far more widely used than the above statistics, based on the notation, indicate. That is, I have heard the sixth clearly *raised* in numbers of songs where the key signature called for a flatting.

[2] Observations made in recent years of the folk-tunes in the British Isles show modality to be on the decline. In Germany the modes are already practically gone, with the regular major and minor scales taking their places.

[3] From this statement it will be seen that I hold with those who look on the full diatonic scales as having evolved from the gapped ones, rather than the other way around. This however is still a matter of controversy.

[4] To those who desire to follow in more detail the problem of the essence of the folk-tune, I commend Cecil Sharp's *English Folk-Song, Some Conclusions*, especially chapters VI and VII. Despite Sharp's having come to his "conclusions" thirty years ago and even though they are concerned with the folk-songs of the British Isles only, they have not, to my knowledge, been essentially altered by subsequent thought on the subject; and they apply, by and large, to American folk-tunes as well.

and note it under the proper song in this collection. Such accidents, however, account for but comparatively few of my related-tune discoveries. In most instances they came to light as the result of a methodical comparison made possible by my having catalogued my spiritual folk-tunes and a large number of secular folk-melodies. I shall not go into a detailed explanation of this cataloguing method here, chiefly because it is one which, though it answered my own purposes well, would probably be found inadequate as a tool for students of comparative melody in general. I shall say merely that the catalog was a card index of tune beginnings, all transposed to a key which had two flats as its signature. The arrangement was based on the scale position or relative pitch of the first few tones. At the beginning of the catalog were those tunes which began on *b*-flat, then came those beginning on *c* and so on. The arrangement among those tunes beginning on any one tone, followed the same pitch sequence, from lowest to highest, taking into consideration the second, third, and more notes of the tune beginnings where necessary. That is, my lexicographical arrangement was like that of the dictionary, but with notes on a regular staff taking the place of letters, and with the scale steps taking the place of alphabetical sequence.

The actual working out of this scheme may be observed in the arrangement of tunes in this collection. In each of the three parts the tunes appear in their catalog sequence.[1]

Through a consistent comparison of the tunes in this catalog with those in secular tune files made on the same plan, I have been able to discover the organic relationship of upwards of 150 melodies in this collection to an even greater number of traditional folk-tunes associated with *secular* texts. This greater number is explained by the fact that one and the same tune in this collection was often found related to a number of worldly songs. To one tune 'Pilgrim', for example, I discovered 17 secular related melodies. The relationship runs in degree all the way from one which is barely recognizable to one which consists in an almost note-for-note identity.

The catalogs were also of distinct value in bringing to light scores of inter-related tunes *within* the collection, and thus in bringing to light the tune families mentioned on page 14 above.

The search for kindred secular tunes was most fruitful in the case of the ballads and somewhat less so for the hymns. Among the spiritual songs the search yielded surprizingly meager results. The reason lay probably in the nature of

[1] A real defect of this system of cataloguing inheres in the difficulty, sometimes the impossibility, of determining the proper key signatures of gapped tunes. And the difficulty is augmented by the tendency of all the old recorders to regard dorian tunes as natural minor ones (or aeolian). I have reproduced all such doubtful tunes here just as I found them. I have catalogued them, however, (and inserted them here serially according to that catalog arrangement) in an order which is determined by what has seemed to be their proper modal form. Among the songs which are touched by this modal (and hence key-signature) uncertainty are Nos. 20, 21, 22, 37, 51, 87, 88, 89, 90, 91, 97, 115, 144, 148, 236, 237, 249, and 250.

the spiritual-song tunes themselves. These tunes — whatever their source — were often altered through the arbitrary intrusion of refrains and choruses. Among these tunes, therefore, my finding of secular analogies was limited usually to melodic *parts* instead of whole tunes.

To be sure, the tune relationships, religious to secular, which I have pointed out, touch little more than half the songs under scrutiny. But when it is taken into consideration that the related secular tunes were all found in a body of British Isles-American melodies not much greater than that of the spiritual tunes themselves, then it would not seem unreasonable to assume that a complete catalog of American worldly folk-tunes would reveal cognates to many more, possibly to all of the tunes presented here. The kinships already discovered, however, warrant the assumption that *these spiritual tunes are part and parcel of the ancestral folk-melodism of the English-speaking peoples.*

The worldly-religious tune comparison has also shed more light on the motives which led the revival folk to borrow from the store of secular melody and on the manner of that borrowing. We have indicated above our belief that one motive was the crying need for rousing and familiar tunes. Another reason seems to have been the mere fact that the borrowed tunes *were* worldly. Worldliness was of itself an asset. Fighting the devil with his own weapons had its distinct advantages in revival technics. But just how and why a *particular* secular tune came into the religious atmosphere is not always evident. In some instances, however, the examination of the secular original song makes this clear.

When the revivalist heard the Scottish-American sing

Will you go, Lassie, go
To the braes o' Balquhidder?

he evidently saw at once the possibilities of turning the text to his own evangelistic purposes, and wasted little time in making it over into 'Sinner's Invitation:'

Sinners go, will you go
To the highlands of heaven?

which he sang to the same tune.

The ballad tune to

O'Reilly on the rolling sea
Bound for Amerikee

went over easily into the song which told of the Christian voyager who was 'Bound for Canaan.'

The old ballad 'Geordie' begins

As I walked over London bridge.

The revival singers took this hint, with its tune phrase, and produced, in 'Victoria':

I have but one more river to cross.

In the traditional ballad 'In Seaport Town' there is a recurring phrase:

Till at last they came to that lonesome valley.

This "valley" suggested to the religious mind the emotional depression of the almost converted mourner as well as the valley of death; and thus came into existence the beautiful spiritual 'Lonesome Valley':

You got to go that lonesome valley,
You got to go there by yourself

whose tune is closely related to that of the secular song.

The 'Poor Stranger' of the English secular ballad who appeared also as "poor strange girl," a "roving soldier," and a "rebel soldier," all of whom are "far from my home," exerted both melodic and textual influence on the 'Heaven-Born Soldier' who urges his comrades to

Come along and shout along
And pray by the way.

The melody which Johann Sebastian Bach, the great adapter of folk-tunes, made a peasant sing in his *Cantata* 'Mer hahn en neue Oberkeet' spread to England and became there the setting of a number of popular texts in the first half of the eighteenth century. One of these songs, dating from 1772, was 'Farewell, Ye Green Fields and Sweet Groves' which gave birth, probably also in England, to the religious song 'Green Fields', found in every old southern fasola book. Its opening lines are

How tedious and tasteless the hours
When Jesus no longer I see.
Sweet prospects, sweet birds and sweet flowers
Have all lost their sweetness to me.

With 'Saw Ye my True Love' as a model, the task of making the religious text 'Saw Ye My Savior,' sung to the same tune, was a grateful one.

The happy inebriate who is his own hero in 'Way Up On Clinch Mountain' is reformed and regretful in 'John Adkins' Farewell' where he gives warning to other alcoholics in the same melodic strain.

From the above examples it would seem that the secular text contained often some hint which led the religious adapter in making his new poetic lines; and that the secular tune usually followed as a matter of course.

The comparison of tunes shed no actually new light on the age of the tunes. But it made clear the fact that the folk's stock of melodies is assembled from divers times. The tunes of two songs in this collection, 'New Orleans', and 'Hark my Soul', have tonal trends strikingly similar to that of melodies found in the eleventh and early thirteenth centuries respectively. From the early seventeenth century we find 'Mourner's Lamentation' which was in those earlier times 'Wae is Me for Prince Charley', a Jacobite song about Charles II of England. 'The Beggar' is a remake of 'A-Begging We Will Go' which has been traced back to 1611. 'Captain Kidd' or 'Kidd', as it is disguised in the fasola books, dates from the first part of the eighteenth century. It is significant that most of the tunes mentioned in the above paragraphs are comparatively modern in their musical aspects. This fact leads to the suspicion that the really old-sounding tunes, those in the antique modes — dorian, phrygian, and the like, especially in their gapped forms — originated in still earlier times. Here is an inviting field for the student of comparative folk-melodism.

Conclusion

I have been impressed, as I have come to know these tunes better, with their variety and beauty. They are believed, by the country folk who still sing them, to be "the most beautiful music on earth." When I first heard this sweeping judgment I put it down as emanating from an understandable though extravagant zeal, one which was all the greater perhaps since the singers, mostly oldsters, felt they were fighting for the very life of a dying cause. But I now see I was mistaken. The songs are living vigorously without being fought for. The country folk clearly realized — however they may have expressed the realisation — that the "good old songs" were ingrained in their racial souls and that for this reason it was the most completely soul-satisfying of all music from whatever source.

If this was and still is the firm belief of those uncounted thousands who know and sing the country songs, those who are still carrying on the tradition for the sheer love of it and the joy they get out of it; then is there not an inspiration for us? Is that picture not an incentive to look into, to learn to know this *tonal tradition*, the chief one in our ethnic background? This quest might well lead to an examination of our other *acquired*, not *inherited*, musical concepts and judgments, in search for reasons why, in acquiring them, we have ignored the simpler art of the past. And from this approach we might open the question as to whether these reasons are valid, — wise or unwise.

American folk-music, basing squarely on that of the British Isles, is purer, I assert, and more completely representative of the *peoples* among whom it has developed, and less representative of *individual* creative activity than is the folk-music of other Western peoples. As evidence of this I present this collection, commending it to the serious consideration of those interested in fundamental phases of American culture.

This collection challenges, I feel, the attention also of those interested in the songs of the churches. Urban congregational singing depends on hymnals. Hymnals are made by successions of revision committees. These committees have been either hostile to, or incognisant of, American folk-hymns. The perusal of almost any protestant hymn-and-tune book will prove this. Thus we have the strange anomaly: *groups whose prime purpose is to induce more general singing by the masses, refusing recognition, in their books of songs, to the melodism of those masses and putting in its place the tonal products of individuals.*

There are of late some exceptions to this attitude. In the *Christian Science Hymnal*, where one finds numerous folk-tunes from many other lands, there are two variants of melodies to be found in the present collection, that is, of 'Pilgrim' and 'Marion'. The editors found these tunes, however, not in America but in the British Isles.

The Methodists who were, as we have seen, originally largely responsible for the appearance of folk-tunes in the American religious environment, have for the past fifty years progressively eliminated them from their authorized hymnals. But their latest revised edition of 1935 indicates that this tendency has been checked. I find in that volume seven tunes which are identical with melodies in the present collection, namely, with 'Green Fields', 'New Britain', 'Beloved', 'Nettleton', 'Friends of Freedom', 'Plenary', and 'Romish Lady', There are also five other tunes in the Hymnal called "early American melodies" which I have not been able to identify as folk-melodies.

In England the evangelical protestant hymnal makers seem now to be folk-minded. The English Methodists, at least, have welcomed into their latest *Hymn Book* no less than 43 traditional folk-tunes of the British Isles. They have even used two tunes — 'Rhode Island' and 'Pisgah' — the latter of which appears in the present collection, and have called them "American", even though one of them, 'Pisgah', came hither from England, as Miss Gilchrist has pointed out.

Then there are the folklorists. How will they greet this collection? My stressing of tunes and saying little about texts will be regarded by some of the old-line folklorists — especially those who still conceive all such material as "popular poetry" — with disapproval. Others, those who are sure that folk-song is dying out and therefore see the collector's duty simply as that of retrieving the last bits of it, may greet the present collection as a new acquisition to the museums. Such a response would arouse in me no enthusiasm and little satisfaction; for I demur completely from narrow interpretations of the status, meaning, import, and destiny of folk-lore, folk-songs, *these* folk-songs. I do not participate in the pessimism of the folk-song fatalists.

The lore of a folk comprehends, as I understand it, the whole of its basic cultural accomplishments. Understood in this broadest and deepest sense, a folk-lore is truer, more vital and more significant than an art-lore. It is a clearer mirror of a people's past, a more reliable interpreter of its present trends, and a safer prophet of its culture to come. It is all this because it is the body and soul of that culture, where art is merely a vestment. The art which fits best this body and soul, this basic ethnic character, is the best art. The art of ancient Greece was great for this reason. All students of esthetics since Lessing and Winckelmann have recognized this. They have recognized also that the great periods in the art of any enduring people are those when its gifted creators are in closest harmony with the genius of their race; and that its barren periods are those when the masters have been faithless to their own and have sought afar "the good which lies so near."

Acknowledgements

I wish to express here my deep gratitude to Mr. Hilton Rufty for his generous help in verifying the musical aspects of this collection and in helping me solve many a knotty problem in interpreting the tunes which I have transcribed from the old singing-school books. Mr. John Powell has earned my sincere thanks for reading critically the entire manuscript, calling my attention to a number of inaccuracies, and to many secular melodies related to those in this volume.

The present collection would have been far less comprehensive without the use of a number of unique source books placed at my disposal by friends. I wish therefore to acknowledge gratefully the co-operation of Mr. Will H. Ruebush for providing me with *The Olive Leaf* and *The Social Harp;* Mrs. Annabel Morris Buchanan for *The Union Harmony* (Hendrickson); Mr. E. S. Lorenz for *The Revivalist* and *Songs of Grace;* Mr. John Lair for the *Scots Musical Museum;* The Lawson McGhee Library (Knoxville, Tennessee) for *The Church Harmony* and *The Supplement to the Kentucky Harmony;* Mr. W. E. Bird for *The Southern and Western Pocket Harmonist;* and Miss Lucille Wilkin for *The Western Harmony.* The University of North Carolina Press has kindly allowed me to reproduce several songs from *White Spirituals in the Southern Uplands.* For this I wish to express my sincere thanks.

I wish also to thank those who have furnished mewith songs from oral tradition. Among such helpful contributors are Professor Donald Davidson, Mr. Don West, Mr. Samuel E. Asbury, Mr. Francis Arthur Robinson, and Miss Will Allen Dromgoole. My gratitude is hereby expressed also to Dr. Carleton Sprague Smith. Chief of the Music Division of the New York Public Library, and to Dr. Oliver Strunk, Chief of the Music Division of the Library of Congress for their helpfulness.

My daughter, Frances Helen Parker, and my sisters, Carol Jackson Ransom and Genevieve Jackson Beckwith, have given me invaluable help in preparing this book for the printer and in correcting the proofs. For this I am deeply and lastingly grateful to them.

George Pullen Jackson
Vanderbilt University

Nashville, Tennessee, April 10, 1937

Opened, *The Original Sacred Harp*, 1911 edition, (above) measures twenty inches across. On the left hand page is a "fuguing" song composed in Alabama in 1908 in the eighteenth-century New England manner. 'Jester' on the right hand page is a typical camp-meeting spiritual song.

Fifty-one
Religious Ballads

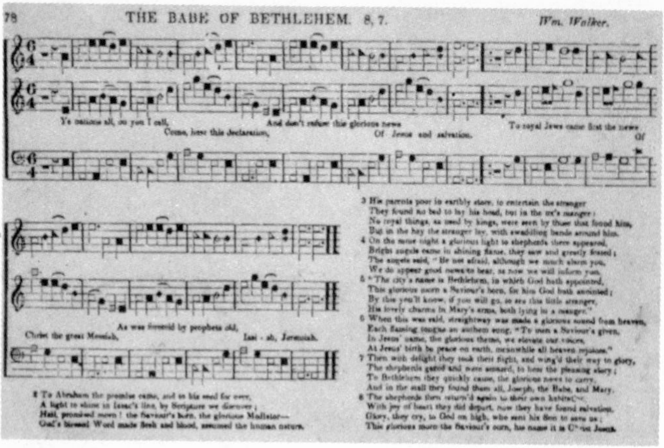

THE SOLE OCCURRENCE OF 'THE BABE OF BETHLEHEM', a carol, is in *The Southern Harmony,* 1835. William (Singin' Billy) Walker recorded it evidently from oral tradition and added a treble and a bass part, in the four-shape notation.

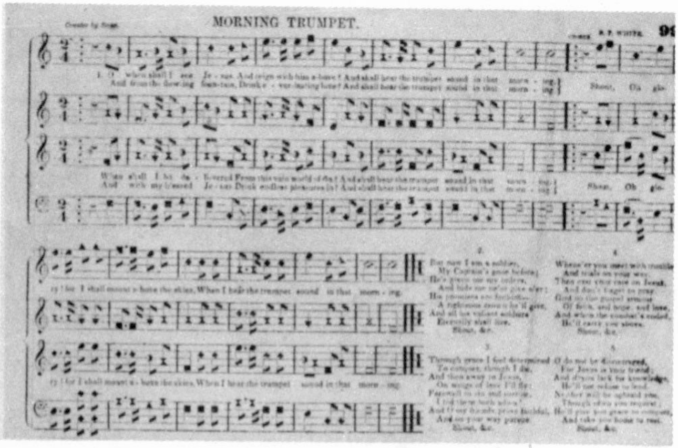

THE 'MORNING TRUMPET' is a spiritual song in the unique seven-shape notation of *The Harp of Columbia,* 1855.

No. 1

ROMISH LADY, HH 257

Pentatonic, mode 3 (I II III — V VI —)

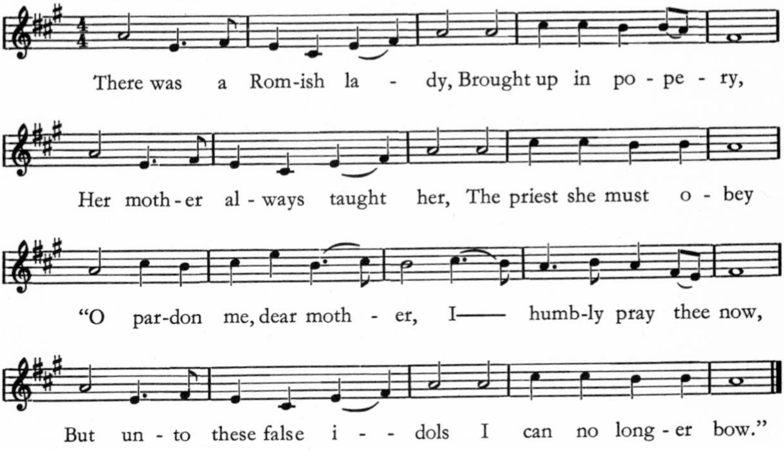
There was a Rom-ish la - dy, Brought up in po - pe - ry,
Her moth - er al - ways taught her, The priest she must o - bey
"O par-don me, dear moth - er, I—— humb-ly pray thee now,
But un - to these false i - - dols I can no long - er bow."

Assisted by her handmaid, a bible she conceal'd,
And there she gain'd instruction, till God his love reveal'd.
No more she prostrates herself to pictures deck'd with gold;
But soon she was betrayed and her bible from her stole.

"I'll bow to my dear Jesus, I'll worship God unseen,
I'll live by faith forever, the works of men are vain.
I cannot worship angels nor pictures made by men:
Dear Mother, use your pleasure, but pardon if you can."

With grief and great vexation her mother straight did go
T' inform the Roman clergy, the cause of all her wo.
The priests were soon assembled, and for the maid did call,
And forced her in the dungeon to fright her soul withal.

The more they strove to fright her, the more she did endure;
Although her age was tender, her faith was strong and sure.
The chains of gold so costly, they from this lady took,
And she, with all her spirits, the pride of life forsook.

Before the pope they brought her, in hopes of her return,
And there she was condem-ned in horrid flames to burn.
Before the place of torment they brought her speedily;
With lifted hands to heaven she then agreed to die.

There being many ladies assembled at the place,
She raised her eyes to heaven and begged supplying grace:
"Weep not, ye tender ladies, shed not a tear for me,
While my poor body's burning, my soul the Lord shall see.

"Yourselves you need to pity, and Zion's deep decay;
Dear ladies, turn to Jesus, no longer make delay."
In comes her raving mother, her daughter to behold,
And in her hand she brought her the pictures deck'd with gold.

"O take from me these idols, remove them from my sight;
Restore to me my bible, wherein I take delight! —
Alas, my aged mother, why on my ruin bent?
'Twas you that did betray me, but I am innocent.

"Tormentors, use your pleasure, and do as you think best;
I hope my blessed Jesus will take my soul to rest."
Soon as these words were spoken, up steps the man of death,
And kindled up the fire to stop her mortal breath.

Instead of golden bracelets, with chains they bound her fast;
She cried, "My God give power, now must I die at last?
With Jesus and his angels forever I shall dwell;
God pardon priest and people, and so I bid farewell."

The text — undoubtedly of Inquisition times origin — indicates the age of the ballad. It is to be found in the *Roxburghe Ballads*, i., 43. It is mentioned in Beaumont and Fletcher's "Knight of the Burning Pestle" (1613). A parody on the opening words:

There was a moanish lady
Lived in a moanish land;
She had a moanish daughter
Could moan at the Lord's command *etc.*

is in Sandburg's *American Songbag*, p. 11. Another echo of this ballad text is:

The Romish Lady, she had babes,

in 'The Wife of Usher's Well', Sharp, i., 159. I recorded the tune in Dayton, Virginia; see *White Spirituals*, 202. *The Methodist Hymnal* (1935, No. 436) has a variant of the tune which it calls a "traditional English carol".

No. 2

BEGGAR or TO BEGGING I WILL GO, SOC 212.

Heptatonic ionian, mode 3 A + b (I II III IV V VI VII)

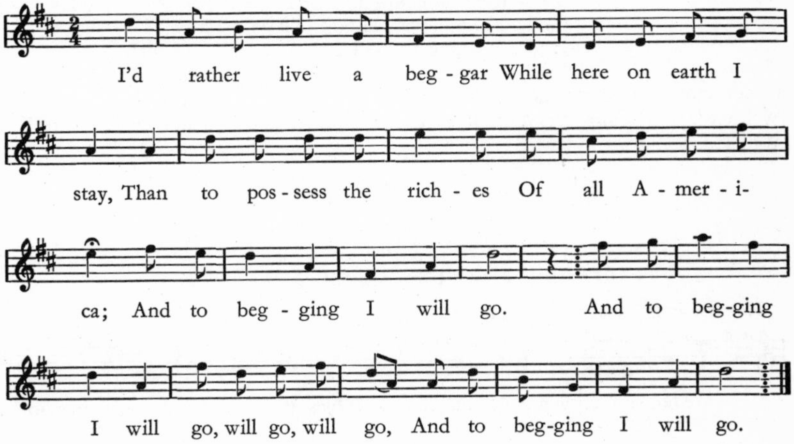
I'd rather live a beg - gar While here on earth I
stay, Than to pos - sess the rich - es Of all A - mer - i-
ca; And to beg - ging I will go. And to beg-ging
I will go, will go, will go, And to beg-ging I will go.

With thoughts of keen emotion our hearts are running o'er,
While parting from the friends we love for China's distant shore,
We're off for China's shore.
We're off for China's shore, China's shore,
We're off for China's shore.

We need your prayers, your sympathies more now than e'er before,
For few the friends and hard the task on China's distant shore;
We're off for China's shore.
We're off *etc.*

We'll heed our Master's call; He is with us ever more;
Then farewell, dear friends, adieu, we're off for China's shore;
We're off for China's shore.
We're off *etc.*

A close tune variant is 'Lost City', or 'To Glory I Will Go' in this collection. Tune and words are a parody of 'A-Begging We Will Go' which was widely popular in the latter part of the seventeenth century and traces of whose existence are found as early as 1611.

See Chappell's *Old English Popular Music*, ii., 42—43.

The first stanza of the song as it appeared in *Choyce Ayres* etc., 1676, runs:

There was a jovial beggar,
He had a wooden leg,
Lame from his cradle and forced for to beg.
And a begging we will go, we'll go, we'll go,
And a begging we will go.

Other songs for which the early song became the prototype were 'A Bowling We Will Go', 'A Fishing We Will Go', 'A Hawking We Will Go' and 'A Hunting We Will Go.'

No. 3
REVEREND JAMES AXLEY'S SONG, OL 369

Hexatonic, mode 4 A (I II — IV V VI 7)

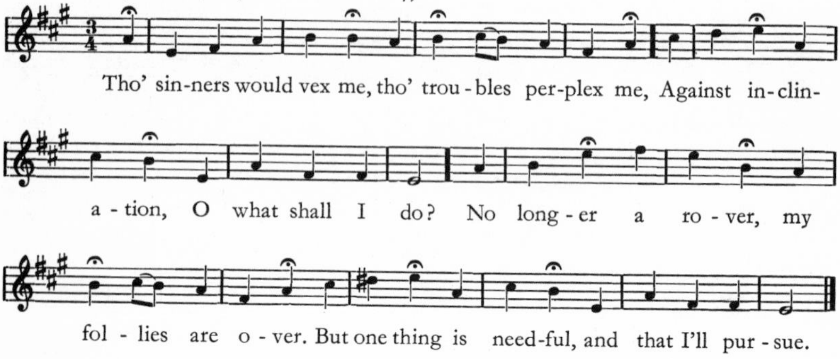
Tho' sin-ners would vex me, tho' trou-bles per-plex me, Against in-clin-
a-tion, O what shall I do? No long-er a ro-ver, my
fol-lies are o-ver. But one thing is need-ful, and that I'll pur-sue.

Vain pleasure is deceitful, and sin is all hateful,
But genuine pleasure in Jesus I find:
This world is a bubble, a life full of trouble;
My thoughts now fly upward, and leave all behind.

I hear the bells tolling; and wheels are now rolling;
Some gallant, gay, fair one goes to her long home:
If dead out of Jesus — the Lord will not save us,
And to him in glory we never can come.

Oh! pray for conversion; shun foolish diversion;
Adopt self-denial, and take up your cross:
These do for a season, and use your own reason,
And you will see clearly you suffer no loss.

Your time is a treasure (there's none in vain pleasure),
Then look up to Jesus with faith's steadfast eye:
Oh, haste to believe in the crucified Savior,
For time flies apace, and eternity's nigh!

My soul starts with wonder, to think how God's thunder,
Will shake all creation at Gabriel's call!
When time is no longer, the aged and younger,
Before the great Judge, in their trouble, will fall.

The Judgment decided, friends now are divided;
And all the ungodly are turned into hell:
But glory to Jesus! believing, He'll save us,
With angels in glory his praises to swell.

The Olive Leaf arranger spoiled the tune's apparent mixolydian purity by changing the *d*'s to *d*-sharps. As to title and source the editor says: "Reverend James Axley was one of the pioneer preachers of the Holston Conference, and a very holy, laborious, and successful minister. I learned this tune and song of Reverend Russell Reneau, who died in Arkansas during our late unhappy Civil War. Crude as the song is, I choose to preserve it in memory of Mr. Axley and Mr. Reneau." The tune is a variant of 'Christian Warfare', GOS 603. Further information as to the Reverend James Axley, whose period of activity in the methodist conferences of Tennessee, Kentucky and other states was during the first decades of the nineteenth century, may be found in Peter Cartwright's *Autobiography*, p. 62 and elsewhere.

No. 4

HICKS' FAREWELL, SOH 19

Pentatonic, mode 2 (I — 3 IV V — 7)

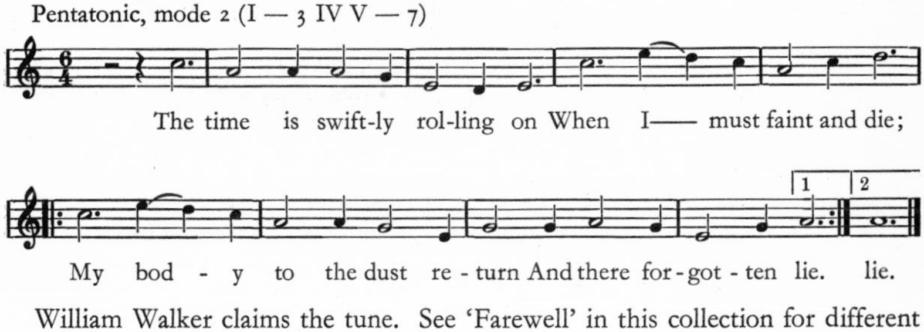

The time is swift-ly rol-ling on When I— must faint and die;
1
2
My bod - y to the dust re - turn And there for-got - ten lie. lie.

William Walker claims the tune. See 'Farewell' in this collection for different melodies associated with this text. Cecil Sharp recorded five versions of the song as he heard them in the Appalachian Mountains in 1916 and 1918. See Sharp, ii., 142—143. The text (given more fully under 'Farewell') was written by the Reverend B. Hicks of South Carolina. See *White Spirituals*, 202ff.

No. 5

FREE SALVATION, *Wesleyan Psalmist*

Pentatonic, mode 3 (I II III — V VI —)

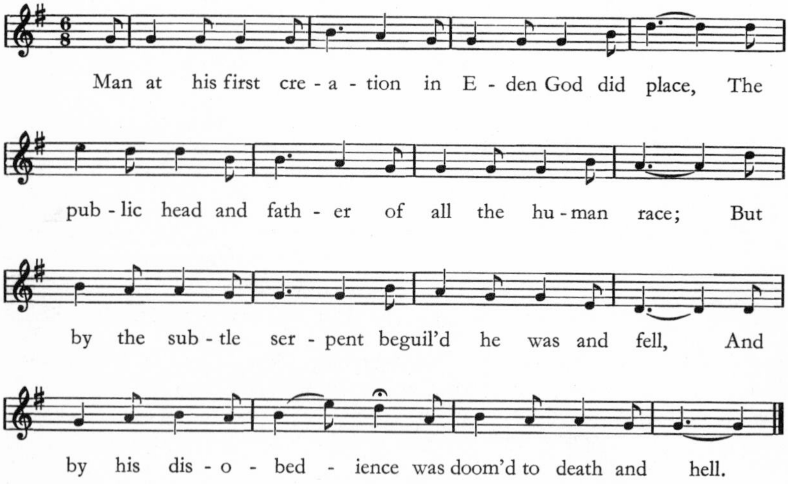
Man at his first cre - a - tion in E - den God did place, The
pub - lic head and fath - er of all the hu - man race; But
by the sub - tle ser - pent beguil'd he was and fell, And
by his dis - o - bed - ience was doom'd to death and hell.

While in this situation a promise there was made,
The offspring of the woman should bruise the serpent's head,
Against the power of Satan that man might only feel
The malice of the serpent enraging at his heel.

Now at the time appointed Jesus unveiled his face,
Assumed our human nature and suffered in our place;
He suffered on Mount Calvary and ransomed all for me,
The law demands attention, to pay the penalty.

They laid him in a sepulchre, it being near at hand,
The grave could not now hold him, nor death's cold iron hand;
He burst them all asunder and pulled their kingdoms down,
He's overcome his enemies and wears a starry crown.

Miss Gilchrist finds this "reminiscent of the old Cornish 'When God at first had Adam made', and of the style of the Manx-Gaelic carvals." See JFSS, viii., 83.

No. 6

SAILOR'S HOME, SOH 182

Hexatonic, mode 3 A (I II III — V VI VII)

When for e - ter - nal worlds we steer, And seas are calm and
And faith in live - ly ex - er - cise, And dis-tant hills of
skies are clear;
Ca - naan rise;
The soul for joy then claps her wings, And loud her
lovely son - net sings, I'm go - ing home, I'm go - ing home
—; And loud her love - ly son - net sings, I'm go - ing home.

With cheerful hope his eyes explore
Each landmark on the distant shore;
The trees of life, the pasture green,
The crystal stream, delightful scene.
Again for joy she plumes her wings,
And loud her lovely sonnet sings:
I'm almost home, I'm almost home!
And loud her lovely sonnet sings:
I'm almost home.

The nearer still she draws to land,
More eager all her pow'rs expand;
With steady helm and free bent sail,
Her anchor drops within the vale.
And now for joy she folds her wings
And her celestial sonnet sings:
I'm home at last, I'm home at last!
And her celestial sonnet sings:
I'm home at last!

She meets with those who're gone before,
On heaven's high and genial shore
Around the dear Redeemer's feet,
— — — — — — — —
And loud they shout: Our God and King!
And ceaseless hallelujahs sing,
We're safe at last! We're safe at last!
And ceaseless hallelujahs sing,
We're safe at last!

The song is attributed in the *Southern Harmony* to Wm. M. Caudill and Wm. Walker. The tune bears some resemblance to 'Liverpool' in this collection. The song is found also in REV 396, entitled 'Sonnet'.

No. 7

LIVERPOOL or SOLEMN ADDRESS TO YOUNG PEOPLE, OSH 37

Hexatonic, mode 3 A (I II III — V VI VII)

Young peo-ple all at - ten - tion give, And hear what I shall say;
1
2
I wish your souls with Christ to live In ev - er - last-ing day. day.

Remember you are hastening on
To death's dark gloomy shade;
Your joys on earth will soon be gone,
Your flesh in dust be laid.

Death's iron gate you must pass through,
Ere long, my dear young friends;
With whom then do you think to go,
With saints or fiery fiends?

Pray meditate before too late,
While in a gospel land;
Behold! King Jesus at the gate
Most lovingly doth stand.

Young men, how can you turn face
From such a glorious friend;
Will you pursue your dang'rous ways?
O don't you fear the end?

Will you pursue that dang'rous road
Which leads to death and hell?
Will you refuse all peace with God,
With devils for to dwell?

Young women too, what will you do,
If out of Christ you die?
From all God's people you must go,
To weep, lament and cry.

Where you the least relief can't find,
To mitigate your pain;
Your good things all be left behind,
Your souls in death remain.

Young people all, I pray then view
The fountain open'd wide;
The spring of life open'd for sin,
Which flow'd from Jesus' side.

There you may drink in endless joy,
And reign with Christ, your king,
In his glad notes your souls employ,
And hallelujahs sing.

The earliest appearance of the text is in *Mercer's Cluster*, a collection of rurally used hymns (not tunes) by Jesse Mercer, benefactor of Mercer University, who lived in Powellton, Georgia, in the 1820's. The editor of the *Sacred Harp* attributes the tune to M. C. H. Davis, a southern rural. The song is found also UH 27, HH 83, HOC 113, WP 36, SOC 76, SOH 1 and CHH 58. The tune is a member of the 'Lord Lovel' family mentioned in the introduction, p. 14, and is closely related to 'Mermaid', Sharp, i., 291, and to 'The Broom of Cowdenknows', SMM No. 3, and its seventeenth-century country-dance form 'The Bonny Bonny Broome', Playford's *The English Dancing Master*, p. 74. For a list of other members of the 'Lord Lovel' tune family see 'Dulcimer' in this collection.

No. 8

LITTLE FAMILY, WS 195 ff.

Pentatonic, mode 1 (I II — IV V VI —)

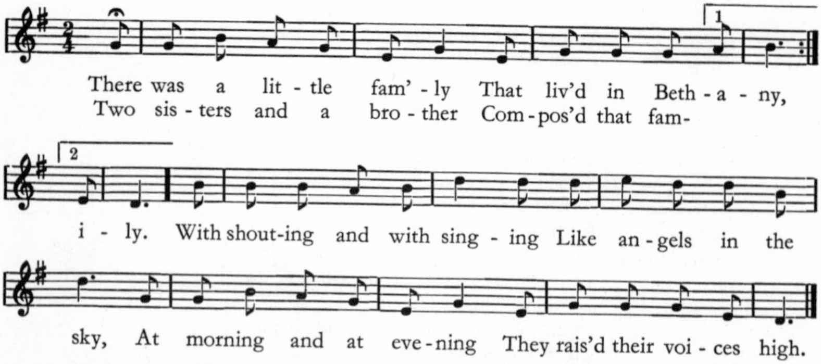
There was a lit - tle fam' - ly That liv'd in Beth - a - ny,
Two sis - ters and a bro - ther Com - pos'd that fam-
1
2
i - ly. With shout-ing and with sing - ing Like an - gels in the
sky, At morning and at eve - ning They rais'd their voi - ces high.

See *White Spirituals* for the full text of seven stanzas about the raising of Lazarus. For references see JAFL, xxv., 17, and xxix., 182.

Almost the same tune is 'Johnny German', Sharp, ii., 256. 'Joe Bowers', Cox, 527, is also similar. Another spiritual ballad using this tune in variant form is 'Wedlock (A)', in this collection.

No. 9

MISS HATAWAY'S EXPERIENCE, HH 421

Heptatonic ionian, Mode 3 A + b (I II III IV V VI VII)

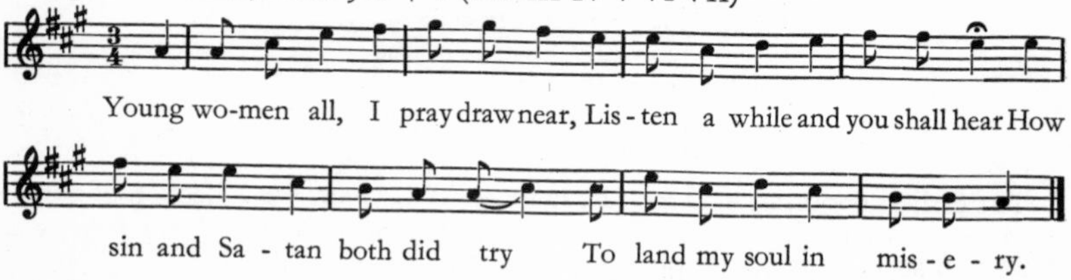
Young wo-men all, I pray draw near, Lis - ten a while and you shall hear How
sin and Sa - tan both did try To land my soul in mis - e - ry.

The full text is reproduced in *White Spirituals*, 186 f. The tune is closely related to 'McAfee's Confession', Sharp, ii., 15 and 16. John Powell notes in connection with this song: "I have collected this tune often as 'Young People Who Delight in Sin' and it is always mixolydian." He then makes the suggestion: "Why not take out the *g*-sharp from the signature? In that case the modal indication would be heptatonic mixolydian, mode 3 a + b (I II III IV V VI 7)."

No. 10

DYING CALIFORNIAN, OSH 410

Hexatonic, mode 3 A (I II III — V VI VII)

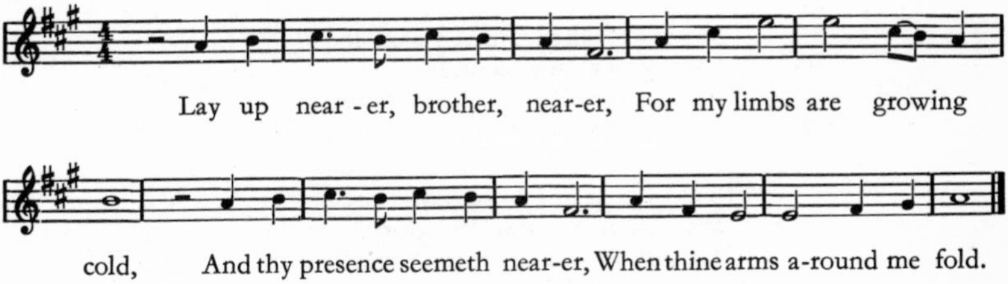
Lay up near - er, brother, near-er, For my limbs are growing
cold, And thy presence seemeth near-er, When thine arms a-round me fold.

I am dying, brother, dying;
Soon you'll miss me in your berth,
For my form will soon be lying
'Neath the ocean's briney deep.

I am going, surely going,
But my hope in God is strong;
I am willing, brother, knowing
That he doth nothing wrong.

Tell my father, when you greet him,
That in death I prayed for him,
Prayed that I might only meet him
In a world that's free from sin.

Tell my mother, — God assist her,
Now that she is growing old, —
That her child would glad have kissed her
When his lips grew pale and cold.

Listen, brother, catch each whisper,
'Tis my wife I'll speak of now;
Tell, O tell her how I missed her,
When the fever burned my brow.

Tell her she must kiss my children,
Like the kiss I last impressed;
Hold them as when last I held them,
Folded closely to my breast.

Give them early to their maker,
Putting all her trust in God;
And he never will forsake her,
For he's said so in his word.

Oh! my children, Heaven bless them,
They were all my life to me;
Would I could once more caress them
Before I sink beneath the sea.

'Twas for them I crossed the ocean,
What my hopes were I'd not tell,
But they gained an orphan's portion, —
Yet he doth all things well.

Listen, brother, closely listen,
Don't forget a single word,
That in death my eyes did glisten
With the tears her memory stored.

Tell them I never reached the haven,
Where I sought the precious dust,
But I've gained a port called heaven
Where the gold will never rust.

Tell my sisters I remember
Every kind and parting word,
And my heart has been kept tender
By the thoughts its memory stirred.

Urge them to secure an entrance,
For they'll find a brother there.
Faith in Jesus and repentance
Will secure for them a share.

Hark! I hear my Savior speaking;
'Tis — I know his voice so well,
When I'm gone, O don't be weeping,
Brother, hear my last farewell.

The song seems to have been inspired by the fate of one of the "forty-niners." It made its first appearance in fasola circles in the 1859 edition of the *Sacred Harp* where it is attributed to Ball and Drinkard. For references as to its origin see Hudson, *Folksongs of Mississippi*, 221.

No. 11

JOHN ADKINS' FAREWELL, SOC 200

Hexatonic, mode 3 b (I II III IV V VI —)

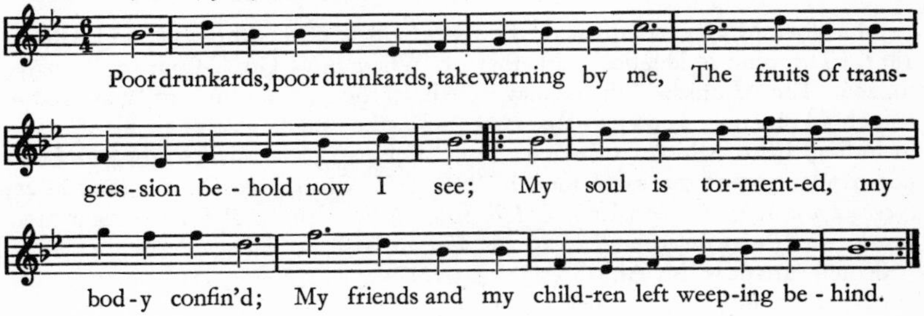
Poor drunkards, poor drunkards, take warning by me, The fruits of trans-
gres-sion be-hold now I see; My soul is tor-ment-ed, my
bod-y confin'd; My friends and my child-ren left weep-ing be-hind.

Much intoxication my ruin has been,
And my dear companion I've barbarously slain;
In yonder cold graveyard her body doth lie,
And I am confined and must shortly die.

A solemn death warning to drunkards I leave,
While my poor body lies cold in the dark grave;
Remember John Adkins, his death and reform,
Lest justice o'ertakes you and sorrow comes on.

A whole life of sorrow can never atone,
For that cruel murder that my hands have done;
I am justly condemned, it's right that I should die,
Therefore, let all drunkards take warning hereby.

Farewell, my dear children, wherever you be;
Though quite young and tender and dear unto me;
I leave you exposed in nature's wide field,
In which God is able poor orphans to shield.

No mother to teach you, no mother to guide
Your tender affections from sin's awful tide;
No portion to shun you from hunger or cold,
My poor little orphans are cast on the world.

When sorrows oppress you and sickness comes on,
You'll cry for your mother, but, oh, she is gone;
Your father, in anger, struck her on the head,
She bled, groan'd, and languish'd, and now she is dead.

My heart swells with sorrow, my eyes overflow,
Soon, oh my dear children, I'll bid you adieu;
Oh may my kind neighbors your guardians prove,
And heaven, kind heaven, protect you above.

My soul to His pleasure I humbly submit,
And with my last burthen fall down at His feet;
To plead for His mercy that flows from above,
That pardons poor drunkards, and crowns them above.

John G. McCurry, compiler of the *Social Harp*, claims this song and dates it 1851. The tune is identical with that of 'When Boys Go A-Courting', Sharp, ii., 206. The "drunkard" theme may have been the textual source of 'Way Up On Clinch Mountain', where, to the same tune, the singer glories in his excesses including that of whiskey drinking. See Sandburg, 307. Miss Scarbrough has a negro adoption of the same tune in 'Noble Skewball'; see *On the Trail of the Negro Folk-Song*, 63. An English folk-song 'Sweet England' has a variant tune. See *English Folk-Songs for Schools*, 46. For an Irish variant see Petrie, No. 1172. A Scotch variant is 'My Ain Fireside', *Lyric Gems of Scotland*, 186, which in turn borrowed its tune from 'Todlen Hame'.

No. 12

REDEMPTION (C), KHN 185

Heptatonic ionian, mode 3 A + b (I II III IV V VI VII)

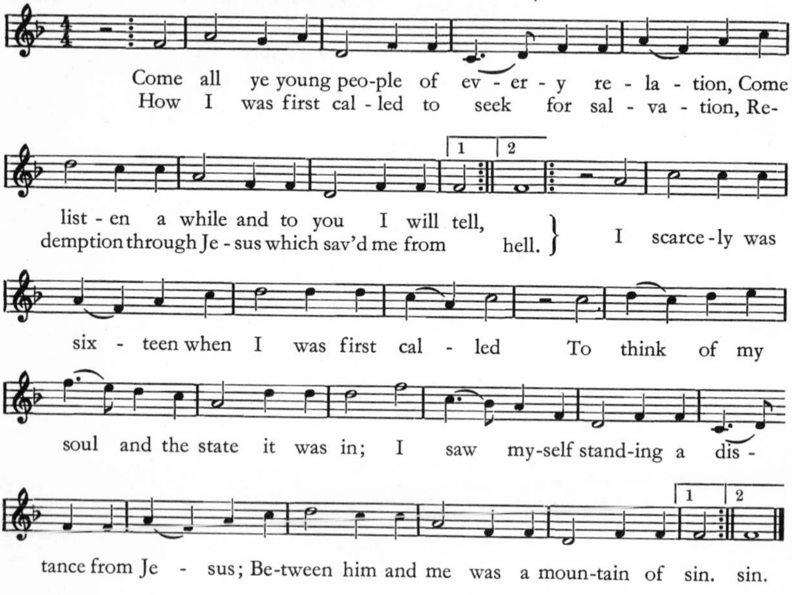
Come all ye young peo-ple of ev - er - y re - la - tion, Come
How I was first cal - led to seek for sal - va - tion, Re-
list - en a while and to you I will tell,
demption through Je - sus which sav'd me from hell.
I scarce-ly was
six - teen when I was first cal - led To think of my
soul and the state it was in; I saw my-self stand-ing a dis -
tance from Je - sus; Be-tween him and me was a moun-tain of sin. sin.

The devil perceived that I was convicted,
And strove to persuade me that I was too young,
That I would get wearied before my days ended,
And wish that I had not so early begun;
Sometimes he persuaded me that Jesus was partial,
When he was a-setting of poor sinners free,
That I was forgotten and was reprobated,
And there was no mercy at all for poor me.

But glory to Jesus, his love's not confined,
To princes or men of a nobler degree;
His love it is boundless to all human creatures,
He died for poor sinners when nail'd to the tree.
For while I lay groaning in sad lamentation,
My soul overwhelmed in sorrow and grief,
He drew near in mercy, looked on me in pity,
He pardon'd my sins and he gave me relief.

The tune is practically the same as 'Grenadier and the Lady', JFSS, viii., 194.

No. 13

WEDLOCK (A), SOC 188

Heptatonic ionian, mode 3 A+b (I II III IV V VI VII)

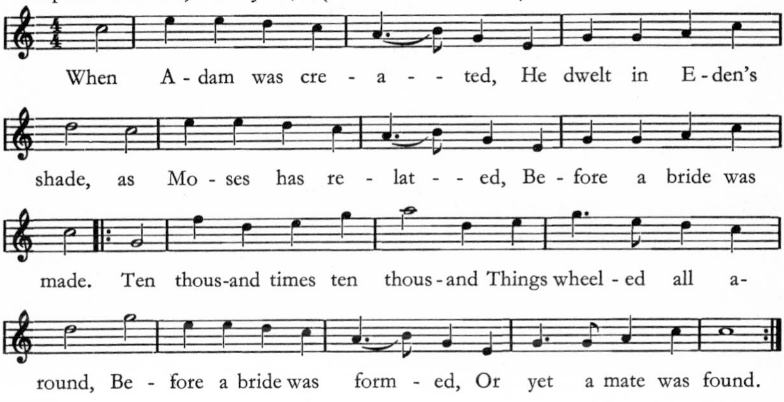
When A - dam was cre - a - - ted, He dwelt in E - den's
shade, as Mo - ses has re - lat - - ed, Be - fore a bride was
made. Ten thous-and times ten thous - and Things wheel - ed all a-
round, Be - fore a bride was form - ed, Or yet a mate was found.

Another tune and additional stanzas of the text are given in this collection under the title 'Wedlock (B)'. The song is attributed, in the *Social Harp*, to Henry F. Chandler and is dated 1854. The tunes of 'Johnny German', Sharp, ii., 256; 'I Rode My Little Horse', Baring-Gould, *Songs of the West*, No. 101; 'The Auld

House', *Lyric Gems of Scotland*, 49; and 'Joe Bowers', are similar to the above air. Another ballad in this collection using this tune in variant form is 'Little Family'. Stephen Foster's song 'Virginia Belle' leans melodically on 'Wedlock (A)'. (See my article in *The Musical Quarterly*, xxii., No. 2.)

No. 14
PATTON, OL 40

Hexatonic, mode 3 A (I II III — V VI VII)

Young peo - ple all, at - ten - tion give, While I ad - dress you
You who in sin and fol - ly live, Come hear the coun - sel
in God's name,
of a friend.
I sought for bliss in glit - t'ring, toys, And
ranged th'al - lur - ing scenes of vice, But nev - er found sub-
stan - tial joys Un - til I heard my Sav - ior's voice.

He spake at once my sins forgiven
And wash'd my load of guilt away;
He gave me glory, peace and heaven,
And thus I found the heav'nly way.
And now with trembling sense I view
The billows roll beneath your feet;
For death eternal waits for you
Who slight the force of gospel truth.

Youth, like the spring, will soon be gone
By fleeting time or conquering death;
Your morning sun may set at noon
And leave you ever in the dark.
Your sparkling eyes and blooming cheeks
Must wither like the blasted rose;
The coffin, earth and winding-sheet
Will soon your active limbs enclose.

Ye heedless ones that wildly stroll,
The grave will soon become your bed,
Where silence reigns and vapors roll
In solemn darkness round your head.
Your friends will pass the lonesome place
And with a sigh move slow along;
Still gazing on the spires of grass
With which your graves are overgrown.

The compiler of *Olive Leaf* gives the following notes: "From McAnally's *Western Harp*" and "Called after the late Wm. Patton, of Mo. Heard him sing it, first, at a camp-meeting, North Cove, Burk Co., N. C., in 1831 or 1832. Published by the admirable A. S. Hayden, perhaps in 1829." The Celtic melodic influence is clearly felt in the above tune.

No. 15

DYING BOY, OSH 398

Hexatonic, mode 3 A (I II III — V VI VII)

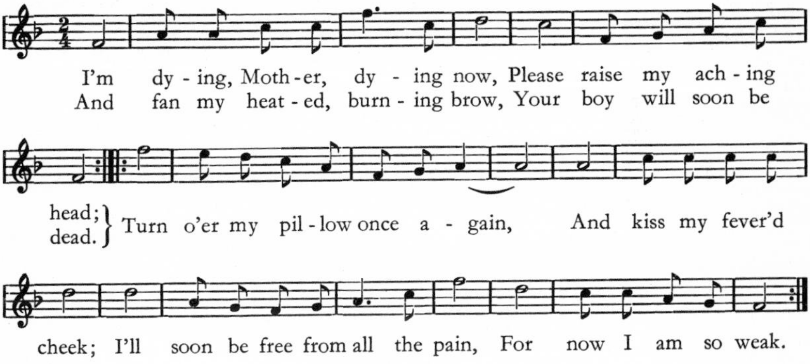
I'm dy - ing, Moth - er, dy - ing now, Please raise my ach - ing
And fan my heat - ed, burn - ing brow, Your boy will soon be
head; dead. Turn o'er my pil - low once a - gain, And kiss my fever'd
cheek; I'll soon be free from all the pain, For now I am so weak.

Now light the lamps, my mother dear,
The sun has pass'd away;
I soon must go, but do not fear,
I'll live in endless day.
I'm sinking fast, my mother dear;
I can no longer dwell;
Yet I'll be with you, do not fear;
But now, O now, farewell.

A band of angels beckon me,
I can no longer stay;
Hark! how they sing: "We welcome thee;
Dear brother, haste away."
The hour has come, my end is near;
My soul is mounting higher.
What glorious strains salute my ear
From heaven's angelic choir.

Their flowing robes in brightness shine;
A crown is on each head;
Say, mother, will not such be mine
When I am with the dead?
Then do not weep, sweet mother, now,
'Twill break this body frail;
Those burning tears fall o'er my brow,
Farewell, O fare thee well.

The *Sacred Harp* says this was "composed by H. S. Rees, 1859". Is it perhaps a parody of Wm. Haines Lytle's 'I'm Dying, Egypt, Dying'? Lytle was a cousin of Stephen Collins Foster whose own song 'For the Dear Old Flag I Die' shows close kinship in words and tune to 'Dying Boy'. (See my article in *The Musical Quarterly*, xxii., No. 2.) There is a resemblance also between the 'Dying Boy' tune and a seventeenth century psalm tune called variously 'Bella', 'Leeds', 'Needham' and 'Derby'; see *Hymns Ancient and Modern*, Historical ed., London, Clowes, 1909, p. 79.

No. 16

SAW YE MY SAVIOR, CH 42

Heptatonic ionian, mode 1 A+B (I II III IV V VI VII)

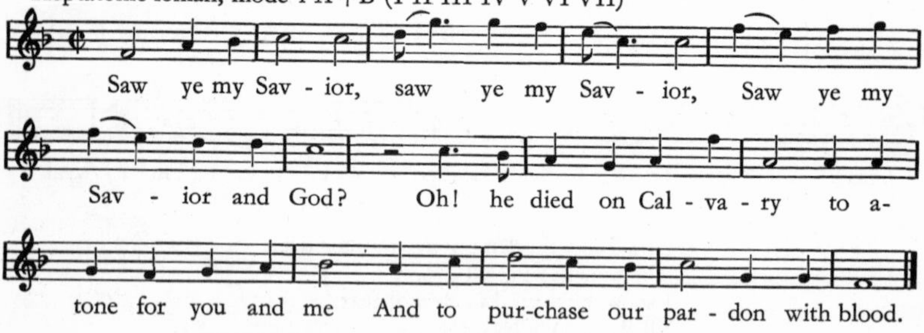
Saw ye my Sav - ior, saw ye my Sav - ior, Saw ye my
Sav - ior and God? Oh! he died on Cal - va - ry to a-
tone for you and me And to pur-chase our par - don with blood.

He was extended, he was extended,
Painfully nailed to the cross;
Then he bowed his head and died, thus my Lord was crucified,
To atone for a world that was lost.

Jesus hung bleeding, Jesus hung bleeding,
Three dreadful hours in pain;
Whilst the sun refused to shine, when his majesty divine
Was derided, insulted and slain.

Darkness prevail-ed, darkness prevail-ed,
Darkness prevailed through the land;
Oh, the solid rocks were rent, through creation's vast extent
When the Jews crucified the God-Man.

When it was finish'd, when it was finish'd,
And the atonement was made;
He was taken by the great, and embalmed in spices sweet,
And was in a new sepulchre laid.

Hail, mighty Savior, hail mighty Savior!
Prince and the Author of peace!
Oh, he burst the bars of death, and triumphing left the earth,
He ascended to mansions of bliss.

Now interceding, now interceding,
Pleading that sinners might live;
Saying, "Father, I have died, (O, behold my hands and side!)
To redeem them, I pray thee, forgive."

"I will forgive them, I will forgive them,
When they repent and believe;
Let them now return to thee, and be reconciled to me,
And salvation they all shall receive."

This song occurs also in *Olive Leaf*, p. 203, where it is called "a Scotch air". Miss Gilchrist tells us, in the article often cited here, that 'Saw Ye My Savior' is 'Saw Ye My Father', or 'The Grey Cock', found in both Scotch and English versions. A text is in Herd's collections of 1769 and 1772, and another with the tune, in Chappell's *Popular Music*. Chappell's version begins:

Saw you my father, saw you my mother,
Saw you my true love John?
He told his only dear that he would soon be here,
But he to another is gone.

The melodic phrase above, which coincides with the text "Oh . . me", is used to build up the tune for 'Simple Ploughboy', Sharp, i., 369. As to the influence of this impressive text on the crucifixion songs of the negroes, see *White Spirituals*, 277. Stephen Foster seems to have been influenced by the 'Saw Ye My Savior' tune or its secular relatives in composing his 'Old Black Joe'. (See my article in *The Musical Quarterly*, xxii., No. 2.) For further references as to 'The Grey Cock' see *British Ballads from Maine*, 310ff.

No. 17

ESTER, OSH 437

Pentatonic, mode 3 (I II III — V VI —)

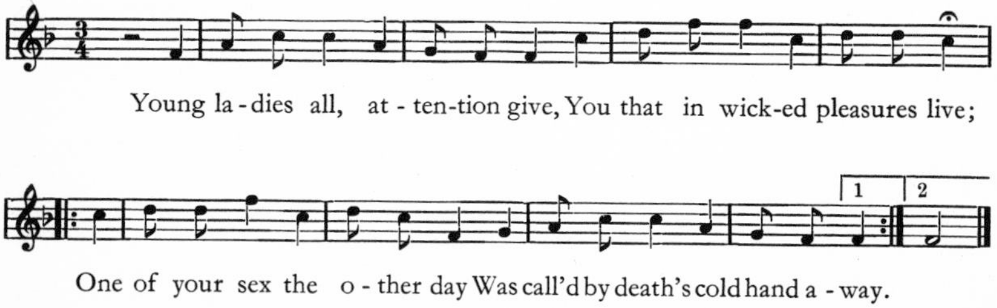
3
4
Young la-dies all, at-ten-tion give, You that in wick-ed pleasures live;
1
2
One of your sex the o-ther day Was call'd by death's cold hand a-way.

This lesson she has left for you,
To teach the careless what to do;
To seek Jehovah while you live
And everlasting honors give.

Her honored mother she addrest,
While tears were streaming down her breast;
She grasped her tender hands and said,
"Remember me when I am dead."

She called her father to her bed,
And thus in dying anguish said:
"My days on earth are at an end,
My soul is summoned to attend;

Before Jehovah's awful bar,
To hear my awful sentence there;
And now, dear father, do repent,
And read the holy testament."

The *Sacred Harp* ascribes the song to John S. Terry and dates it 1869. Terry was a singing-school teacher of Georgia and later lived in Alabama. The singing-school teacher took for his warning song the 'Lord Lovel' tune type that has been used for many secular ballads. Among them are 'Barbara Allen', Sharp, i., 195, tune O; 'Gypsy Laddie', Sharp, i., 237, tune F; 'Come all Ye Fair and Tender Ladies', Sharp, ii., 135, tune P. For other tunes of the same type see 'Dulcimer' in this collection.

No. 18

LONE PILGRIM, SOH 256

Hexatonic, mode 3 A (II II III — V VI VII)

I came to the place where the lone pil-grim lay, And
pen - sive - ly stood by the tomb, When in a low whis-per I
heard some-thing say, "How sweet-ly I sleep here a - lone."

"The tempest may howl and the loud thunder roar,
And gathering storms may arise,
Yet calm is my feeling, at rest is my soul
The tears are all wiped from my eyes.

"The cause of my master compelled me from home,
I bade my companions farewell;
I blessed my dear children who now for me mourn, —
In far distant regions they dwell.

"I wandered an exile and stranger from home,
No kindred or relative nigh;
I met the contagion and sank to the tomb,
My soul flew to mansions on high.

"O tell my companion and children most dear,
To weep not for me now I'm gone;
The same hand that led me through scenes most severe,
Has kindly assisted me home.

"And there is a crown that doth glitter and shine,
That I shall for evermore wear;
Then turn to the Savior, his love's all divine,
All you that would dwell with me there."

The text is attributed, by the 1911 editor of the *Sacred Harp*, to B. F. White, original compiler of that book. He wrote it "on the lone prairie in Texas", while standing "at the grave of a friend who once lived in Georgia". In *Folksongs of Mississippi* Hudson gives a variant text from oral tradition and tells of a local legend as to its source which agrees in the main with that given in the *Sacred Harp* which book, I suspect, was the source of the Mississippi legend.

The tune, variously claimed in the fasola books, is identical with the 'Braes o' Balquhidder'. See Gilchrist, JFSS, viii., 77. Other derivatives of the same tune are 'Sinner's Invitation', 'Florence', and 'Orphan Girl' in this collection. In *The Musical Quarterly*, xxii., No. 2, I have shown the relationship between this tune and Stephen Foster's 'Linda Has Departed'.

No. 19
ORPHAN GIRL, CSH 506

Pentatonic, mode 3 (I II III — V VI —)

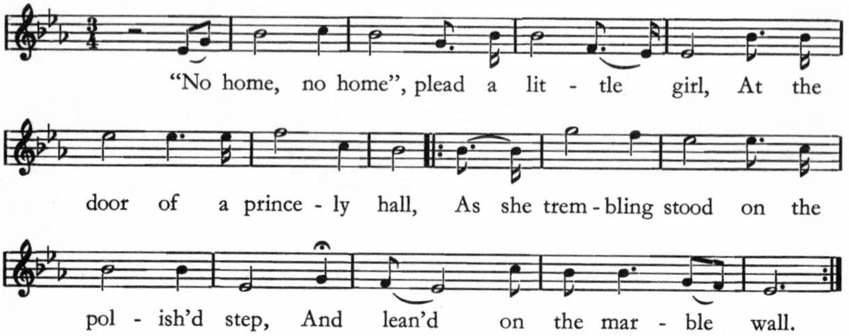
"No home, no home", plead a lit - tle girl, At the
door of a prince - ly hall, As she trem - bling stood on the
pol - ish'd step, And lean'd on the mar - ble wall.

"My father, alas, I never knew",
And a tear dimmed her eyes so bright;
"My mother sleeps in a new-made grave,
'Tis an orphan begs tonight".

Her clothes were thin and her feet were bare,
But the snow had covered her head;
"O! give me a home", she feebly said,
"A home and a bit of bread".

The night was dark and the snow fell fast,
But the rich man closed his door;
And his proud face frowned as he scornfully said:
"No room, no bread for the poor".

The morning dawned, and the orphan girl
Still lay at the rich man's door;
But her soul had fled to a home above,
Where there's room and bread for the poor.

The Cooper edition of the *Sacred Harp* gives the note: "Music by Eld. C. G. Keith, Nov. 1, 1906." See Henry, JAFL, vl., 66f, for further references as to its occurrence. The tune is a derivative of 'The Braes o' Balquidder'. See 'Lone Pilgrim' for references to related tunes in this collection.

No. 20

PARALYTIC, REV 4

Heptatonic aeolian; mode 4 a + b (I II 3 IV V 6 7)

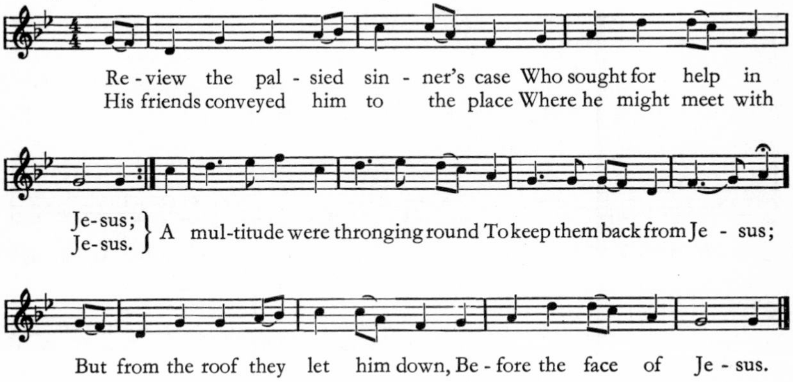
Re - view the pal - sied sin - ner's case Who sought for help in
His friends conveyed him to the place Where he might meet with
Je-sus;
Je-sus.
A mul-titude were thronging round To keep them back from Je - sus;
But from the roof they let him down, Be - fore the face of Je - sus.

Thus fainting souls by sin diseased,
There's none can save but Jesus;
With more than plague or palsy seized
Oh! help them on to Jesus.
Oh! Savior, hear their mournful cry,
And tell them thou art Jesus;
Oh! speak the word, or they must die,
And bid farewell to Jesus.

Now let them hear thy voice declare,
Thou sin-forgiving Jesus,
That thou didst die to hear their prayer,
And give them help in Jesus.
The great Physician now is near,
The sympathizing Jesus;
He speaks the drooping heart to cheer,
Oh! hear the voice of Jesus.

All glory to the dying Lamb,
I now believe in Jesus;
I love the blessed Savior's name,
I love the name of Jesus.
And when to that bright world above
We rise to see our Jesus,
We'll sing around the throne of love
The blessed name of Jesus.

The author of the text is given as Wm. Hunter. The tune is a variant of 'London Pride', Sharp, *Morris Dances*, Set vii, No. 6. Its proper mode would seem to be dorian and its correct signature therefore one flat.

No. 21

VILLULIA or BARTIMEUS, OSH 331

Pentatonic, mode 4 (I II — IV V — 7)

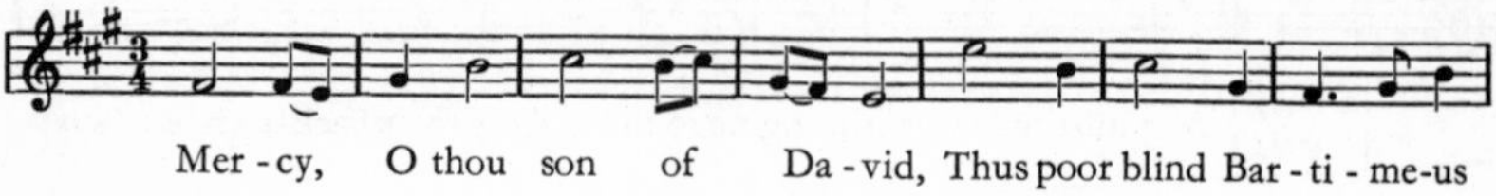
Mer - cy, O thou son of Da - vid, Thus poor blind Bar - ti - me-us

pray'd; Oth-ers by thy grace are sav-ed, Now to me af-ford thine aid.

Money was not what he wanted,
Though by begging used to live;
But he asked and Jesus granted
Alms which none but he could give.

"Lord, remove this grievous blindness;
Let mine eyes behold the day."
Straight he saw and, won by kindness,
Followed Jesus by the way.

Tune attributed to J. M. Day, a Georgian. Doubt as to the correctness of this source is cast by the appearance of both tune and text in the *Christian Lyre* of 1830, No. 4. Variants are 'Invocation', GOS 67, and 'Lord Revive Us', PB 198. The *Sacred Harp* editor evidently looked upon this tune as one in *a*-minor, whereas it is probably a dorian melody with *f*-sharp as its tonic, and should have also a *d*-sharp in its key signature.

No. 22

MOULDERING VINE, UH 101

Heptatonic aeolian, mode 4 a + b (I II 3 IV V 6 7)

Hail! ye sigh - ing sons of sor - row, Learn from me your cer - tain doom;
Learn from me your fate to - mor - row, Dead per- haps laid in your tomb.
1
2
See all na - ture fa - ding, dy - ing, sil - ent all things seem to pine; Life from veg - e- ta - tion fly - ing, Brings to mind the moul - d'ring vine.

See in yonder forest standing
Lofty cedars, how they nod!
Scenes of nature how surprising,
Read in nature, nature's God.
Whilst the annual frosts are cropping
Leaves and tendrils from the trees,
So, our friends are early dropping,
We are like to one of these.

Hollow winds about me roaring,
Noisy waters round me rise,
Whilst I sit my fate deploring,
Tears fast streaming from mine eyes.
What to me is autumn's treasure,
Since I know no earthly joy?
Long I've lost all youthful pleasure,
Time must youth and health destroy.

The tune was recorded, from oral tradition evidently, by William Caldwell (of eastern Tennessee) in the 1830's. His source was doubtless some variant of 'Banks of Inverary'. Cf. JFSS, viii., 198.

The unique opening melodic phrase is to be found also in 'Young Beeham' or 'Ship's Carpenter', Cox 528. Another tune variant in the fasola environment is 'Sons of Sorrow', OSH 332.

No. 23

CONVERTED THIEF (A), COH 147

Hexatonic, mode 4 A (I II — IV V VI 7)

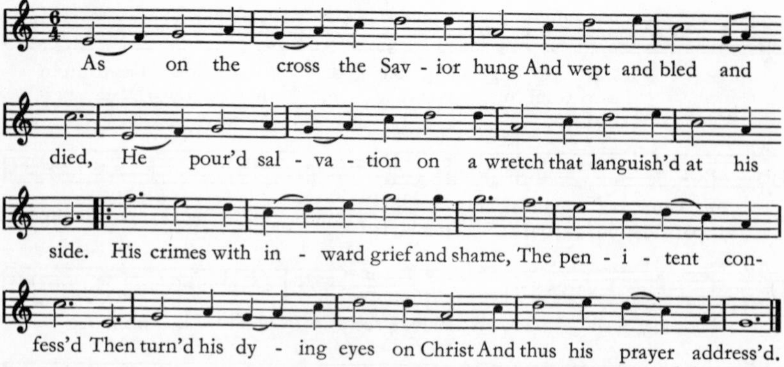
As on the cross the Sav - ior hung And wept and bled and
died, He pour'd sal - va - tion on a wretch that languish'd at his
side. His crimes with in - ward grief and shame, The pen - i - tent con-
fess'd Then turn'd his dy - ing eyes on Christ And thus his prayer address'd.

The poem, given in full under 'Converted Thief (B)', is attributed to Stennett. William Moore of Tennessee, compiler of *Columbian Harmony*, lays claim to the tune, and probably did record it from oral sources. Found also SOH 9, OSH 44, GOS 140. The tune is a member of the 'Hallelujah' family. See the song with that title in this collection.

No. 24

TENNESSEE, HH 140

Hexatonic, mode 3 A (I II III — V VI VII)

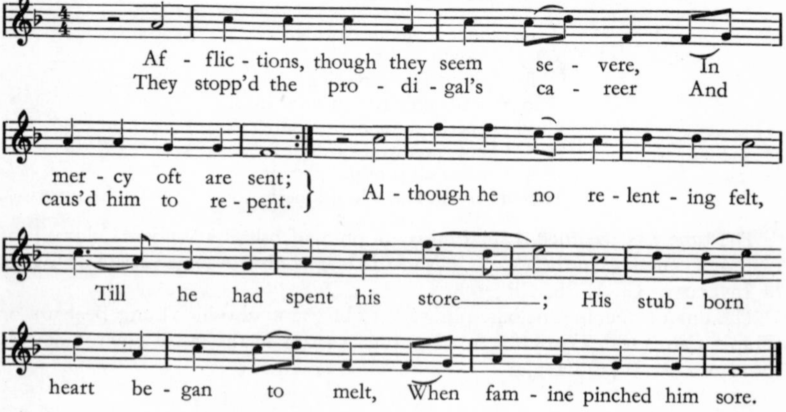
Af - flic - tions, though they seem se - vere, In
They stopp'd the pro - di - gal's ca - reer And
mer - cy oft are sent;
caus'd him to re - pent.
Al - though he no re - lent - ing felt,
Till he had spent his store——; His stub - born
heart be - gan to melt, When fam - ine pinched him sore.

"What have I gained by sin?" he said,
"But hunger, shame, and fear?
My father's house abounds with bread,
While I am starving here.

"I'll go and tell him all I've done
And fall before his face;
Unworthy to be called his son,
I'll seek a servant's place."

His father saw him coming back;
He saw and ran and smiled,
And threw his arms around the neck
Of his repenting child.

"Father, I've sinned, but O forgive!"
"Enough," the father said;
"Rejoice, my house, my son's alive,
For whom I mourned as dead.

"Now let the fatted calf be slain;
Go spread the news around;
My son was dead, but lives again,
Was lost, but now is found."

'Tis thus the Lord his love reveals,
To call his children home;
More than a father's love he feels,
And bids the needy come.

The tune is a member of the 'Roll Jordan' family which is described under the song by that name in this collection. The 'Tennessee' tune's resemblance to Foster's 'Susanna' is evident. The melody, or some near relative of it, may well have furnished Foster with his inspiration in composing the latter. It had been sung widely in America for at least fifty years before the Pittsburgh composer published his minstrel song. (See the author's article 'Stephen Foster's Debt to American Folk-Song', *The Musical Quarterly*, xxii., No. 2.

That the 'Tennessee' tune was "unwritten music" in the South, and therefore free for all, is indicated by the many claimants to its authorship; Chapin, J. Robertson, L. P. Breedlove, William C. Davis, and William Walker were among them. In various forms and with different texts the tune is found also, CHI 84 (published in 1805), SKH 23, GCM 134, SOH 28, GOS 229, HOC 114, WP 96, TZ 94, SOC 78, SOC 81, SOC 145, SOH 105, OSH 501, SKH 23. The second part of the tune is similar to 'Jamaica', Sharp, *Country Dances*, Set IV, No. 12.

No. 25

FAREWELL, HOC 32

Hexatonic, mode 3 b (I II III IV V VI —)

The time is swift - ly roll - ing on, When I must faint and die, My
bo - dy to the dust re - turn, And there for - got - ten lie——,
And there for - got - ten lie————, And there for - got - ten lie, My
bo - dy to the dust re - turn, And there for - got - ten lie.

Through heats and colds I've ofttimes went,
I've wandered in despair,
To call poor sinners to repent
And seek their Savior dear.

My brother preachers, boldly speak
And stand on Zion's wall;
Confirm the drunk, confirm the weak
And after sinners call.

My loving wife, my bosom friend,
The object of my love,
The time's been sweet I've spent with you,
My sweet and harmless dove.

My little children near my heart
My warm affections know.
Fer each the path will I attend.
O from them can I go?!

O God, a father to them be
And keep them from all harm,
That they may love and worship Thee
And dwell upon thy charm.

How often you have looked fer me
And often seen me come;
But now I must depart from thee
And nevermore return.

My loving wife, don't grieve fer me,
Neither lament nor mourn;
Fer I will with my Jesus be,
And dwell upon his charm.

The tune is attributed in the *Harp of Columbia* to W. Atchley. It belongs to what I have called (Introduction, p. 14) the 'Hallelujah' type of melody. See 'Hallelujah' for other related spiritual tunes. A secular song using the same melodic formula is 'Virginia Lover', Sharp, ii., 150. The text of 'Farewell' is recorded from oral tradition and reproduced from *White Spirituals*, p. 202. See 'Hicks' Farewell' in this collection as to the authorship of the words.

No. 26
WICKED POLLY, WS 190

Hexatonic mode 4, b (I II 3 IV V — 7)

Young people who delight in sin, I'll tell you what has lately been: A
wo - man who was young and fair Died in sin and deep des-pair.

For the full text and much data as to the source and occurrence of this song, see *White Spirituals*, 189—193. A tune variant is 'Supplication', in this collection. Another is 'Lord Bateman', Sharp *One Hundred English Folksongs*, No. 6.

No. 27
MOSES

Hexatonic, mode 1 A (I II III IV V VI —)

An' Pha - re - oh's daugh-ter went down to thee wa - ter An'
foun' there thee beau-tee - ful child, A - mong thee tall bush - es thee
reeds an' thee rush - es Thee ba - bee look'd sweet - lee an' smil'd.

Recorded from singing of Miss Will Allen Dromgoole, Nashville, Tennessee, as she remembered it sung in 1890 by Mr. Tate, stage driver from Beersheba to Beersheba Springs on Cumberland Mountain in Tennessee. The unusual spelling is an attempt at reproducing the emphatic rhythmic pronunciation of Mr. Tate. The one stanza given above was all Miss Dromgoole remembered. The full text, however, was recorded by Mr. Fred Haun of Newport, Tennessee, from the singing of his mother, Mrs. Maggie Haun, and placed at my disposal by Miss Mildred Haun, his sister. This rather defective text is as follows:

The ladies were wending their way
As Pharo's daughter stepped down to the water
To bathe in the cool of the day.
Before it was dark she opened the ark
And found the sweet infant was there.

She took him in pity and thought him so pretty;
That made little Moses so glad.
She called him her own, her beautiful son,
And sent for a nurse that was near.

By the side of the river so clear
They carried that beautiful child
To his own tender mother, his sister and brother;
Little Moses looked happy and smiled.

His mother so good done all that she could
To hear [rear?] him and teach him with care.
Then away by the sea that was red
Stood Moses the servant of God.

While in him confided the deed [sea?] was divided
While upward he lifted his rod.
The Jews safely crossed while Pharo's host
Was drounded in the water and lost.

Then away by the mountain so high
Stood Moses with trembling an' awe;
With lightning and thunder, great signs and wonders,
While God was giving the law.
He wrote it down on two tables of stone
Before he returned to the sky.

Then away on the mountain so high
Stood the last one he ever might see.
While Isreal victorious, his hope was most gloriest,
Would soon over Jordan be free.
His neighbors did cease, he departed in peace,
And rest-es in heaven above.

No. 28

MOURNER'S LAMENTATION or CHURCH'S DESOLATION, CHH 265

Pentatonic, mode 1 (I II — IV V VI —)

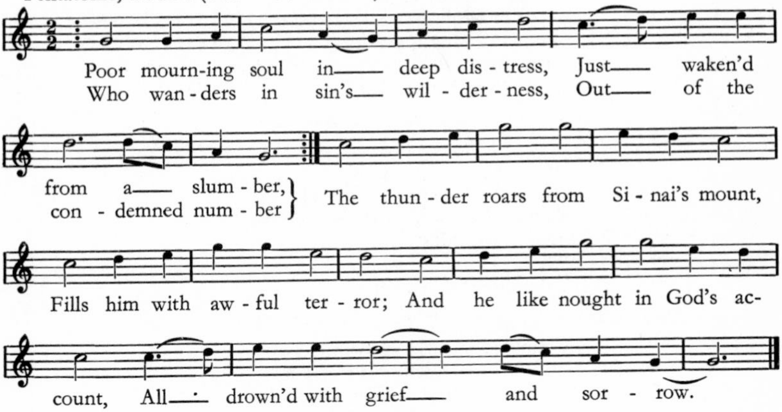
Poor mourn-ing soul in— deep dis - tress, Just— waken'd
Who wan - ders in sin's— wil - der - ness, Out— of the
from a— slum - ber,
con - demned num - ber
The thun - der roars from Si - nai's mount,
Fills him with aw - ful ter - ror; And he like nought in God's ac-
count, All— drown'd with grief— and sor - row.

Oh, woe is me that I was born,
Or after death have being;
Fain would I be some earthly worm,
Which has no future being;
Or had I died when I was young,
Oh, what would I have given!
Then might with babes my little tongue,
Been praising God in heaven.

But now may I lament my case,
Just worn away by trouble;
From day to day I look for peace,
But find my sorrow double.
Cries Satan, "Desp'rate is your state,
Time's been you might repented,
But now you see it his too late,
So make yourself contented!"

How can I live, how can I rest
Under this sore temptation,
Fearing the day of grace is past,
Lord, hear my lamentation!
For I am weary of my life,
My groans and bitter crying;
My wants are great, my mind's in strife,
My spirit's almost dying.

Without relief I soon shall die,
No hope of getting better;
Show pity, Lord, and hear the cry
Of a distress-ed sinner.
For I'm resolv-ed here to trust
At thy footstool for favor,
Pleading for life, though death be just,
Make haste, Lord, to deliver.

"Come, hungry, weary, naked soul,
For such I ne'er rejected;
My righteousness sufficient is,
Though you have long neglected.
Come, weary soul, for right you have,
I am such soul's protector;
My honor is engaged to save
All under this character.

"I came to seek, I came to save,
I came to make atonement,
I lived, I died, laid in the grave
To save you from the judgment."
By faith, my glorious Lord I see;
Oh, how it doth amaze me
To see him bleeding on the tree,
From death and hell to raise me.

The above homespun text points to the rural preacher or revival song leader of the late eighteenth century as its source. It is a conversion story in dramatic form, the Savior, the Sinner and the Devil having parts in the drama.

The earliest known occurence of the tune is in the Vermont book, Ingalls' *Christian Harmony* of 1805, p. 77. In the *Sacred Harp* of 1844, p. 89, it is found with a different text and is entitled 'Church's Desolation'. It is claimed there by J. T. White, and in the *Christian Harmony* of 1866, by William Walker. Both were South Carolinians, from which territory Reed Smith recorded the tune in 1913 as one of the 'Barbara Allen' settings; SCB 130. This tune was probably adopted for 'Church's Desolation' and for the 'Barbara Allen' ballad from the Scotch ballad 'Wae's me for Prince Charlie'. See Kennedy's *Handbook of Scottish Song*, p. 20 The London *Era* in the early 1860's speaks of this as the "celebrated Jacobite song." The 'Prince Charlie' of the song is Charles II of England. Hence the song, the text at least, is nearly 300 years old. The same tune is used also for 'Geordie', *Last Leaves*, p. 133; 'Locks and Bolts', Sharp, ii., 19; 'Lazarus', Sharp, ii., 30; an old Irish tune in Petrie, No. 363; 'Johnny Fa'', SMM, No. 62; and 'Hynd Horn', Motherwell, Appendix, *Musick*, No. 13.

The noted composer of hymn tunes, J. B. Dykes, was influenced by the 'Prince Charlie' melody in the building up of 'Lindisfarne'; see *Hymns Ancient and Modern*, No. 156, second tune.

No. 29

ADDRESS FOR ALL, CHH 101

Hexatonic, mode 1 b (I II — IV V VI 7)

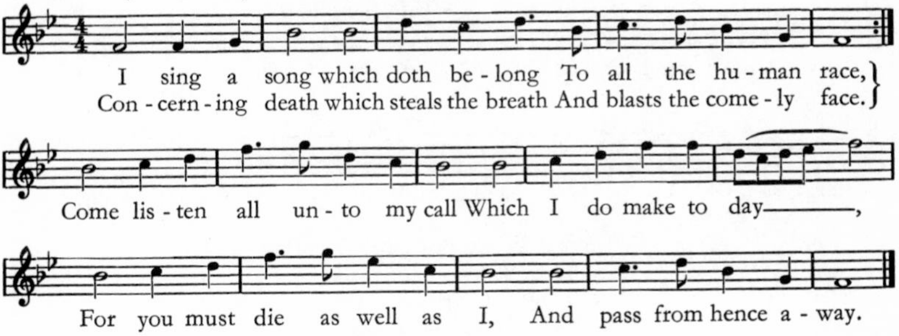
I sing a song which doth be - long To all the hu - man race,
Con - cern - ing death which steals the breath And blasts the come - ly face.
Come lis - ten all un - to my call Which I do make to day——,
For you must die as well as I, And pass from hence a - way.

No human power can stop the hour
Wherein a mortal dies;
A Caesar may be great today,
Yet death will close his eyes.
Though some do strive and do arrive
To riches and renown,
Enjoying health and swim in wealth,
Yet death will bring them down.

Though beauty grace your comely face
With roses white and red,
A dying fall will spoil it all,
For Absalom is dead.
Though you acquire the best attire,
Appearing fine and fair,
Yet death will come into the room
And strip you naked there.

The princes high and beggars die
And mingle with the dust,
The rich, the brave, the negro slave,
The wicked and the just.
Therefore prepare to meet thy God
Before it be too late,
Or else you'll weep, lament and cry,
Lost in a ruin'd state.

William Walker claims this song. See 'Church's Desolation', a variant of the tune, for source references. See also 'Sweet William and Lady Margery' (Wyman and Brockway, p. 94) for a secular tune variant.

No. 30

CONDESCENSION, GOS 656

Hexatonic, mode 1 b (I II — IV V VI 7)

How con-de-scend-ing and how kind Was God's e - ter - nal Son! Our
mis - 'ry reach'd his heav'n-ly mind— And pi - ty brought him down.
1
2

When justice by our sins provoked,
Drew forth its dreadful sword,
He gave his soul up to the stroke,
Without a murmuring word.

Here we behold his bowels roll,
As kind as when he died;
And see the sorrows of his soul
Bleed through his wounded side.

This was compassion like a God,
That when the Savior knew
The price of pardon was his blood,
His pity ne'er withdrew.

Now though he reigns exalted high,
His love is still as great;
Well he remembers Calvary,
Nor let his saints forget.

Here let our hearts begin to melt,
While we his death record,
And with our joy for pardoned guilt,
Mourn that we pierced the Lord.

The words are attributed to Isaac Watts. I have supplied the second and third stanzas from *The Olive Leaf*, p. 129. The tune is from the eighteenth century; found also OSH 286, PB 38, HH 63, UHH 13. The tune's frame is found with the text of 'Good Morning, My Pretty Little Miss', Sharp, ii., 90, also in 'Ibby Damsel', Sharp, ii., 137. I surmise that we have, in the last line of the second stanza above, the source of the negro spiritual refrain:

An' he never said a mumblin' word.

No. 31

GOOD PHYSICIAN, SOH 49

Pentatonic, mode 2 (I — 3 IV V — 7)

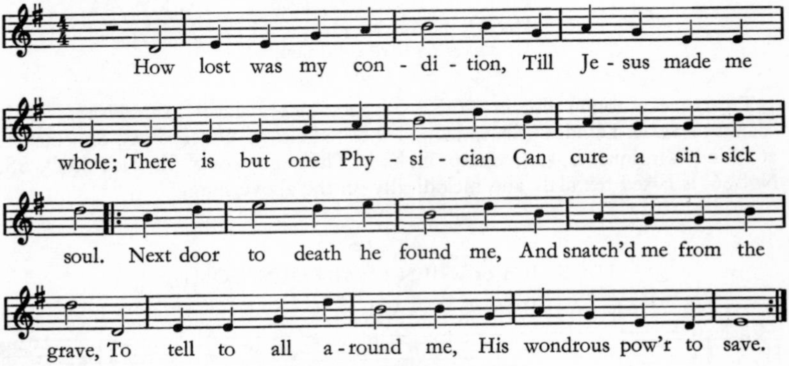
How lost was my con - di - tion, Till Je - sus made me
whole; There is but one Phy - si - cian Can cure a sin - sick
soul. Next door to death he found me, And snatch'd me from the
grave, To tell to all a - round me, His wondrous pow'r to save.

The worst of all diseases
Is light compared with sin;
On every part it seizes,
But rages most within.
'Tis palsy, plague, and fever,
And madness, all combin'd;
And none but a believer
The least relief can find.

From men great skill professing,
I thought a cure to gain;
But this proved more distressing
And added to my pain.
Some said that nothing ail'd me.
Some gave me up for lost;
Thus every refuge fail'd me,
And all my hopes were cross'd.

At length this great Physician
(How matchless is his grace!)
Accepted my petition
And undertook my case.
First gave me sight to view him,
For sin my eyes had seal'd;
Then bid me look unto him,
I look'd, and I was heal'd.

A dying, risen Jesus,
Seen by the eye of faith,
At once from anguish frees us
And saves the soul from death.
Come, then, to this Physician,
His help he'll freely give;
He makes no hard condition,
'Tis only — look and live.

This tune is found also in GOS, No. 227. A remake is in OSH 176. It is 'Banks of Sweet Dundee', Sharp i., 399. Related also to 'Pinery Boy', Shoemaker, 262; and 'Virginian Lover', Sharp, ii., 150. The negro song 'Sin-Sick Soul', SS, No. 66, is based textually and melodically on the above song.

No. 32

LOOK OUT or WHEN I WAS YOUNG, OSH 90

Hexatonic, mode 3 A (I II III — V VI VII)

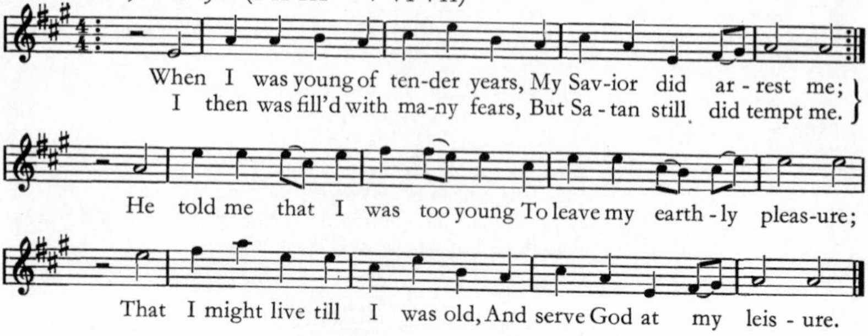
When I was young of ten-der years, My Sav-ior did ar - rest me;
I then was fill'd with ma-ny fears, But Sa - tan still did tempt me.
He told me that I was too young To leave my earth - ly pleas-ure;
That I might live till I was old, And serve God at my leis - ure.

Again the spirit came one day
With his almighty power,
Which caused me to forsake my way
And tremble every hour;
And he caused me to weep and mourn,
Saying, Lord Jesus, save me,
If mercy thou canst me afford,
And to thy glory raise me.

When Jesus heard the rebel cry,
He sent his kind compassion;
Down at his feet my soul did lie,
There pleading for a blessing.
My heart was filled with tenderness.
My mouth was filled with praises,
While Abba, Father, I did cry,
And glory to my Savior.

B. F. White, compiler of the *Sacred Harp*, is given as the composer. It is dated 1842. The text is supplied from *Good Old Songs*, No. 154. A secular setting is 'Three Crows', Davis, p. 562, tune "P". Both 'Look Out' and 'Three Crows' are adaptations of 'Ye Banks and Braes', or 'Bonnie Doon', see Kennedy, *Handbook of Scottish Song*, p. 27. In *Church Harmony*, p. 134, we find the 'Bonnie Doon tune in its original form under the little 'Star of Bethlehem'. A variant tune in this collection is 'Tis a Wonder'.

No. 33

SAINT'S REQEST, OSH 286

Pentatonic, mode 3 (I II III — V VI —)

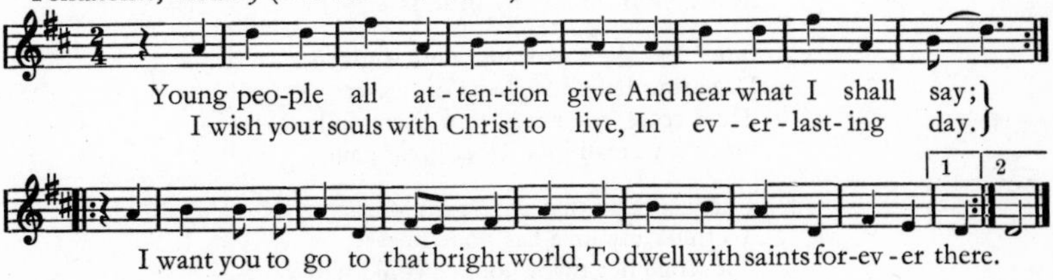
Young peo-ple all at-ten-tion give And hear what I shall say;
I wish your souls with Christ to live, In ev - er - last- ing day.
1 2
I want you to go to that bright world, To dwell with saints for-ev - er there.

The *Sacred Harp* gives but one stanza of this ballad. The rest of the text is to be found in *Zion Songster*. The tune is widely used among the secular ballads. See 'Barbara Allen', Sharp, i., 183; 'Geordie', Sharp, i., 240; 'False Young Man', Sharp, ii., 52; 'Lord Thomas and Fair Eleanor', Smith, 115; 'True Lover's Farewell', Sharp, ii., 114; 'Lizzie Wan', Sharp, i., 89; and 'Little Musgrave and Lady Barnard', Sharp, i., 164 and 166.

No. 34

NEWBERRY or LONESOME GROVE, SOC 131

Pentatonic, mode 3 (I II III — V VI —)

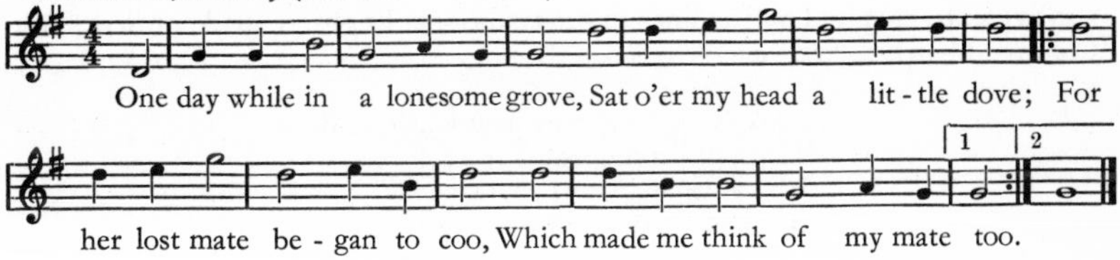
One day while in a lonesome grove, Sat o'er my head a lit - tle dove; For
1 2
her lost mate be - gan to coo, Which made me think of my mate too.

Ah! little dove, you're not alone,
For I, like you, can only mourn;
I once, like you, did have a mate,
But now, like you, am desolate.

Consumption seized my love severe
And preyed upon her one long year,
Till death came at the break of day,
And my poor Mary he did slay.

Her sparkling eyes and blooming cheeks
Withered like the rose and died;
The arms that once embraced me round
Lie mould'ring under the cold ground.

But death, grim death, did not stop here;
I had one child, to me most dear;
He, like a vulture, came again
And took from me my little Jane.

But, bless the Lord, his word is given,
Declaring babes are heirs of heaven.
Then cease, my heart, to mourn for Jane,
Since my small loss is her great gain.

I have a hope that cheers my breast,
To think my love has gone to rest;
For while her dying tongue could move,
She praised the Lord for pardoning love.

Shout on, ye heavenly pow'rs above,
While I this lonesome desert rove;
My master's work will soon be done,
And then I'll join you in your song.

O hasten on that happy day,
When I must leave this clod of clay,
And soar aloft o'er yon blest plain
And there meet Mary and my Jane.

The song is attributed in the *Social Harp* to Wm. C. Davis. The first stanza was evidently inspired by the lines in the traditional English ballad entitled 'Giles Collins', Sharp, i., 196, which reads:

Look away, look away, that lonesome dove
That sails from pine to pine;
It's mourning for its own true love
Just like I mourn for mine.

Four recently recorded (1917 and 1918) variants of the 'Newberry' tune, with one stanza of text each are in Sharp, ii., 197f. See also JAFL, xxv., 276. 'Lonesome Dove', Thomas, 162, has the same text but a different tune. 'Heavenly Dove' in this collection is a variant tune, but it is more closely related to the 'Barbara Allen' tune in Sharp, i., 183ff. 'Newberry' belongs to the 'Lord Lovel' type of tune mentioned in the Introduction, p. 14. Other melodies of the same type are listed under 'Dulcimer' in this collection.

No. 35

DEEP SPRING or CONVERTED THIEF (B), KNH 90

Pentatonic, mode 3 (I II III — V VI —)

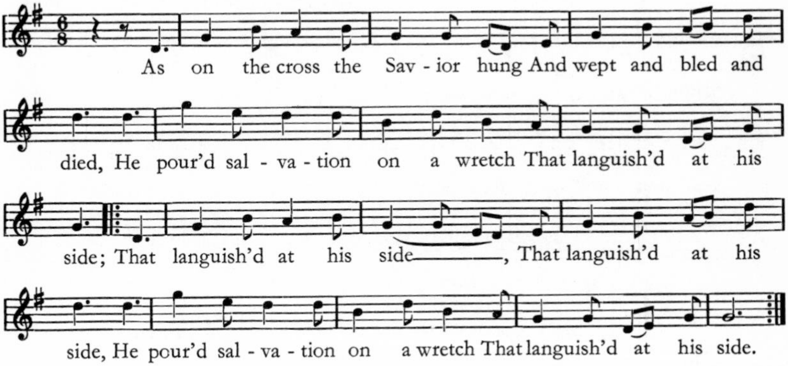

His crimes, with inward grief and shame, the penitent confess'd;
Then turn'd his dying eyes to Christ and thus his prayer address'd:

"Jesus, thou son and heir of heaven! Thou spotless lamb of God!
I see thee bathed in sweat and tears and welt'ring in thy blood.

"Yet quickly from those scenes of wo, in triumph thou shalt rise,
Burst through the gloomy shades of death and shine above the skies.

"Amid the glories of that world, dear Savior, think on me,
And in the vict'ries of thy death let me a sharer be."

His prayer the dying Jesus hears and instantly replies:
"Today thy parting soul shall be with me in paradise."

The tune is found also UH 89, SOC 249, HOC 93, OSH 44. It is reminiscent of 'Little Musgrave and Lady Barnard', Sharp, i., 166; 'Lord Thomas and Fair Eleanor', Sharp, i., 118; and 'O Land of Rest' in this collection.

No. 36

SALUTATION or GOOD MORNING BROTHER PILGRIM, GOS 298

Hexatonic, mode 2 A (I II 3 IV V — 7)

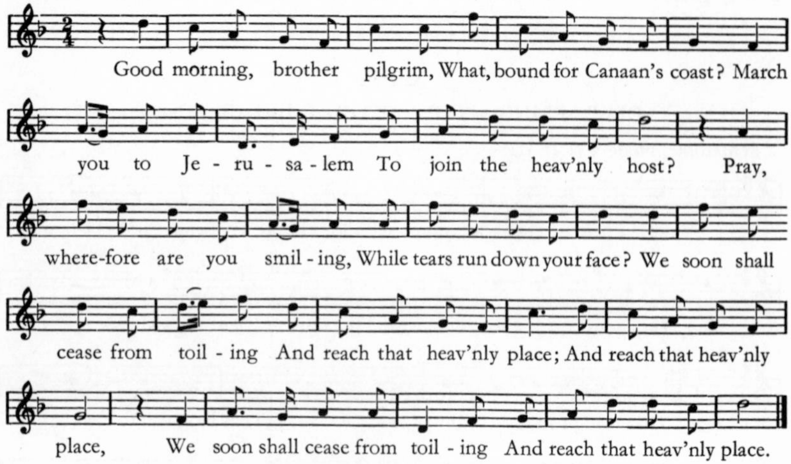
Good morning, brother pilgrim, What, bound for Canaan's coast? March
you to Je - ru - sa - lem To join the heav'nly host? Pray,
where-fore are you smil - ing, While tears run down your face? We soon shall
cease from toil - ing And reach that heav'nly place; And reach that heav'nly
place, We soon shall cease from toil - ing And reach that heav'nly place.

To Canaan's coast we'll hasten, to join the heavenly throng;
Hark, from the banks of Jordan, how sweet the pilgrims' song!
Their Jesus they are viewing, by faith we see him, too,
We smile and weep and praise him, and on our way pursue;
(repeated as above)

Though sinners do despise us and treat us with disdain,
Our former comrades slight us, esteem us low and mean;
No earthly joy shall charm us while marching on our way,
Our Jesus will defend us in the distressing day.

The frowns of old companions we're willing to sustain,
And, in divine compassion, to pray for them again;
For Christ, our loving Savior, our Comforter and Friend,
Will bless us with his favor and guide us to the end.

With streams of consolation, we're filled as with new wine,
We die to transient pleasures, and live to things divine,
We sink in holy raptures, while viewing things above,
While, glory to my Savior, my soul is full of love.

This is evidently a marching tune and from the eighteenth century vintage. It occurs also OSH 153, SOC 216, HH 387. 'Walking on the Levy' (Newell, *Games and Songs of American Children*, p. 231) has a similar beginning. Echoes of the text are found in Dett, p. 8:

> Good mornin', brother trav'ler,
> Pray tell me where you're bound,
> I'm bound for Canaan's happy land,
> And de enchanted ground.

Stephen Foster's 'Farewell My Lily Dear' and 'The Soldier's Home' show relationship to the tune. (See my article in *The Musical Quarterly*, vol. xxii., No. 2. For the English source of this *dialogue* type of song, see the note under 'Warrenton' in this collection.

No. 37
HEAVENLY UNION or EXPERIENCE, REV 42

Heptatonic aeolian, mode 1 A + b (I II 3 IV V 6 7)

Come, saints and sin - ners, hear me tell, The won-ders of Im-
man - u - el Who saved me from a burn - ing hell, And
brought my soul with him to dwell, And gave me heav'n-ly un - ion.
Un - ion, un - ion, Who sav'd me from a burn-ing hell, And
brought my soul with him to dwell, And gave me heav'n-ly un - ion.

> When Jesus saw me from on high,
> Beheld my soul in ruin lie,
> He looked on me with pitying eye,
> And said to me as he passed by:
> "With God you have no union."

Then I began to weep and cry;
And looked this way and that to fly;
It grieved me so that I must die;
I strove salvation then to buy,
But still I had no union.

But when I hated all my sin,
My dear Redeemer took me in,
And with his blood he washed me clean;
And oh! what seasons I have seen
Since first I felt this union.

I now with saints can join to sing,
And mount on faith's triumphant wing
And make the heavenly arches ring
With loud hosannas to our King,
Who brought our souls to union.

The tune seems dorian in character. If so classed, the key signature should be natural. A variant of tune and text is in CHI 30 and SWP 69.

No. 38

MARION or I'LL RAMBLE AND I'LL ROVE, SOC 228

Pentatonic, mode 2 (I — 3 IV V — 7)

I have a lov-ing old fa-ther at home, I've cost him ma-ny a tear;
And to make la-ment to him, I'll tra-vel ten thousand year. I'll ramble and I'll
rove and I'll call up-on my God. They may all say what they will, Re-
solv'd as I am so long as I live, For to be a ro-ver still.

Further stanzas are made merely by the substitution of "mother" etc. for "father". The song, tune and words, was probably parodied from 'Seven Long Years'. See Sharp, ii., 79. From the latter song I quote the second stanza.

I have a good old father at home,
And I've cost him many a pound,
And now to make amends for this,
I'll travel the whole world round.
Chorus I'll romp and I'll rave, and I'll call for my bode,
They may all say what they will;
Resolved as I am, just as long as I can,
For to drink good liquor still.

Compare also 'Lord Thomas and Fair Eleanor', Sharp, i., 124, tune 'N'. 'Marion' belongs to the 'Babe of Bethlehem' group of tunes. See the song by that title in this collection. 'Kingsfold', No. 270 in the *Christian Science Hymnal* is the same. In the English *Methodist Hymn Book*, 'Kingsfold' is given as a traditional melody of England. See also Petrie, Nos. 193 and 863.

No. 39
UNION, OSH 116

Heptatonic aeolian, mode 2 A+b (I II 3 IV V 6 7)

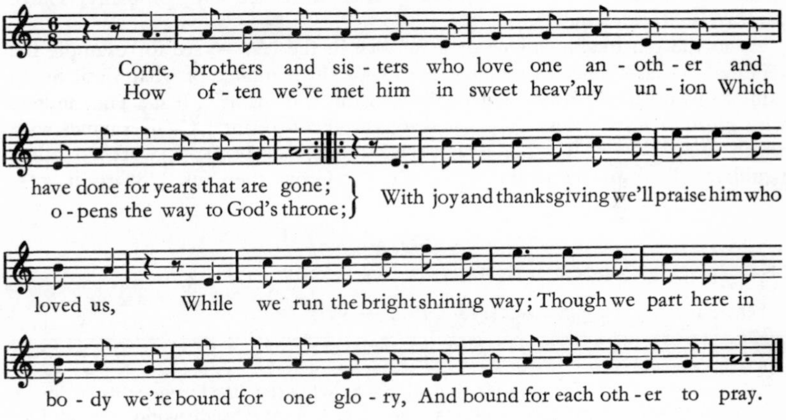
Come, brothers and sis - ters who love one an - oth - er and
How of - ten we've met him in sweet heav'nly un - ion Which
have done for years that are gone;
o - pens the way to God's throne;
With joy and thanksgiving we'll praise him who
loved us, While we run the bright shining way; Though we part here in
bo - dy we're bound for one glo - ry, And bound for each oth - er to pray.

There was Joshua and Joseph, Elias and Moses,
That pray'd, and God heard from his throne;
There was Abraham, and Isaac, and Jacob, and David,
And Solomon, and Stephen, and John,
There was Simeon, and Anna, and I don't know how many,
That pray'd as they journey'd along;
Some cast among lions, some bound with rough irons,
Yet glory and praises they sung.

Some tell us that praying, and also that praising
Is labor that's all spent in vain;
But we have such a witness that God hears with swiftness,
From praying we will not refrain.
There was old father Noah, and ten thousand more,
That witness'd that God heard them pray;
There was Samuel and Hannah, Paul, Silas, and Peter,
And Daniel and Jonah, we'll say.

That God, by his spirit, or an angel doth visit
Their souls and their bodies while praying,
Shall we all go fainting, while they go on praising,
And glorify God in the flame?
God grant us to inherit the same praying spirit,
While we are journeying below,
That when we cease praying, we shall not cease praising,
But round God's white throne we shall bow.

James, editor of the *Original Sacred Harp*, 1911, says: "The hymn is from a very old edition, 1820. It is not in any of the hymn books found since that date." The quick triple time of the tune indicates Irish influence and, probably, source Similar is 'Royal Band', OSH 360.

As to the remarkable rhyme or assonance in the text — see for example the repeated "o" assonance in the first lines — I am reminded of what Cecil Sharp said of this feature in Anglo-Irish ballads of this sort, namely, that "They imitate with more or less success in an alien tongue the assonantal Caelic rhymes with which their makers, whether hedge-schoolmasters or peasants, were doubtless familiar." The same metrical trend is in 'Green Grows the Laurel', Sharp, ii., 211.

No. 40

POOR WAYFARING STRANGER, GOS 714

Pentatonic, mode 2 minorized (I — 3 IV V — VII)

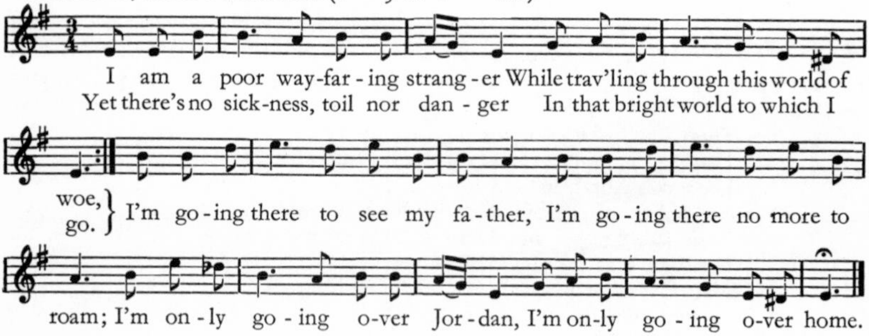
I am a poor way-far - ing strang - er While trav'ling through this world of
Yet there's no sick-ness, toil nor dan - ger In that bright world to which I
woe, go.
I'm go - ing there to see my fa - ther, I'm go - ing there no more to
roam; I'm on - ly go - ing o-ver Jor - dan, I'm on-ly go - ing o-ver home.

I know dark clouds will gather round me,
I know my way is rough and steep;
Yet beauteous fields lie just before me
Where God's redeem'd their vigils keep.
I'm going there to see my mother,
She said she'd meet me when I come;
I'm only going over Jordan,
I'm only going over home.

I'll soon be freed from every trial,
My body sleep in the church-yard;
I'll drop the cross of self-denial
And enter on my great reward.
I'm going there to see my class-mates,
Who've gone before me one by one;
I'm only going over Jordan,
I'm only going over home.

I want to wear a crown of glory,
When I get home on that good land;
I want to shout salvation's story,
In concert with the blood-wash'd band;
I'm going there to see my Savior,
To sing his praise forever more;
I'm only going over Jordan,
I'm only going over home.

This is a comparatively recent recording (around the beginning of the present century) of an extremely widely sung folk-tune. It appears in *Good Old Songs* as a bare melody, no harmonic parts. I suggest, as an explanation of the *d*-flat in the fifth measure from the end, the intrusion of dorian influence. The earliest known recording among the fasola folk was in the first edition of the *Sacred Harp*, 1844. The negro adoptions and adaptations are reviewed WS 251ff.

The tune is quite evidently borrowed from secular environment. I list here a number of secular songs whose tunes are variously related: 'Barbara Allen', Sharp, i., 194 and 195; 'In Old Virginny', Sharp, ii., 232—234; 'Come All Ye Fair and Tender Ladies', Sharp, ii., 128—136; 'Katie Morey', Sharp, ii., 120; 'Dear Companion', Sharp, ii., 109; 'George Reilly', Sharp, ii., 26; 'Awake, Awake', Sharp, i., 358—364, and Petrie, Nos. 1222 and 265.

A note on this song in the *Social Harp* says that the compiler, John G. McCurry, Hartwell, Georgia, "when eight years old, learned the air of this tune from Mrs. Catherine Penn." That was therefore in the year 1829.

Text passages in the secular ballads which remind of those in the fasola song are seen in 'In Old Virginny', where we read:

I am a man of constant sorrow,
I have seen troubles all my days.
I'll bid farewell to old Virginia,
The place where I was partly raised.

We see also in 'Awake, Awake', how the poor wayfaring stranger appears as "your true love" who "is going away."

No. 41

ZION'S SOLDIER, SWP 118

Heptatonic aeolian, mode 4 a+b (I II 3 IV V 6 7).

Christ is set on Zi - on's hill; He re - ceiv - eth sin - ners still:
Who will serve this bles - sed King? Come, en - list, and help me sing.
This sol - dier sure will be Hap - py in e - ter - ni - ty,
This sol - dier sure will be Hap - py in e - ter - ni - ty.

I by faith enlisted am in the service of the Lamb;
Present pay I now receive, future happiness he'll give.
This soldier *etc.*

Zion's King my Captain is, conquest I shall never miss;
Let the fiends of hell engage, fret and fume and roar in rage.

Let the world their forces join, with the feinds of hell combine;
Greater is my King than they, through him I shall win the day.

Wicked men I scorn to fear, though they persecute me here;
True, they may my body kill, but my King's on Zion's hill.

What a Captain I have got! Is not mine a happy lot?
Hear, ye worldlings, hear my song, this the language of my tongue.

When this life's short space is o'er, I shall live to die no more;
Therefore will I take the sword, fight for Jesus Christ, my Lord.

Come, ye worldlings, come enlist; 'tis the voice of Jesus Christ:
Whosoever will may come; Jesus Christ refuseth none.

Jesus is my Captain's name, now, as yesterday, the same;
In his name I notice give, all who come he will receive.

Be persuaded, take his pay, all your sins he'll wash away;
Now in Jesus' name believe; future happiness he'll give.
(last chorus)
Yes! in heaven you sure will be praising God eternally. *(repeat)*

For a related chorus text see 'O Ye Young and Gay and Proud' in this collection. The tune, claimed by William Walker, is keyed in the natural minor (aeolian) of *a*. I suggest the signature of one sharp, bringing the tune into the dorian mode, as more natural.

No. 42

FEMALE CONVICT, SOH (1835) 160

Heptatonic aeolian, mode 4 a+b (I II 3 IV V 6 7)

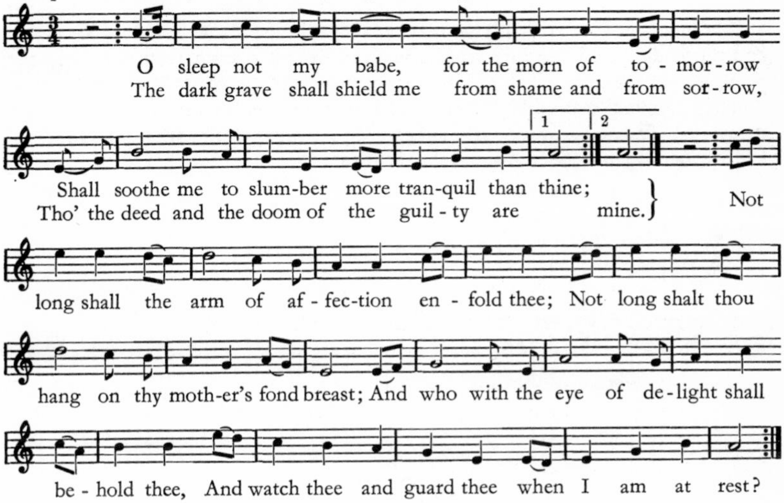
O sleep not my babe, for the morn of to - mor - row
The dark grave shall shield me from shame and from sor - row,
1
2
Shall soothe me to slum-ber more tran-quil than thine;
Tho' the deed and the doom of the guil - ty are mine.
Not
long shall the arm of af - fec-tion en - fold thee; Not long shalt thou
hang on thy moth-er's fond breast; And who with the eye of de - light shall
be - hold thee, And watch thee and guard thee when I am at rest?

And yet it doth grieve me to wake thee, my dearest,
The pangs of thy desolate mother to see;
Thou wilt weep when the clank of my cold chains thou hearest;
And none but the guilty should weep over me.
And yet I must wake thee, and whilst thou art weeping,
To calm thee I'll stifle my tears for a while.
Thou smil'st in thy dreams whilst thus placidly sleeping,
And O how it wounds me to gaze on thy smile.

Alas, my sweet babe, with what pride I had press'd thee
To the bosom that now throbs with terror and shame,
If the pure tie of virtue's affection had bless'd thee,
And hail'd thee the heir of thy father's high name.
But now with remorse that avails not I mourn thee,
Forsaken and friendless as soon thou wilt be,
In a world, if they cannot betray, that will scorn thee,
Avenging the guilt of thy mother on thee.

And when the dark thought of my fate shall awaken
The deep blush of shame on thy innocent cheek,
Then by all but the God of the orphan forsaken,
A home and a father in vain thou wilt seek.
I know that the base world will seek to deceive thee
With falsehood like that which thy mother beguiled;
Deserted and helpless, with whom can I leave thee?
O God of the fatherless, pity my child!

The tune shows remarkable similarity to 'As I Was A-Walking' or 'Grenadier and the Lady', see JFSS viii., 194; also to 'Westron Wynde' from the early 16th century, see Jackson, *English Melodies from the 13th to the 18th Century*, p. 11. 'Female Convict' was widely sung in the early nineteenth century. The full title reads: "A Female Convict, After receiving pardon in the sight of God, thus addrest her infant. Set to music by R. Boyd."

No. 43

WEDLOCK (B), OSH 115

Heptatonic aeolian, mode 2 A+b (I II 3 IV V 6 7)

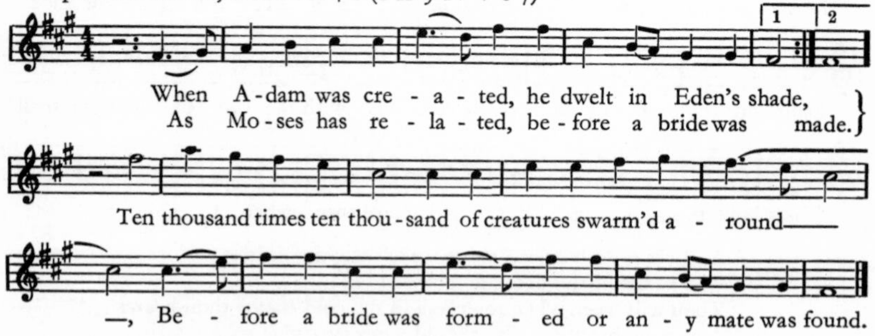
1
2
When A-dam was cre - a - ted, he dwelt in Eden's shade,
As Mo-ses has re - la - ted, be-fore a bride was made.
Ten thousand times ten thou-sand of creatures swarm'd a - round——
—, Be - fore a bride was form - ed or an - y mate was found.

He had no consolation, but seemed as one alone,
Till, to his admiration, he found he'd lost a bone.
This woman was not taken from Adam's head, we know;
And she must not rule o'er him, 'tis evidently so.

This woman she was taken from near to Adam's heart,
By which we are directed that they should never part.
The book that's called the bible, be sure you don't neglect,
For in every sense of duty, it will you both direct.

The woman is commanded to do her husband's will,
In everything that's lawful, her duty to fulfill.
Great was his exultation to see her by his side;
Great was his elevation to have a loving bride.

This woman she was taken from under Adam's arm;
And she must be protected from injury and harm.
This woman was not taken from Adam's feet, we see;
And she must not be abus-ed, the meaning seems to be.

The husband is commanded to love his loving bride,
And live as does a Christian, and for his house provide.
The woman is commanded her husband to obey,
In everything that's lawful, until her dying day.

Avoiding all offenses, not sow the seed of strife,
These are the solemn duties of every man and wife.

A variant of the third line of the first stanza, found in SOC 188, reads:

Ten thousand times ten thousand things wheel-ed all around.

The tune is especially announced in the *Sacred Harp* as "original" and by Elder E. Dumas, a Primitive Baptist. And it is dated 1869. An older tune to the same text is given in this collection as 'Wedlock (A)'. See also 'Wedlock', Sharp, ii., 272. 'The Banks of Newfoundland', a capstan shanty, is essentially the same tune. See JFSS, v., 300.

No. 44
LEP'ROUS JEW, SWP 43

Heptatonic aeolian, mode 2 A+b (I II 3 IV V 6 7)

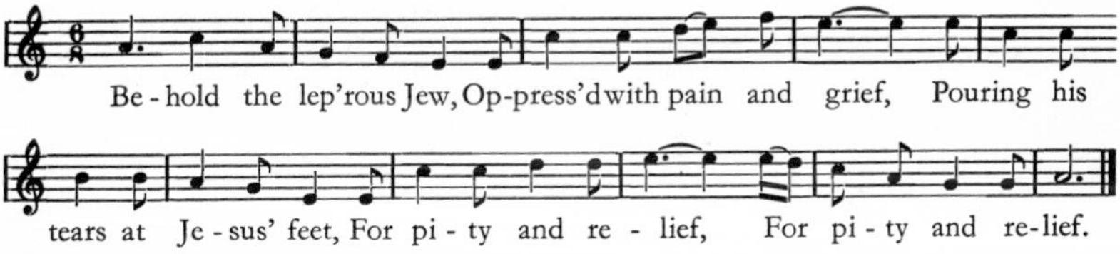
Be-hold the lep'rous Jew, Op-press'd with pain and grief, Pouring his
tears at Je-sus' feet, For pi-ty and re-lief, For pi-ty and re-lief.

"O speak the word," he cries, "and heal me of my pain:
Lord, thou art able, if thou wilt, to make a leper clean,
To make a leper clean."

Compassion moves his heart, he speaks the gracious word;
The leper feels his strength return, and all his sickness cured,
And all his sickness cured.

To thee, dear Lord, I look, sick of a worse disease;
Sin is my painful malady, and none can give me ease,
And none can give me ease.

But thy almighty grace can heal my lep'rous soul;
O bathe me in thy precious blood and that will make me whole,
And that will make me whole.

A tune quite similar to the one above, though cast in two-four time, is 'Dependence', HH 250.

No. 45

SPRING PLACE or CHURCH OF MY YOUTH, GOS 44

Hexatonic, mode 2 b (I — 3 IV V 6 7)

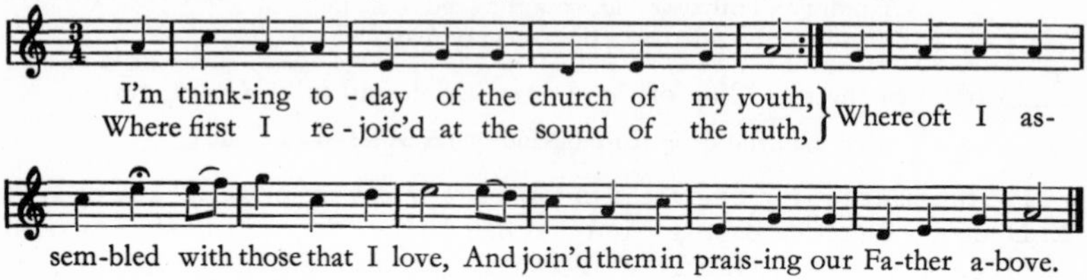
I'm think-ing to - day of the church of my youth,
Where first I re - joic'd at the sound of the truth,
Where oft I as-
sem-bled with those that I love, And join'd them in prais-ing our Fa-ther a-bove.

Ah! well I remember, when youthful and gay,
In mirthfulness sporting while time sped away,
With my parents went to the house of the Lord,
And wonder'd what made them rejoice in His word.

But when my dear Savior, so precious to me,
My blind eyes did open, my sins all to see,
With fearfulness, trembling, too great to express,
I went to that house fill'd with woe and distress.

When Jesus, my blessed Redeemer and Friend,
Reveal'd that He was the Beginning and End,
I long'd for the season of worship once more,
That I might join His saints, His dear name adore.

And when in that dear place of worship and praise,
My voice with His saints I endeavor'd to raise,
My heart fill'd with love and my hope bright and clear,
I thought surely trouble could no more appear.

When deeply impress'd with a sense of His love,
When this world could no more a resting place prove,
I went with a feeling I could not control,
And told what my Savior had done for my soul.

With loving caresses they welcomed me home,
And bade me no longer in darkness to roam;
The great joy of that hour I never can tell,
When I with such friends was permitted to dwell.

Though now sunder'd far from that blessed abode,
I feel, that I'm still with the children of God.
Dear brethren, I love you in deed and in truth,
Yet my heart oft goes to the church of my youth.

Ah! well I remember their kindness to me,
In my memory now their kind deeds I can see;
Wherever my lot is to publish the truth,
I'll never forget the church of my youth.

The oldest occurrence of the text seems to be in the *Hesperian Harp*, 1848. This song is a parody (words and music) of 'In the Days of My Youth', *Beggars Opera*, No. 42; Act 3, Scene 1. The tune there was that sung earlier to 'A Shepherd Kept Sheep'.

No. 46

REDEMPTION (B), OSH 501

Hexatonic, mode 2 A (I II 3 IV V — 7)

Come, friends and re - la-tions, let's join hearts and hands; The voice of the
tur - tle is heard in the land. Let's all walk to- geth- er and
fol-low the sound, And march to the place where re-demp-tion is found.

The place it is hidden, the place it is seal'd,
The place it is hidden till it is reveal'd;
The place is in Jesus, to Jesus we'll go,
And there find redemption from sorrow and wo.

That place it is hidden by reason of sin;
Alas! you can't see the sad state you are in!
You're blind and polluted, in prison and pain;
O how can such rebels redemption obtain!

But if you are wounded and bruised by the fall,
Then up and be doing! For you he doth call;
And if you are tempted to doubt and despair,
Then come home to Jesus, redemption is there.

And you, my dear brethren, that love my dear Lord,
Have witness for pardon, thro' faith in his blood;
Let patience attend you wherever you go,
Your Savior has purchased redemption for you.

The tune of 'Redemption (C)' is a variant of the above, as is also that of 'Redemption (A)'. See the last named song for mention of its tune relationship to the 'Grenadier and the Lady'.

No. 47

WEEPING MARY (B), SWP 102

Hexatonic, mode 2 A (I II 3 IV V — 7)

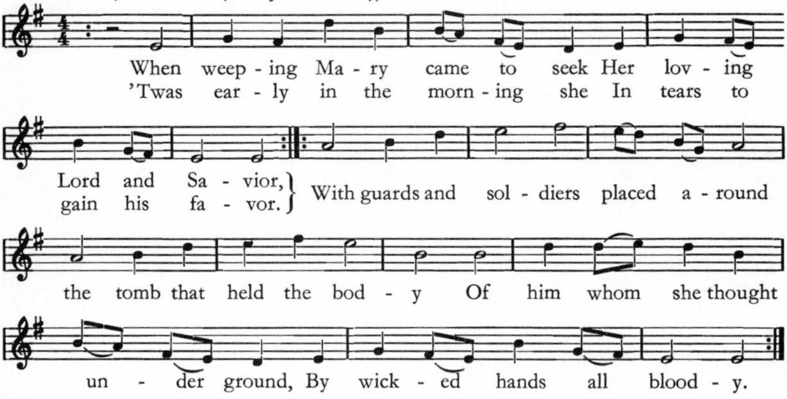
When weep - ing Ma - ry came to seek Her lov - ing
'Twas ear - ly in the morn - ing she In tears to
Lord and Sa - vior,
gain his fa - vor.
With guards and sol - diers placed a - round
the tomb that held the bod - y Of him whom she thought
un - der ground, By wick - ed hands all blood - y.

But how her aching heart was torn,
To find the tomb was empty,
In solemn silence did she mourn,
As onward she did venture.
'Twas angels in bright raiment shone,

Anticipate [imagine?] her sorrow,
And said, why doth this creature mourn,
And why this gloomy horror.

Whom seek'st thou, Mary, they did say,
And why this solemn mourning?
Because they've took my Lord away,
I thought to see this morning.
He, standing by her, though unknown,
She thought it was the gardener;
In flowing tears she made her moan,
Not knowing 'twas her partner.

I'll grieve, and my poor Mary said,
'Till I know where they laid him;
And quickly turning round her head,
Began for to upbraid him.
Whom seek'st thou, Mary? said the Son;
She then perceived her Savior,
And quickly to his feet she run,
Not fearing harm or danger.

And now, like Mary, let us go
And kiss the feet of Jesus,
That we may hear his word also,
Which he delights to give us.
From God we have the word of life,
Through Christ the Mediator;
Like him we hope to die and rise,
And dwell with the Creator.

A version of both tune and words is found in Ingalls' *Christian Harmony* of 1805, p. 73. Its seventh and eighth stanzas, reminding of the above text, are:

When weeping Mary came to seek
Her Lord with a perfume,
The napkin and the sheet she found
Together in the tomb.

The angels said, he is not here;
He's risen from the dead;
And streams of grace to sinners flow,
As free as did his blood.

The tune shows unmistakable family resemblance to a number of secular folk-melodies. See for example the score of 'Daemon Lover' tunes, Sharp, i., pp. 244—258; 'Lady Maisry', Sharp, i., 97; 'Locks and Bolts', Sharp, ii., 17; 'Betty Anne', Sharp, ii., 37; 'Swing a Lady', Sharp, ii., 379.

No. 48

REDEMPTION (A), WH 101

Heptatonic aeolian, mode 4 a+b (I II 3 IV V 6 7)

Come, friends and re - la-tions, let's join heart and hand, The voice of the
tur - tle is heard in our land. Let's all join to - geth - er and
fol - low the sound, And march to the place where re-demp-tion is found.

The tune was perhaps the inspiration of R. Boyd in making the melody for 'Female Convict', which is in this collection. (Or did the influence flow in the opposite direction?) The 'Grenadier and the Lady', as sung in England, is practically the same tune. See JFSS, viii., 194. Full text and a variant melody are given under 'Redemption (B)'. An ancestor of all these tunes seems to be 'Westron Wynde' of the early part of the sixteenth century. See Jackson, *English Melodies from the 13th to the 18th Century*, p. 11.

No. 49

PRODIGAL, SKH 35

Heptatonic aeolian, mode 2 A+b (I II 3 IV V 6 7)

1
2
Af - flictions, tho' they seem severe, Are oft in mer - cy sent;
They stopt the pro - di - gal's ca-reer And caused him to re - pent,
Al - tho' he no re - lent - ing felt Till he had spent his store -
—; His stubborn heart be - gan to melt When famine pinch'd him sore.

What have I gain'd by sin, he said, but hunger, shame and fear;
My father's house abounds with bread, while I am starving here.
I'll go and tell him all I've done, fall down before his face;
Unworthy to be called his son, I'll seek a servant's place.

The father saw him coming back, he looked, he ran, he smiled;
He throws his arms around the neck of his rebellious child.
Father, I've sinned, but O forgive; enough, the father said..
Rejoice, my house, my son's alive for whom I mourn'd as dead.

Now let the fatted calf be slain, go spread the news around;
My son was dead, but lives again, was lost but now is found.
'Tis thus the Lord his love reveals, to call poor sinners home.
More than a father's love he feels and welcomes all that come.

Davisson, the compiler of the SKH, claimed this tune. It functioned as the melodic material out of which the "fuguing" tune 'Alabama', in the *Sacred Harp*, was built.

No. 50

HAPPY SOULS (A), OL 145

Hexatonic, mode 4 A (I II — IV V VI 7)

O hap - py souls, how fast you go, And leave me far be-hind!
Don't stay for me, for now I see, The Lord is good and kind.
Go on, go on, my soul says go; And I'll come af - ter you
—; Tho' I'm be - hind, I feel in-clin'd To sing hos - an - na too.

God give you strength your race to run
And keep your footsteps right;
Though fast you go and I so slow,
You are not out of sight.
When you get to that world above,
And all God's glory see,
On that bright shore, your journey o'er,
Then look you out for me.

I'm coming on fast as I can.
Nor toil nor danger fear;
God give me strength! — — may I at length
Be one among you there.

Then alltogether we shall meet —
Together we will sing;
Together we will praise our God
And everlasting King.

The tune is one of the comparatively few correct dorian recordings — not minorized — in the fasola song books. The compiler of the *Olive Leaf* gives the following note below the song: "I learned this air of Rev. Samuel Anthony, of Georgia, more than thirty years ago, Wm. Hauser, M. D., March, 1878." See Introduction, p. 14, as to the 'Babe of Bethlehem' tune family to which 'Happy Souls' belongs. An Irish variant is 'The Peevish Child', Petrie, No. 591.

No. 51
BABE OF BETHLEHEM, SOH 78

Hexatonic, mode 4 a (I II — IV V 6 7)

Ye na - tions all, on you I call, Come hear this
de - clar - a - - tion, And don't re - fuse this glo-rious news, Of
Je - sus and sal - va - tion. To roy - al Jews came
first the news Of Christ the great Mes - - si - - ah, As
was fore - told by prophets old, I - sai - ah, Je - re - mi - ah.

To Abraham the promise came,
And to his seed forever,
A light to shine in Isaac's line,
By scripture we discover;
Hail, promised morn, the Savior's born,
The glorious Mediator —
God's blessed word made flesh and blood,
Assumed the human nature.

His parents poor in earthly store,
To entertain the stranger
They found no bed to lay his head,
But in the ox's manger;
No royal things, as used by kings,
Were seen by those that found him,
But in the hay the stranger lay,
With swaddling bands around him.

On the same night a glorious light
To shepherds there appeared,
Bright angels came in shining flame,
They saw and greatly feared;
The angels said, "Be not afraid,
Although we much alarm you,
We do appear good news to bear,
As now we will inform you.

"The city's name is Bethlehem,
In which God hath appointed,
This glorious morn a Savior's born,
For him God hath anointed;
By this you'll know, if you will go
To see this little stranger,
His lovely charms in Mary's arms,
Both lying in a manger."

When this was said, straightway was made
A glorious sound from heaven,
Each flaming, tongue an anthem sung,
"To men a Savior's given,
In Jesus' name, the glorious theme,
We elevate our voices,
At Jesus' birth be peace on earth,
Meanwhile all heaven rejoices."

Then with delight they took their flight,
And wing'd their way to glory,
The shepherds gazed and were amazed,
To hear the pleasing story;
To Bethlehem they quickly came,
The glorious news to carry,
And in the stall they found them all,
Joseph, the Babe, and Mary.

The shepherds then return'd again,
To their own habitation,
With joy of heart they did depart,
Now they have found salvation.
Glory, they cry, to God on high,
Who sent his son to save us,
This glorious morn the Savior's born,
His name it is Christ Jesus.

The tune, evidently dorian, is of a type that was widely used and varied by folk singers. I mentioned this type in the Introduction, page 14, and called it the 'Babe of Bethlehem' family of tunes because the above seems to have been one of its best members. Other members, in either the dorian or the aeolian mode, are 'Happy Souls (A)', 'Marion', 'Atonement', and 'Enquirer' in this collection; related spiritual tunes not included here are 'Help me to Sing', OSH 376; 'Staunton', SKH 26; 'Melody', PB 313; 'Brownson', OL 259; 'Howland', REV 73; and 'Sweet Prospect', OSH 65.

Related worldly songs are 'The Peevish Child', Petrie, No. 591; a song without title, Petrie, No. 193; 'When First I Left Old Ireland', Petrie, No. 863; 'Lowlands of Holland', Sharp, i., 200; 'Virginian Lover', Sharp, ii., 149; and 'The Little Red Lark of the Mountain', Petrie, No. 383. John Powell has set 'Babe of Bethlehem' in a beautiful dorian-mixolydian form for mixed chorus. It is published by J. Fischer and Brother, New York.

Ninety-eight Folk-Hymns

Benjamin Franklin White, and Thurza Golightly White, of Hamilton, Georgia. White was a life-long singing school master and folk-song collector who little dreamed of the immeasurable value his labors were to become to singers and folklorists of posterity. His compendium of tunes, wedded to spiritual texts and provided with simple harmonies, bore the name, *The Sacred Harp.*

In the shade of spreading magnolias and beneath this memorial erected by kinspeople and devoted *Sacred Harp* singers in the Oakland Cemetery in Atlanta, the revered master of singing rests besides his wife.

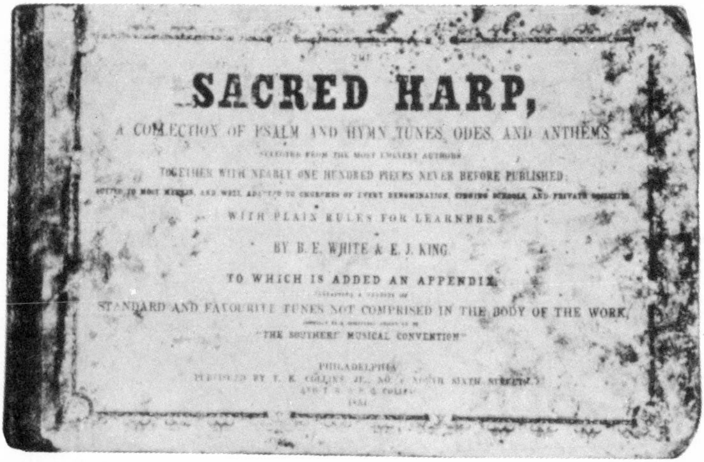

SACRED HARP,

A COLLECTION OF PSALM AND HYMN TUNES, ODES, AND ANTHEMS

TOGETHER WITH NEARLY ONE HUNDRED PIECES NEVER BEFORE PUBLISHED;

WITH PLAIN RULES FOR LEARNERS.

BY B. F. WHITE & E. J. KING.

TO WHICH IS ADDED AN APPENDIX

STANDARD AND FAVOURITE TUNES NOT COMPRISED IN THE BODY OF THE WORK,

"THE SOUTHERN MUSICAL CONVENTION"

PHILADELPHIA

THE SACRED HARP appeared in 1844. Its most recent edition came out in 1936. It was the source of sixty-seven songs in the present collection.

No. 52
WASHINGTON, OSH 147

Heptatonic aeolian, mode 2 A+b (I II 3 IV V 6 7)

Dis-miss us with thy blessing, Lord, Help us to feed up-on thy word.
All that has been a-miss for-give, And let thy truth within us live.
Tho' we are guil-ty, thou art good, Wash all our works in Je-sus' blood;
Give ev-ery fet-ter'd soul re-lease And bid us all de-
part in peace. Give ev-ery fetter'd soul release And bid us all de-part in peace.

The text is credited to Joseph Hart, tune to Munday, in the *Original Sacred Harp*. Melodic relationship is to be seen between this and 'Ye Mariners of England'. See Dolph, *Sound Off*, p. 228.

No. 53
STEPHENS, PB 338

Pentatonic, mode 3 (I II III — V VI —)

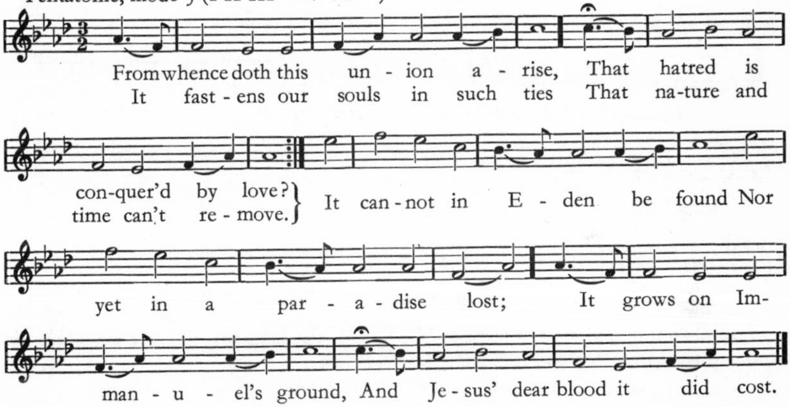
From whence doth this un-ion a-rise, That hatred is
It fast-ens our souls in such ties That na-ture and
con-quer'd by love?
time can't re-move.
It can-not in E-den be found Nor
yet in a par-a-dise lost; It grows on Im-
man-u-el's ground, And Je-sus' dear blood it did cost.

My friends are so precious to me,
Our hearts all united in love;
Where Jesus is gone we shall be,
In yonder blest mansions above.
O! why then so loath for to part,
Since we shall ere long meet again,
Engraved on Immanuel's heart,
At distance we cannot remain.

And when we shall see that bright day,
And join with the angels above,
Leaving these vile bodies of clay,
United with Jesus in love.
With Jesus we ever shall reign,
And all his bright glories shall see,
Singing hallelujah, Amen,
Amen, even so let it be.

This is probably a homespun text. Its tune is called a "popular old melody." I find it almost identical with a 'Kilrush Air' in Petrie, No. 167, and with a close variant of the latter, Petrie, No. 283. Other related tunes are 'Tweed Side', SMM, p. 9; 'Inkle and Yarico', *The English Repository*, p. 226; 'O I'm So Happy', 'Faithful Soldier', and 'Sawyer's Exit' in this collection.

No. 54

SEPARATION, UHH 27

Heptatonic aeolian, mode 2 A+b (I II 3 IV V 6 7)

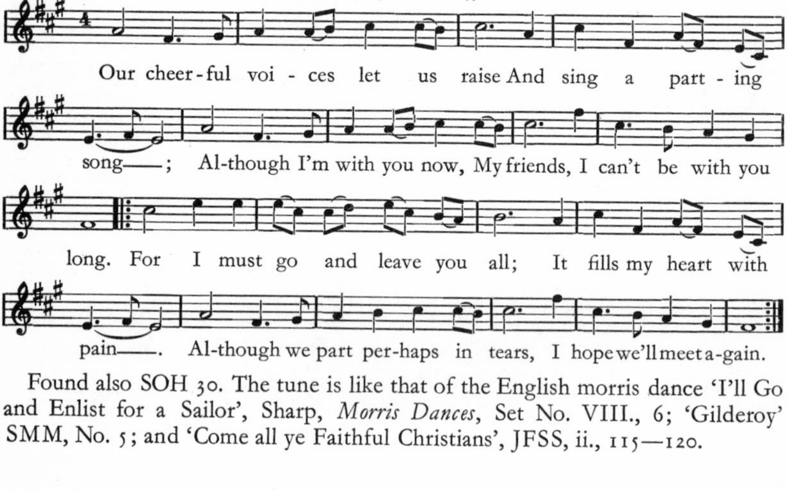
Our cheer-ful voi - ces let us raise And sing a part - ing song——; Al-though I'm with you now, My friends, I can't be with you long. For I must go and leave you all; It fills my heart with pain——. Al-though we part per-haps in tears, I hope we'll meet a-gain.

Found also SOH 30. The tune is like that of the English morris dance 'I'll Go and Enlist for a Sailor', Sharp, *Morris Dances*, Set No. VIII., 6; 'Gilderoy' SMM, No. 5; and 'Come all ye Faithful Christians', JFSS, ii., 115—120.

No. 55

VESPER, *Baptist Hymnal*, No. 65

Hexatonic, mode 3 A (I II III — V VI VII)

The day is past and gone, the evening shades ap-pear; O
may we all re - mem - ber well, the night of death is near.

We lay our garments by, upon our beds to rest;
So death will soon disrobe us all of what we here possess.
Lord, keep us safe this night, secure from all our fears;
May angels guard us while we sleep, till morning light appears.

Miss Gilchrist compares this tune with 'Sprig of Thyme'. See JFSS, viii., 70. Lowell Mason calls it an "Old American Tune" in using if in his *Harp of the South*, p. 123.

No. 56

MISSIONARY'S FAREWELL, OL 333

Hexatonic, mode 3 A (I II III — V VI VII)

Yes, my na - tive land, I love thee; All thy scenes I love them well;
Friends, con-nec-tions, hap - py coun-try, Can I bid you all fare-well!
Can I leave you, can I leave you, Far in heath-en lands to dwell?
Can I leave you, can I leave you, Far in heath-en lands to dwell?

Home, thy joys are passing lovely,
Joys no stranger heart can tell;
Happy home! indeed I love thee;
Can I, can I say, "Farewell!"
Can I leave thee, *etc.*

Scenes of sacred peace and pleasure,
Holy days and Sabbath bell —
Richest, brightest, sweetest treasure —
Can I say a last farewell?
Can I leave you, *etc.*

The words are ascribed to "Rev. Samuel F. Smith, Baptist, Boston, Mass." The tune was "learned [by William Hauser, compiler, of the *Olive Leaf*] in Burke Co, Ga., 1841."

No. 57
KEDRON, SOH 3

Heptatonic aeolian, mode 2 A+b (I II 3 IV V 6 7)

The tune is attributed in the southern books to "Dare". Found also GCM 165, OSH 48, SOC 175, HOC 45, WP 16. The tune is of a type which was widely sung to texts of the extremely solemn sort. The introduction of slight variation in the expression of this melodic idea led to tunes with other titles and various composers (?). I have called this tune family the 'Kedron' group. Its members are 'Distress', OSH 50; 'Solemnity', MOH 40; 'Salem', UH 22; 'French Broad' in this collection; 'Child of Grace', KNH 74; and 'Messiah', VH 30. Secular songs showing the same general melodic trend are 'McAfee's Confession', Sharp, ii., 16, and Cox, p. 525; 'A Brisk Young Sailor', Sharp, *One Hundred English Folksongs*, No. 94; 'Lord Bateman', ibid., No. 6; and 'Samuel Young', Sharp, ii., 271.

No. 58
ALL IS WELL, OSH 122

Hexatonic (6th missing, cannot be classified but obviously ionian) (I II III IV V—VII)

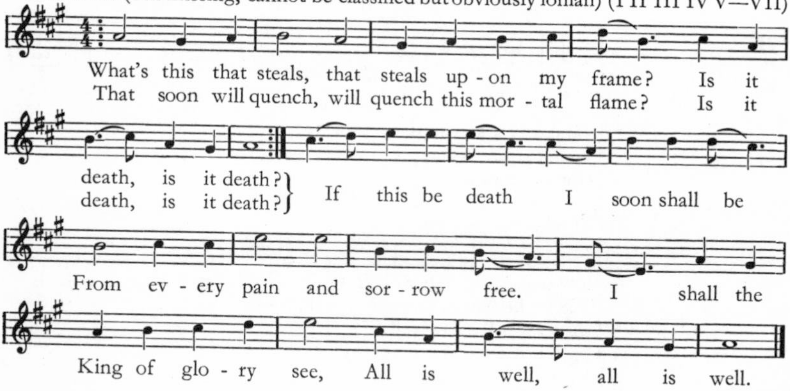

Weep not, my friends, weep not for me,
All is well, all is well!
My sins forgiv'n, forgiv'n, and I am free,
All is well, all is well!
There's not a cloud that doth arise,
To hide my Jesus from my eyes.
I soon shall mount the upper skies,
All is well, all is well!

Tune, tune your harps, your harps ye saints on high,
All is well, all is well!
I too will strike my harp with equal joy,
All is well, all is well!
Bright angels are from glory come,
They're round my bed, they're in my room,
They wait to waft my spirit home,
All is well, all is well.

As to sources we quote the 1911 editor of the *Original Sacred Harp.* After attributing tune and words to J. T. White, nephew of B. F. White, compiler of the 1844 *Sacred Harp*, the editor states: "The tune had been published before it was printed in the [1844] *Sacred Harp.*" A negro version of the song was recently recorded in Texas and appears in the *Publications of the Texas Folk-Lore Society*, vii., 109.

No. 59

FAITHFUL SOLDIER, SOH (1835) 122

Hexatonic, mode 1 A (I II III IV V VI —)

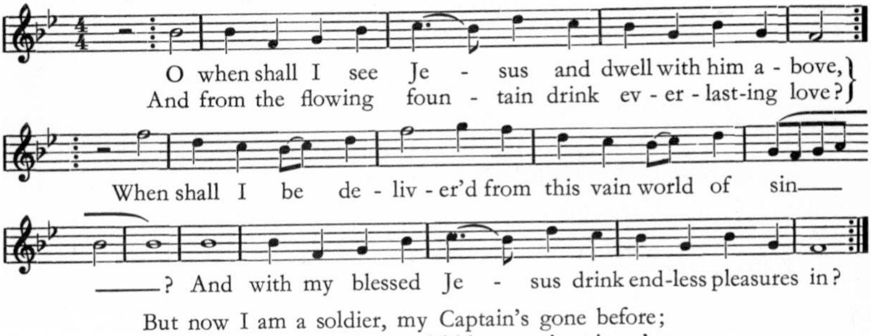
O when shall I see Je - sus and dwell with him a - bove,
And from the flowing foun - tain drink ev - er - last-ing love?
When shall I be de - liv - er'd from this vain world of sin——
——? And with my blessed Je - sus drink end-less pleasures in?

But now I am a soldier, my Captain's gone before;
He's given me my orders and bids me ne'er give o'er;
His promises are faithful — a righteous crown he'll give,
And all his valiant soldiers eternally shall live.

Through grace I am determined to conquer tho' I die,
And then away to Jesus on wings of love I'll fly.
Farewell to sin and sorrow, I bid them both adieu,
And O, my friends, prove faithful, and on your way pursue.

Whene'er you meet with troubles and trials on your way,
Then cast your cares on Jesus and don't forget to pray.
Gird on the gospel armor of faith and hope and love,
And when the combat's ended He'll carry you above.

O do not be discouraged for Jesus is your friend,
And if you lack for knowledge, he'll not refuse to lend.
Neither will he upbraid you, though often you request,
He'll give you grace to conquer and take you home to rest.

And when the last loud trumpet shall rend the vaulted skies,
And bid th' entombed millions from their cold beds arise;
Our ransomed dust, reviv-ed, bright beauties shall put on,
And soar to the blest mansions where our Redeemer's gone.

Our eyes shall then with rapture, the Savior's face behold;
Our feet, no more diverted, shall walk the streets of gold.
Our ears shall hear with transport the hosts celestial sing;
Our tongues shall chant the glories of our immortal King.

William Walker, compiler of the SOH, claims the tune. A recent variant of it, orally transmitted, is 'O I Am So Happy', in this collection. Another variant here is 'Stephens'. All these tunes seem to derive from an old one recorded in Kilrush, Ireland, and found in the Petrie collection in two variants, Nos. 167 and 283. Compare also the similar 'Hallelujah' tune family with its members listed under the tune by that title in this collection.

The text is by John Leland and was uniquely popular — as sung in its purity or associated with various refrains and revival choruses — during the early part of the nineteenth century. The negroes have borrowed freely from this poem in making the texts for their spirituals, especially from the fourth and fifth stanzas. Cf. WS 217ff. and 286.

No. 60

GREEN FIELDS, SOH 71

Hexatonic, mode 3 b (I II III IV V VI —)

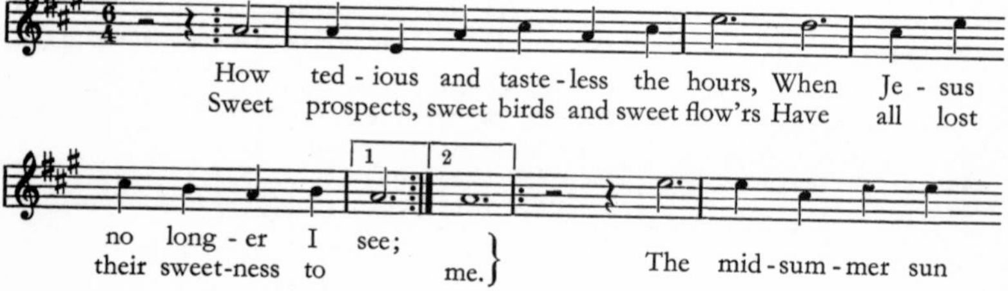

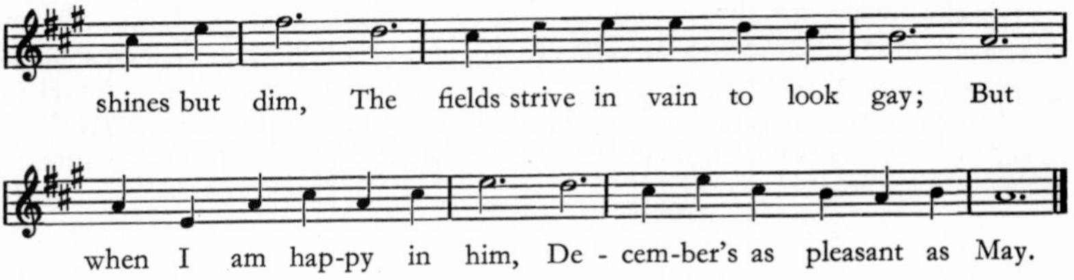
shines but dim, The fields strive in vain to look gay; But
when I am hap-py in him, De - cem-ber's as pleasant as May.

His name yields the richest perfume,
And sweeter than music his voice;
His presence disperses my gloom,
And makes all within me rejoice.
I should, were he always thus nigh,
Have nothing to wish or to fear;
No mortal so happy as I,
My summer would last all the year.

Content with beholding his face,
My all to his pleasure resigned,
No changes of seasons or place,
Would make any change in my mind.
While blessed with a sense of his love,
A palace a toy would appear;
And prisons would palaces prove,
If Jesus would dwell with me there.

The tune is to be found in S. Baring-Gould's *Songs of the West*, No. 100, as recorded before 1890 from the singing of an old man in Lamerton, England. We are informed by the editor of the collection that the song, 'Both Sexes Give Ear to My Fancy' which used this tune, had been very popular with aged people residing in the North of England, but that it was then "long out of print and handed down traditionally". The earliest form of the tune seems to have been 'Es nehme zehn-tausend Ducaten' in Johann Sebastian Bach's cantata *Mer hahn en neue Oberkeet* (Cf. Bach-Gesellschaft, Vol. 29, p. 195). The earliest printed form of the Bach tune in England, according to Baring-Gould, was in *The Tragedy of Tragedies*, or *Tom Thumb*, 1734, as the setting of the song 'In Hurry Posthaste for a License'. The earliest occurrence of the tune with the 'Both Sexes' text was in *The Lady's Evening Book of Pleasure*, about 1740. The air is also found in *Vocal Music, or the Songster's Companion*, second edition, 1782, to the song entitled 'Farewell, Ye Green Fields and Sweet Groves'. This was probably the song whose tune was taken over bodily and whose words were parodied to make the above song 'Green Fields'. The author of the parody text was sometimes given in the fasola books as John Newton. The incidence of the song in southern song books of the first half of the nineteenth century (MOH 52, GCM 144, UH 112, KNH 80, OSH 127, HH 345, SOC 30, CM 24, HOC 16, TZ 237, SKH 18, PB 312, GOS 303, etc.) indicates its one-time wide popularity also on this continent.

No. 61

SAINTS' RAPTURE, REV 17

Heptatonic ionian, mode 3 A + b (I II III IV V VI VII)

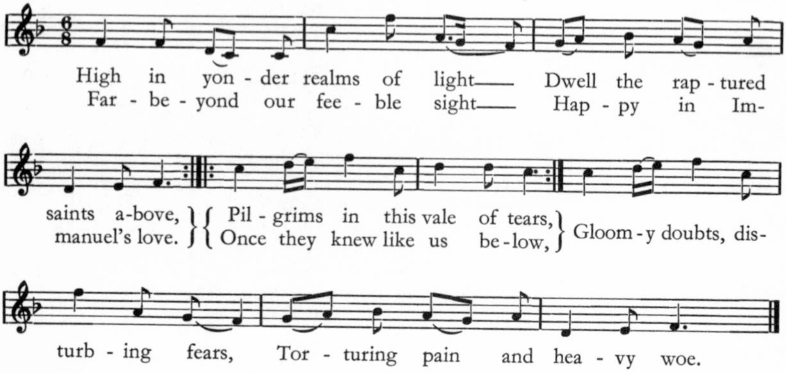
High in yon - der realms of light—— Dwell the rap - tured
Far - be - yond our fee - ble sight—— Hap - py in Im-
saints a-bove,
manuel's love.
Pil - grims in this vale of tears,
Once they knew like us be - low,
Gloom - y doubts, dis-
turb - ing fears, Tor - turing pain and hea - vy woe.

Days of weeping now are o'er,
Past those scenes of toil and pain;
They will feel distress no more,
Never, never weep again.
'Mid the chorus of the skies;
'Mid angelic choirs above;
They now join the songs that rise,
Songs of praise to Jesus' love.

There are two more stanzas of the text in the *Revivalist*. The tune and the text are obviously a parody on 'Reuben, Reuben, I've Been Thinking'.

No. 62

ANIMATION, SOH (1835) 85

Hexatonic, mode 2 A (I II 3 IV V — 7)

Droop-ing souls, no long - er grieve —, Heav - en is pro - pi-
tious; If in Christ you do be - lieve —, You will find him
prec - ious. Je - sus now is pas - sing by, Calls the mourn - er
to— him, Brings sal - va - tion from on high; Now look up and see him.

For the complete text see 'Lebanon' in this collection. This song was taken into the *Southern Harmony* from the *Dover Selection*. The tune is related to 'Maid Freed From the Gallows', Thomas, p. 164, and to the old Irish 'Tell Me Dear Eveleen', in *A Select Collection of Original Irish Airs*, No. 6, composed by Beethoven.

No. 63

INVITATION, OL 247

Hexatonic, mode 3 A (I II III — V VI VII)

Hark, I hear the— harps e - ter - nal Ring-ing on
As I near those swol - len wa - ters With their deep
the far - ther shore,
and sol - emn roar.
Hal - le - lu - jah—, hal - le - lu-
jah, Hal - le - lu - jah—, praise the Lamb; Hal - le - lu-
jah—, hal - le - lu - jah, Glor - y to the GREAT I AM!

And my soul, tho' stain'd with sorrow,
Fading as the light of day,
Passes swiftly o'er those waters,
To the city far away.
Hallelujah *etc.*

Souls have cross'd before me, saintly,
To that land of perfect rest;
And I hear them singing faintly,
In the mansions of the blest.
Hallelujah *etc.*

The compiler of the *Olive Leaf* found this song, as he tells us, in F. R. Warren's *Dream Music*. The tune shows unmistakable family relationships, especially in the chorus, to 'Nettleton' in this collection.

No. 64

HARK MY SOUL, CHH 224

Hexatonic, mode 3 b (I II III IV V VI —)

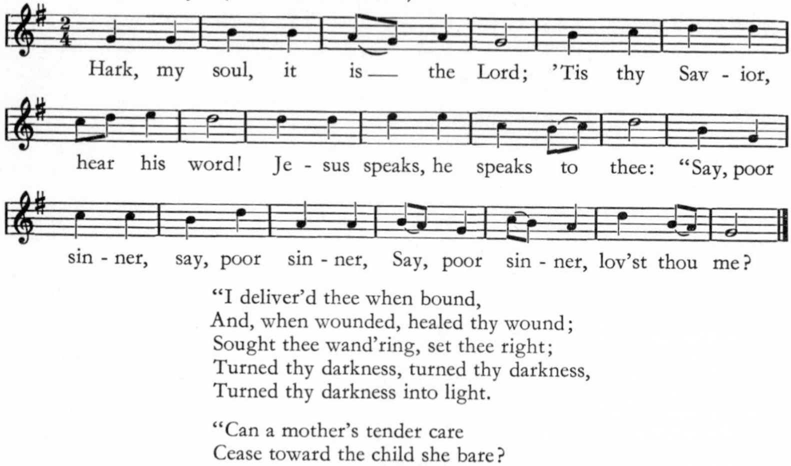
Hark, my soul, it is — the Lord; 'Tis thy Sav - ior,
hear his word! Je - sus speaks, he speaks to thee: "Say, poor
sin - ner, say, poor sin - ner, Say, poor sin - ner, lov'st thou me?

"I deliver'd thee when bound,
And, when wounded, healed thy wound;
Sought thee wand'ring, set thee right;
Turned thy darkness, turned thy darkness,
Turned thy darkness into light.

"Can a mother's tender care
Cease toward the child she bare?
Yes, she may forgetful be,
Yet will I re-, yet will I re-,
Yet will I remember thee.

The song was "Arranged by James Christopher, of Spartansburg, S. C.", according to the *Christian Harmony*. Richardson has a variant of this tune used with a text which is a recent mountain eulogy on the whiskey of the hills under the title 'Moonshine', see *American Mountain Songs*, page 94. A hint of the antiquity of this tune form is given by the 'Ass's Sequence' or 'Orientis partibus' from the beginning of the thirteenth century, a tune which was apparently cast in the folk-manner of that age.

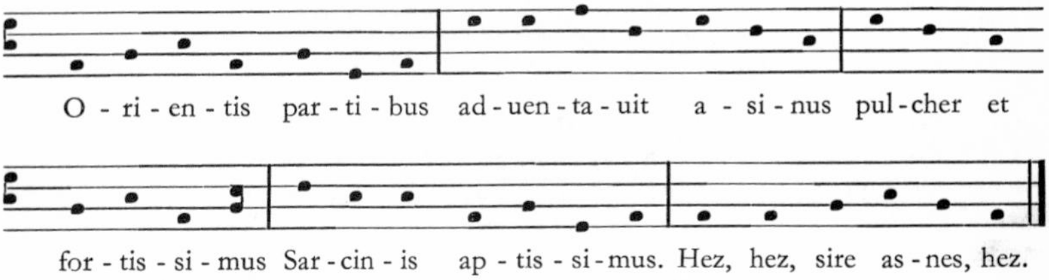
O - ri - en - tis par - ti - bus ad - uen - ta - uit a - si - nus pul - cher et
for - tis - si - mus Sar - cin - is ap - tis - si - mus. Hez, hez, sire as - nes, hez.

Its modern representative is:

See *Hymns Ancient and Modern*, No. 413.

No. 65

FROZEN HEART, OSH 93

Hexatonic, mode 3 A (I II III — V VI VII)

6
4
Lord, shed a beam of heav'n - ly day To melt this
stub-born stone a - way; And thaw, with rays of love di - vine, This
heart, this fro - zen heart of mine; This heart, this fro - zen
heart of mine; This heart, this fro - zen heart of mine.

The rocks can rend; the earth can quake;
The seas can roar; the mountains shake;
Of feeling, all things show some sign,
But this unfeeling heart of mine.

To hear the sorrows thou hast felt,
Dear Lord, an adamant would melt!
But I can read each moving line,
And nothing move this heart of mine.

The text is attributed, in the *Sacred Harp* of 1844, to Joseph Hart and it is dated 1759. The tune is ascribed to E. J. King. The melodic trend of the refrain brings to mind 'The Campbells are Coming'.

No. 66

LEBANON, KNH 88

Hexatonic, mode 5 A (I — 3 IV V 6 7)

Mourning souls, no long - er grieve, Hea - ven is pro - pit - ious;
If on Christ you do be - lieve, You shall find him prec-ious.
Je - sus now is pass - ing by, Calls the mourn - er to—— him;
He hath died for you and I, Now look up and view him.

He has pardons, full and free,
Drooping souls to gladden;
Still he cries: "Come unto me,
Weary, heavy-laden."
Tho' your sins, like mountains high,
Rise and reach to heaven,
Soon as you on him rely
All will be forgiven.

Precious is the Savior's name,
All his saints adore him;
He to save the dying came —
Prostrate bow before him;
Wand'ring sinners, now return;
Contrite souls, believe him!
Jesus calls you — cease to mourn;
Worship him — receive him!

From his hands, his feet, his side, runs the healing lotion;
See the consolating tide, boundless as the ocean!
See the healing waters move for the sick and dying!
Now resolve to gain his love, or to perish trying.

Grace's store is always free, drooping souls to gladden;
Jesus calls: "Come unto me — weary, heavy laden."
Though your sins like mountains high, rise and reach to heaven,
Soon as you on him rely, all shall be forgiven.

Now methinks I hear one say: "I will go and prove him;
If he takes my sins away, surely I shall love him.
Yes, I see the Father smile, now I lose my burden;
All is grace, for I am vile, yet he seals my pardon."

This text is found HH 413, and also COH 122.

No. 67

SOLDIER'S RETURN, SOH 36

Heptatonic ionian, mode 3 A+b (I II III IV V VI VII)

Bright scenes of glo - ry strike my sense, And all my pas - sions
E - ter - nal beauties round me shine, In - fus - ing warm - est
cap - ture;
rap - ture.
I live in pleasures deep and full, In
swel - ling waves of glo - ry. I feel my Sav - ior
in my soul And groan to tell the sto - ry. -ry.
1
2

Further stanzas are given under 'Mecklinburg'. The tune was borrowed from 'When the Wild War's Deadly Blast', SMM, No. 131. See also for melodic similarities 'The Mill Mill O', SMM, No. 157; and 'Blue-Eyed Stranger', Sharp, *The Morris Book*, Part 1, p. 91. See Greig-Keith, *Last Leaves*, p. 181, for the tune's wide use in the British Isles during the eighteenth century.

No. 68

CHRISTIAN SOLDIER, GOS 207

Heptatonic ionian, mode 3 A+b (I II III IV V VI VII)

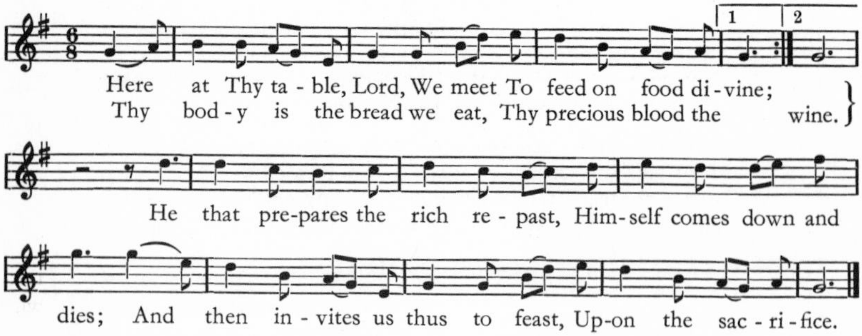
1
2
Here at Thy ta - ble, Lord, We meet To feed on food di - vine;
Thy bod - y is the bread we eat, Thy precious blood the wine.
He that pre-pares the rich re - past, Him-self comes down and
dies; And then in - vites us thus to feast, Up-on the sac - ri - fice.

The bitter torments he endured upon the shameful cross,
For us his welcome guests procured these heart-reviving joys.
His body torn with rudest hands becomes the finest bread,
And with the blessings he commands, our noblest hopes are fed.

His blood that from each opening vein in purple torrents ran
Hath filled this cup with generous wine, that cheers both God and man.
Sure there was never love so free, dear Savior, so divine;
Well thou may'st claim that heart of mine, which owes so much to thine.

The text is one of those which rationalize religious rites; in this case, that of the communion. The tune is credited to Freeman Price. Its second part reminds of 'The Merry, Merry Milkmaids', Sharp, *Country Dances*, Set No. 5.

No. 69

TRIBULATION, MOH 46

Hexatonic, mode 2 A (I II 3 IV V — 7)

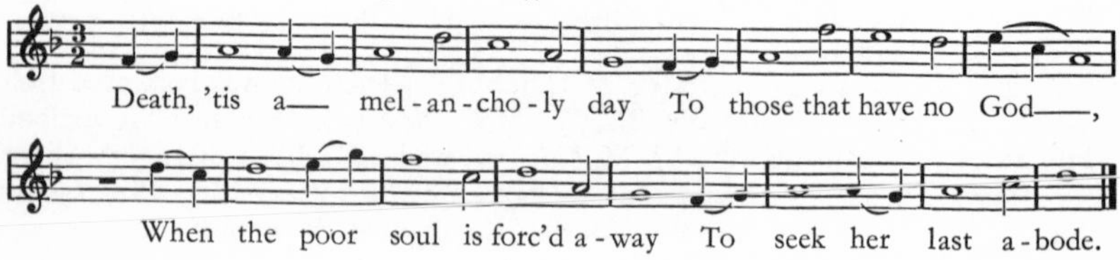
Death, 'tis a— mel - an - cho - ly day To those that have no God—,
When the poor soul is forc'd a - way To seek her last a - bode.

In vain to heaven she lifts her eyes;
But guilt, a heavy chain,
Still drags her downard from the skies
To darkness, fire and pain.

Awake and mourn, ye heirs of hell,
Let stubborn sinners fear;
You must be driv'n from earth and dwell
Alone forewer there.

See how the pit gapes wide for you,
And flashes in your face;
And thou, my soul, look downward too,
And sing recov'ring grace.

The text has been attributed to Watts. Recent hymnals have been purged of this doleful ditty and of all other songs which make hellfire too realistic. The tune was attributed to Chapin in some books and to Davisson in others. Davisson claims it in his *Kentucky Harmony* (1815). It is practically identical with 'Little Musgrave and Lady Barnard', Sharp, i., 182, a tune which Sharp heard in Greenwood, Albemarle County, Virginia, Davisson's own territory and near where he is buried. An early variant which is practically identical with both the Sharp and the Davisson tunes is in Motherwell, Supplement, No. 30, associated with 'The Bonnie Mermaid' text. Found also, KYH 43, SOH 119, UH 37, KNH 38, OSH 29, HH 55.

No. 70

VOLUNTEERS, CHH 110

Hexatonic, mode 3b (I II III IV V VI —)

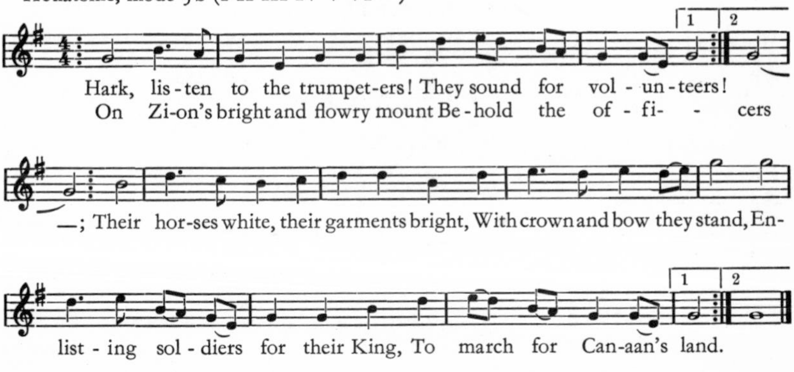
1
2
Hark, lis-ten to the trumpet-ers! They sound for vol - un-teers!
On Zi-on's bright and flowry mount Be-hold the of - fi- - cers
—; Their hor-ses white, their garments bright, With crown and bow they stand, En-
1
2
list - ing sol - diers for their King, To march for Can-aan's land.

It sets my heart all in a flame; a soldier I will be;
I will enlist, gird on my arms and fight for liberty.
They want no cowards in their band (They will their colours fly),
But call for valiant hearted men, who're not afraid to die.

The armies now are on parade, how martial they appear!
All armed and dressed in uniform, they look like men of war;
They follow their great General, the great Eternal Lamb,
His garments stained with his own blood, King Jesus, is his name.

The trumpet sounds, the armies shout, and drive the hosts of hell;
How dreadful is our God in arms! The great Immanuel!
Sinners, enlist with Jesus Christ, th' eternal Son of God,
And march with us to Canaan's land, beyond the swelling flood.

There is a green and flow'ry field, where fruits immortal grow;
There, clothed in white, the angels bright, our great Redeemer know.
We'll shout and sing forever more in that eternal world;
But Satan and his armies too, shall down to hell be hurled.

Hold up your heads, ye soldiers bold, redemption's drawing nigh,
We soon shall hear the trumpet sound; 'Twill shake both earth and sky;
In fiery chariots then we'll fly, and leave the world on fire,
And meet around the starry throne to tune th' immortal lyre.

The tune is attributed to Wm. Bradshaw. Found also HH 159 and SWP 90. Dett, p. 180, and SOH 301, have the same words but different tunes.

No. 71

BACKSLIDER, REV 208

Pentatonic, mode 3 (I II III — V VI —)

How can I vent my grief? My com - for - ter is fled! By
day I sigh with - out re - lief And groan up - on my bed.

How little did I think when first I did begin
To join a little with the world it was so great a sin.

I thought I might conform, nor singular appear,
Converse and dress as others did, but now I feel the snare.

My confidence is gone, I find no words to say,
Barren and lifeless is my soul when I attempt to pray.

The tune is similar to those used with several text variants of 'The Wife of Usher's Well'. Sharp, i., 150ff. The oldest American song book record of the 'Backslider' tune is in Ingalls' *Christian Harmony* of 1805, p. 55, where it is entitled 'The General Doom' and begins:

Behold! with awful pomp,
The Judge prepares to come;
Th'archangel sounds the awful trump
And wakes the general doom.

No. 72

GOOD OLD WAY (B), OL 8

Hexatonic, mode 2 A (I II 3 IV V — 7)

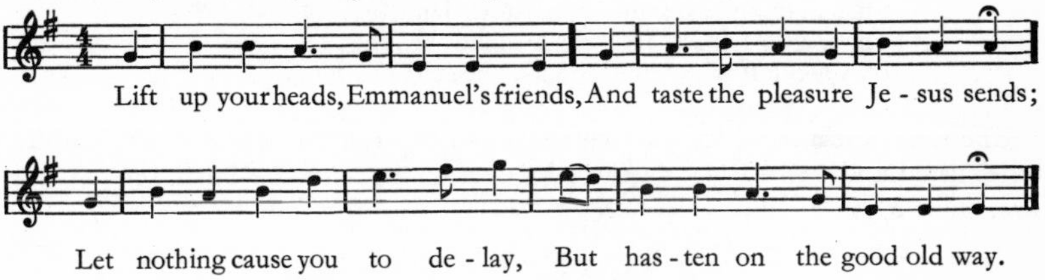
Lift up your heads, Emmanuel's friends, And taste the pleasure Je - sus sends;
Let nothing cause you to de - lay, But has - ten on the good old way.

Our conflicts here, tho' great they be,
Shall not prevent our victory,
If we but watch, and strive, and pray!
Like soldiers in the good old way.

O good old way, how sweet thou art!
May none of us from thee depart;
But may our actions always say
We're marching in the good old way!

"A tune and song [words] of the Granade period", William Hauser, compiler of the *Olive Leaf* suggests. John Adam Granade was an evangelist of the "wild" sort who lived 1775 to 1806. A negro tune which combines elements of the above and 'I Went Down to the Valley', in this collection, is in *Slave Songs*, No. 104.

No. 73

REST IN HEAVEN, OL 358

Hexatonic, mode 2 A minorized (I II 3 IV V — 7 [VII])

My rest is in hea-ven, my rest is not here, Then why should I
mur-mur at tri-als se-vere. Be tran-quil, my spi-rit, the
worst that can come But short-ens thy journey and hast-ens thee home.

Let trouble and danger my progress oppose;
They'll only make heaven more bright at the close;
Come joy, then, or sorrow — whate'er may befall —
One moment in glory will make up for all.

A scrip on my back, and a staff in my hand,
I march on in haste thro' an enemy's land;
The road may be rough, but it cannot be long;
I'll smooth it with hope, and I'll cheer it with song.

The tune is related to 'Begone Unbelief', in this collection, and to the worldly tunes listed under that song. Negro adoptions of the tune are Marsh, pp. 144 and 173, and SS 33.

No. 74

TO DIE NO MORE, GOS 363

Pentatonic, mode 3 (I II III — V VI —)

My heav'nly home is bright and fair, No pain nor death can en-ter
Chorus I'm go-ing home to Christ a-bove, I'm go-ing to the Christian's
D.C. for Chorus
there; Its glitt'ring tow'rs the sun out-shine, I hope that mansion shall be mine.
rest, To die no more to, die no more, I'm go-ing home to die no more.

My Father's house is built on high,
Far, far above the starry sky;
When from this earthly prison free,
I hope that mansion mine shall be.
Chorus

I envy not the rich and great,
Their pomp of wealth and pride of state;
My Father is a richer King,
That heav'nly mansion still I sing.
Chorus

The tune is identical with one used with the worldly ballad 'Three Ravens', see Davis 562.

No. 75
COLUMBUS, OSH 67

Pentatonic, mode 2 (I — 3 IV V — 7)

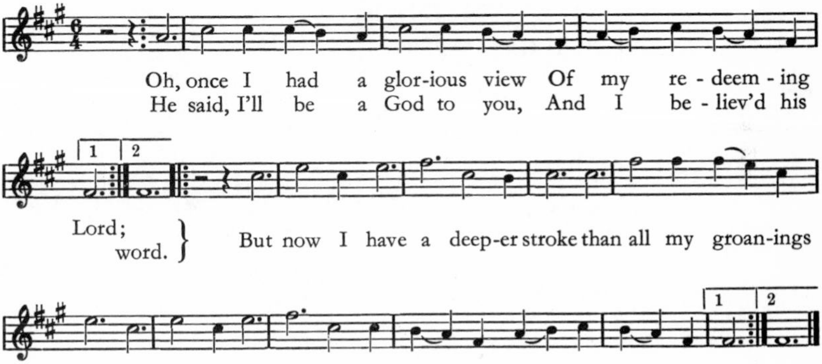
Oh, once I had a glor-ious view Of my re - deem - ing
He said, I'll be a God to you, And I be - liev'd his
Lord;
word.
But now I have a deep-er stroke than all my groan-ings
are; My God has me of late for - sook, He's gone I know not where.

Oh, what immortal joys I felt
On that celestial day,
When my hard heart began to melt,
By love dissolved away!
But my complaint is bitter now,
For all my joys are gone;
I've strayed! I'm left! I know not how;
The light's from me withdrawn.

Once I could joy the saints to meet,
To me they were most dear;
I then could stoop to wash their feet,
And shed a joyful tear;
But now I meet them as the rest,
And with them joyless stay;
My conversation's spiritless,
Or else I've nought to say.

The words appeared in *Mercer's Cluster*, a Georgia hymn and spiritual-song collection of the 1820's. The earliest appearance of the tune seems to have been in the *Southern Harmony* (1835). Found also in HH 128, UH 57, KNH 42, HOC 37, SOC 109, GOS 380, PB 343. The tune is a variant of 'Antioch', in this collection.

For negro tune derivatives see *White Spirituals*, 259. Among the tunes in secular environment, 'Virginian Lover', Sharp, ii., 149, tune B, shows closest relationship to the above. See also 'Flat River Girl', Rickaby, p. 6; and 'Driving Saw Logs on the Plover', Rickaby, p. 89.

No. 76

YONGST, BS 203

Hexatonic, mode 3 b (I II III IV V VI —)

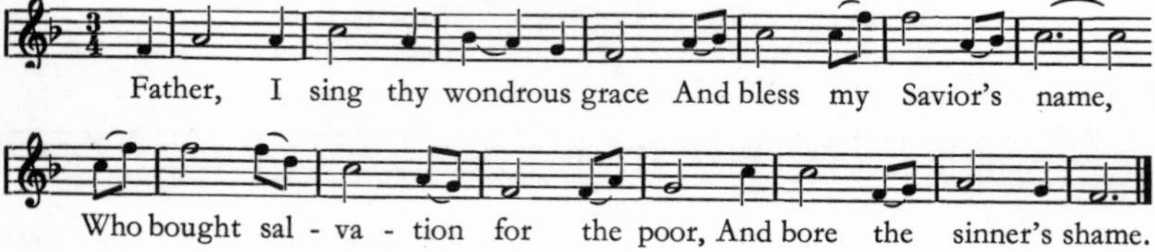
Father, I sing thy wondrous grace And bless my Savior's name,
Who bought sal - va - tion for the poor, And bore the sinner's shame.

His deep distress has raised us high;
His duty and his zeal
Fulfilled the law which mortals broke,
And finished all thy will.

Zion is thine, most holy God;
Thy Son shall bless her gates;
And glory, purchased by his blood,
For thine own Israel waits.

The tune is attributed to W. B. Gillham. It is member of the 'Lord Lovel' group mentioned in the Introduction, page 14. Noteworthy in this connection is a variant of the above tune as sung by a negro in North Carolina; see Scarbrough, p. 55. Further tunes belonging to the 'Lord Lovel' group are listed under 'Dulcimer' in this collection.

No. 77

DOWN IN THE GARDEN, REV 108

Heptatonic ionian, mode 3 A+b (I II III IV V VI VII)

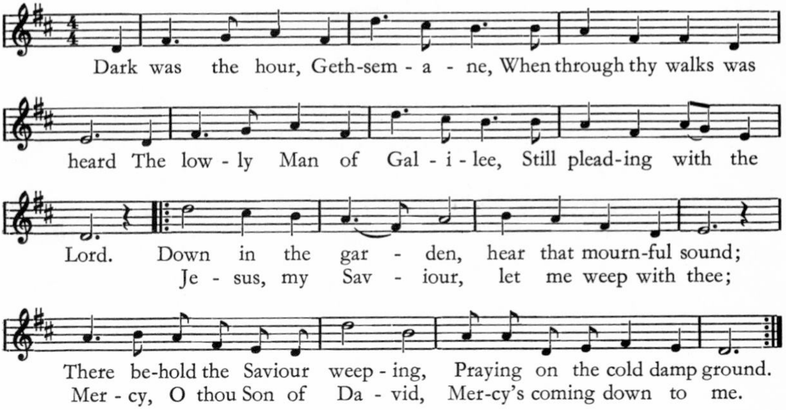
Dark was the hour, Geth-sem - a - ne, When through thy walks was
heard The low - ly Man of Gal - i - lee, Still plead-ing with the
Lord. Down in the gar - den, hear that mourn-ful sound;
Je - sus, my Sav - iour, let me weep with thee;
There be-hold the Saviour weep - ing, Praying on the cold damp ground.
Mer - cy, O thou Son of Da - vid, Mer-cy's coming down to me.

Alone in sorrow see him bow,
As all our griefs he bears;
Not words may tell his anguish now,
But sweat and blood and tears.
Down in the garden *etc.*

Four more stanzas of the text are given in the *Revivalist*. The last part of the tune and the whole text are obvious parodies of the Foster song 'Massa's in the Cold, Cold Ground'. For possible folk sources of Foster's song, see my article "Stephen Foster's Debt to American Folk-Song", *The Musical Quarterly*, xxii (1936), No. 2, p. 159.

No. 78

ALBION, MOH 49

Pentachordal, cannot be classified (I II III IV V — —)

Come, ye that love the Lord, And let your love be known; Join in a song of
sweet — ac-cord And thus sur-round the throne, And thus sur-round the throne.

The sorrows of the mind
Be banished from this place;
Religion never was designed
To make our pleasures less,
To make our pleasures less.

Let those refuse to sing,
Who never knew our God;
But fav'rites of the heav'nly King
May speak their joys abroad,
May speak their joys abroad.

The words are by Watts. The tune is ascribed to R(obert) Boyd. It is found also, KYH 18, GCM 171, SOH 23, UH 21, GOS 126, KNH 51, OSH 52, HH 201, HOC 12. It sounds like one of the old psalm tunes.

No. 79

DUNLAP'S CREEK, SOH 276

Hexatonic, mode 3 A (I II III — V VI VII)

My God, My Por - tion, and my Love, My ev - er - last - ing all,
I've none but thee in heav'n a - bove, Or on this earth - ly ball.

What empty things are all the skies,
And this inferior clod!
There's nothing here deserves my joys,
There's nothing like my God.

In vain the bright, the burning sun
Scatters his feeble light;
'Tis thy sweet beams create my noon;
If thou withdraw, 'tis night.

The words are Watts'. The tune is given as by F(reeman) Lewis. Found also, GCM 63, SOC 238, WP 44, TZ 77, GOS 650, SKH 83, CM 120, *Baptist Hymn and Tune Book* (1857), p. 106, where it is called a 'Western Melody'. It is practically the same as 'Wife of Usher's Well', Sharp, i., 160, Q. See Introduction, page 14, for mention of the 'Lord Lovel' type of tune to which 'Dunlaps' Creek' belongs.

No. 80

SINNER'S INVITATION, OL 211

Pentatonic, mode 3 (I II III — V VI —)

Sin - ner go, will you go To the high - lands of hea - ven,
Where the storms nev - er blow And the long summer's giv - en,
Where the bright bloom-ing flow'rs Are their o - dors e - mit - ting
And the leaves of the bow'rs In the bree - zes are flit - ting.

Where the rich golden fruit
Is in bright clusters pending,
And the deep laden boughs
Of life's fair tree are bending;
And where life's crystal stream
Is unceasingly flowing,
And the verdure is green,
And eternally growing.

The tune and words which are parodied here are those of the 'Braes o' Balquhidder'. The text is attributed, by the compiler of the *Olive Leaf*, to "Rev. Wm. McDonald, I guess". The Scotch song begins:

> Will you go, lassie, go to the braes o'Balquhidder,
> Where the blackberries grow in the bonnie blooming heather.

See Gilchrist, JFSS, viii., 77. Another variant of the 'Braes o' Balquhidder' tune in this collection is 'Lone Pilgrim'. Gilchrist traces the Scotch tune back still farther to 'Brochan Buirn', an old Gaelic air. See JFSS, viii., 76. It influenced Stephen Foster in his making of the tune 'Linda Has Departed'. (See my article in *The Musical Quarterly*, vol. xxii, No. 2.)

No. 81
LAND OF REST, OL 117

Pentatonic, mode 3 (I II III — V VI —)

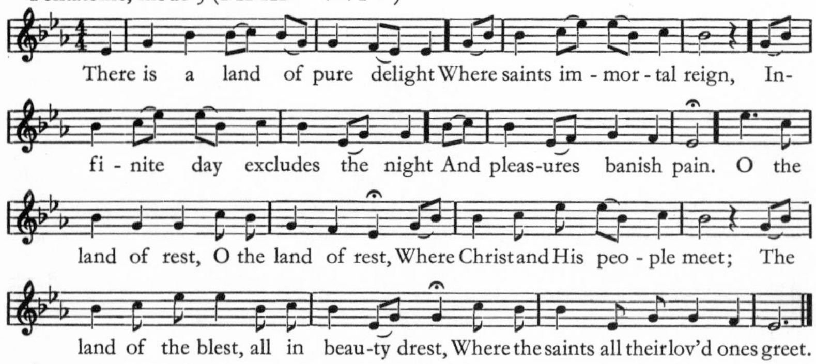

"Inspiration of this tune," says the compiler of the *Olive Leaf*, "caught from a female voice at a distance, at Barbee Hotel, High Point, N. C., June 9th, 1868." The mountain woman must have been singing 'Lord Lovel'; for the tunes of that ballad, as found for example in Davis, p. 574, O; and Sharp, i., 148, are practically the same as 'Land of Rest'. See Introduction, page 14.

No. 82
FLORENCE, OSH 121

Pentatonic, mode 3 (I II III — V VI —)

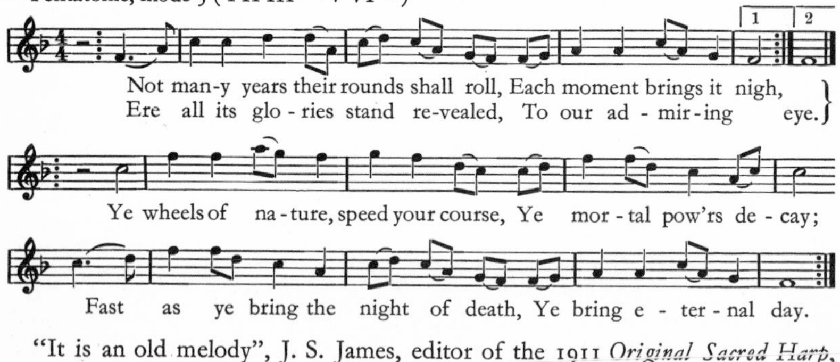

"It is an old melody", J. S. James, editor of the 1911 *Original Sacred Harp*, says. "Prof. T. S. Carter of Georgia took the outlines and arranged it in 1844."

The tune is found also, SOC 77, GOS 178. A variant is GOS 165, entitled 'Lonesome Dove'. Another variant is 'The Weary Soul', OSH 72. I find this tune to be a member of the group which I have called the 'Roll Jordan' family of melodies. See the song with that title in this collection.

No. 83

ALBERT, SOC 153

Heptatonic ionian, mode 3 A+b (I II III IV V VI VII)

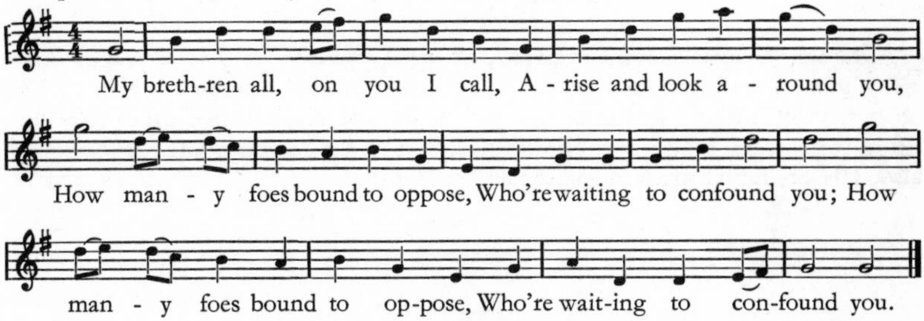
My breth-ren all, on you I call, A - rise and look a - round you,
How man - y foes bound to oppose, Who're waiting to confound you; How
man - y foes bound to op-pose, Who're wait-ing to con-found you.

Credited in the *Social Harp* to E. R. White and dated 1855. The tune is a clear adaptation of 'The Girl I Left Behind Me'.

No. 84

ROYAL PROCLAMATION, SOH 146

Hexatonic, mode 3 A (I II III — V VI VII)

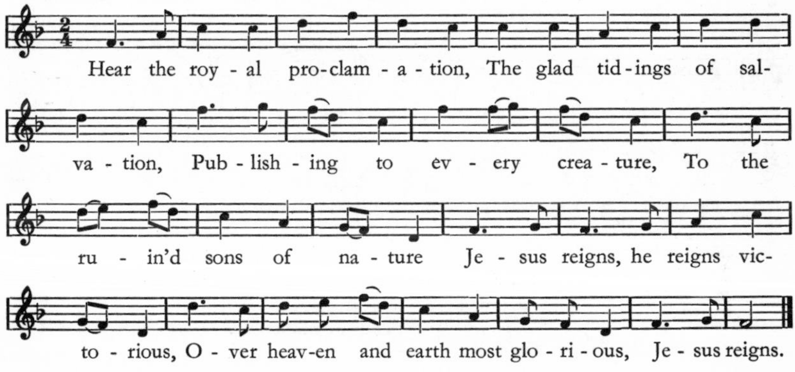
Hear the roy - al pro-clam - a - tion, The glad tid-ings of sal-
va - tion, Pub - lish - ing to ev - ery crea - ture, To the
ru - in'd sons of na - ture Je - sus reigns, he reigns vic-
to - rious, O - ver heav-en and earth most glo - ri - ous, Je - sus reigns.

See the royal banner flying,
Hear the heralds loudly crying:
"Rebel sinners, royal favour
Now is offer'd by the Saviour."
Jesus reigns, *etc.*

Hear, ye sons of wrath and ruin,
Who have wrought your own undoing,
Here is life and free salvation,
Offered to the whole creation.
Jesus reigns, *etc.*

Although Ananias Davisson claims, in the *Supplement to The Kentucky Harmony*, to have made the tune, no subsequent user of the song seems to have looked on him as its author. It has all the earmarks of an eighteenth century fife-and-drum-corps tune which was appropriately set to the religio-martial text. Found also, UH 91, KNH 91, HH 468, SKH 107, GOS 643.

No. 85

CARRY ME HOME or PENICK, OSH 387

Hexatonic, mode 3 b (I II III IV V VI —)

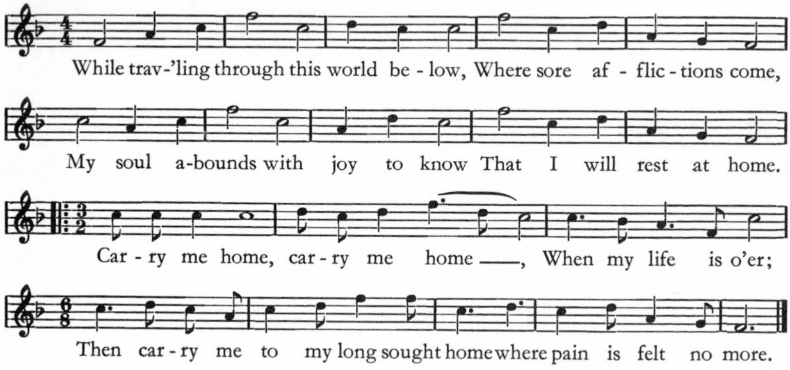
While trav-'ling through this world be - low, Where sore af - flic - tions come,
My soul a-bounds with joy to know That I will rest at home.
Car - ry me home, car - ry me home ——, When my life is o'er;
Then car - ry me to my long sought home where pain is felt no more.

Yes, when my eyes are closed in death,
My body cease to roam,
I'll bid farewell to all below
And meet my friends at home.
Carry me home *etc.*

And then I want these lines to be
Inscribed upon my tomb:
"Here lies the dust of S. R. P.,
His spirit sings at home."
Carry me home *etc.*

The initials in the third stanza belonged to "Professor S. R. Penick, a devoted Christian man, and one who was very fond of music," according to James, 1911 editor of the OSH. But he ascribes tune and words to M. Sikes, a singing-school teacher in Georgia before the Civil War. The tune is a variant of 'Dying Boy' in this collection.

No. 86

JORDAN, SKH 86

Heptatonic ionian, mode 3 A + b (I II III IV V VI VII)

On Jor - dan's storm - y banks I stand And cast a wish - ful eye,
To Canaan's fair and hap - py land Where my pos - ses - sions lie.
O the tran - sport - ing rapt' - rous scene That ri - ses to my
sight, Sweet fields arrayed in liv - ing green And riv - ers of de - light.

There generous fruits that never fail
On trees immortal grow;
There rocks and hills and brooks and vales
With milk and honey flow.

(Four stanzas omitted.)

Soon will the Lord my soul prepare
For joys beyond the skies,
Where never-ceasing pleasures roll,
And praises never die.

The tune belongs to the 'Roll Jordan' group; see Introduction, page 14. See also the song by that title in this collection.

No. 87

ENQUIRER, OSH 74

Hexatonic, mode 4 a (I II — IV V 6 7)

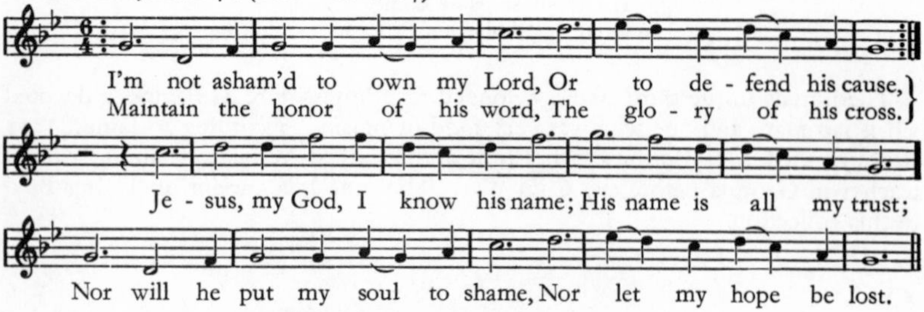
I'm not asham'd to own my Lord, Or to de - fend his cause,
Maintain the honor of his word, The glo - ry of his cross.
Je - sus, my God, I know his name; His name is all my trust;
Nor will he put my soul to shame, Nor let my hope be lost.

Firm as his throne his promise stands,
And he can well secure
What I've committed to his hands,
Till the decisive hour.
Then will he own my worthless name,
Before his Father's face,
And in the new Jerusalem
Appoint my soul a place.

The words are attributed to Isaac Watts; the tune to B. F. White of Georgia, and dated 1844. The tune is a member of the 'Babe of Bethlehem' group. See Introduction, p. 14, and, 'Babe of Bethlehem' in this collection. A secular related tune is 'Lowlands of Holland', Sharp, i., 200. Since the tune has clear dorian implications, its proper key signature is one flat.

No. 88

WONDROUS LOVE, OSH 159

Hexatonic, mode 4 a (I II — IV V 6 7)

What won-drous love is this, O my soul, O my soul; What
won-drous love is this, O my soul; What won-drous love is
this That caused the Lord of bliss To bear the dreadful curse for my
soul, for my soul, To bear the dread-ful curse for my soul.

When I was sinking down, sinking down, sinking down;
When I was sinking down, sinking down;
When I was sinking down beneath God's righteous frown,
Christ laid aside his crown for my soul, for my soul;
Christ laid aside his crown for my soul.

To God and to the Lamb I will sing, I will sing;
To God and to the Lamb I will sing;
To God and to the Lamb who is the great I AM,
While millions join the theme, I will sing, I will sing;
While millions join the theme I will sing.

And when from death I'm free I'll sing on, I'll sing on;
And when from death I'm free I'll sing on.
And when from death I'm free I'll sing and joyful be,
And through eternity I'll sing on, I'll sing on,
And through eternity I'll sing on.

The song is found also, SOH (1854) 252, GOS 436, PB 384, OL 371, and in various tune books of the Baptists up to the present time. The *Southern Harmony* attributes the tune to "Christopher"; *Good Old Songs*, to "J. Christopher"; and the *Hesperian Harp* attributes the words to the "Rev. Alex Means, A. M., M. D., D. D., LL. D.", a Methodist minister of Oxford, Ga. It looks as though tune and words were born together, so beautifully they fit. The stanzaic form is that of the 'Captain Kidd' ballad which has been widely sung and parodied since the beginning of the eighteenth century. A spiritual song tune related to 'Wondrous Love' is 'Villulia' in this collection. I have heard the country folk sing this tune with the dorian raised sixth.

No. 89

SALVATION (A), BS 127

Hexatonic, mode 1 B (I II — IV V VI VII)

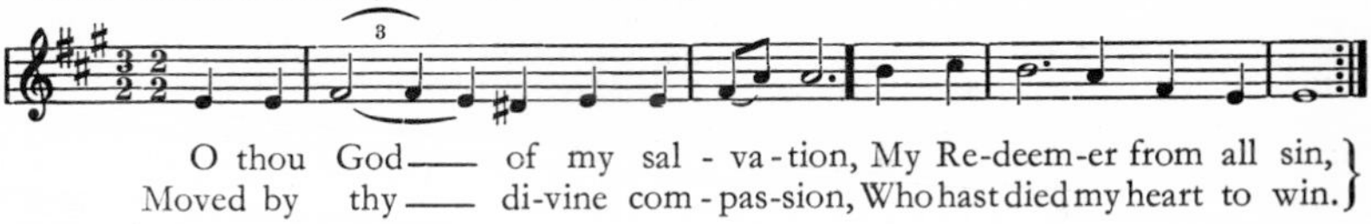
O thou God— of my sal - va - tion, My Re - deem - er from all sin,
Moved by thy— di - vine com - pas - sion, Who hast died my heart to win.

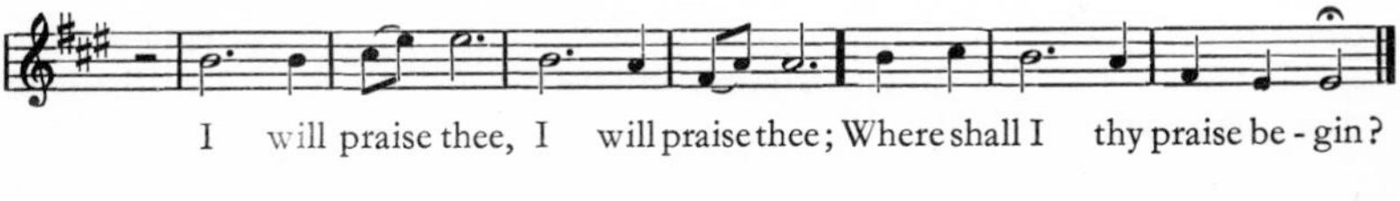
I will praise thee, I will praise thee; Where shall I thy praise be - gin?

Angels now are hov'ring round us,
Unperceived amid the throng;
Wond'ring at the love that crown'd us,
Glad to join the holy song;
Hallelujah, hallelujah,
Love and praise to Christ belong.

The tune is evidently a remake of 'Locks and Bolts'. Compare, for example, Sharp, ii., 19. The difference between the two tunes is probably due in part to their structure, which provided real difficulties for their recorders, and in part to the efforts of the *Bible Songs* arranger to make the apparently dorian tune fit into current scale formulas. Compare also 'Bed of Primroses', Thomas, p. 176.

No. 90

MOUNT WATSON, OL 272

Heptatonic dorian, mode 2 A + B (I II 3 IV V VI 7)

Death shall not des - troy my comfort, Christ shall guide me thro' the gloom;
Chorus O hal-le - lu-jah! how I love my Sav - ior, O hal-le - lu - jah! that I do;
D. C. for Chorus
Down he'll send some heav'n - ly con-voy, To es - cort my spi - rit home.
O hal-le - lu - jah! how I love my Sav-ior! Mourners, you may love him too.

Jordan's stream shall not o'erflow me,
While my Savior's by my side;
Canaan, Canaan lies before me!
Soon I'll cross the swelling tide.
O hallelujah *etc.*

See the happy spirits waiting,
On the banks beyond the stream!
Sweet responses still repeating,
"Jesus! Jesus!" is their theme.
O hallelujah *etc.*

William Hauser, compiler of the *Olive Leaf*, informs us that "this tune [is] called after Rev. John H. Watson, whom, in my youth [in the 1820's], I used to hear sing [it]". It is a variant of the beautiful traditional secular ballad 'The Poor Little Fisherman Girl' or 'Green Willow'.

No. 91

CROSS OF CHRIST, GOS 504

Heptatonic aeolian, mode 2 A + b (I II 3 IV V 6 7)

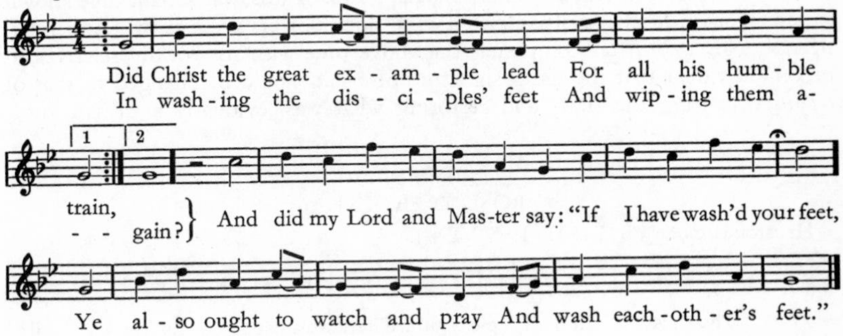
Did Christ the great ex - am - ple lead For all his hum - ble
In wash - ing the dis - ci - ples' feet And wip - ing them a-
1
2
train,
- - gain?
And did my Lord and Mas-ter say: "If I have wash'd your feet,
Ye al - so ought to watch and pray And wash each - oth - er's feet."

O blessed Jesus, at thy board
I have thy children met;
The bread I've broke, the wine I've poured,
We've washed each other's feet.
In imitation of my Lord
Whose blood for me did sweat,
I yield unto his sacred word
And wash the pilgrims' feet.

Yea, blessed Jesus, I, like thee,
Would Christians often meet;
The least of all the flock would be,
And wash his children's feet.
For this let men reproach, defame,
And call me what they will;
I still would follow Christ the Lamb,
And be his servant still.

The loving labor I repeat,
Obedient to his word,
And wash his dear disciples' feet
And wait upon the Lord.
Shall I, a worm, refuse to stoop?
My fellow worm disdain?
I give my vain distinctions up,
Since Christ did wait on man.

The words were quite evidently made to go with the celebration of the foot-washing rite still observed by the Primitive Baptists, from whose hymn book the song is taken. The tune is ascribed to L. P. Breedlove of Georgia. I find it to be a close variant of 'James Harris' (or 'Daemon Lover' or 'House Carpenter') turned around; that is, with the second part of the above tune coming first in the secular ballad tune. For versions of the 'James Harris' tune see Thomas 172, Davis 592—594, Cox 524, and Sharp, i., 244—258. The oldest variant tune known to me is that in Motherwell associated with 'Blue Flowers and Yellow' (Appendix, *Musick*, No. 17.) After comparing the above tune with its worldly relatives, it becomes evident that the GOS signature of *b*-flat should be changed to that of *f*-natural, raising the sixth and restoring what was evidently a dorian tune.

No. 92

ROSE TREE, KNH 165

Hexatonic, mode 3 b (I II III IV V VI —)

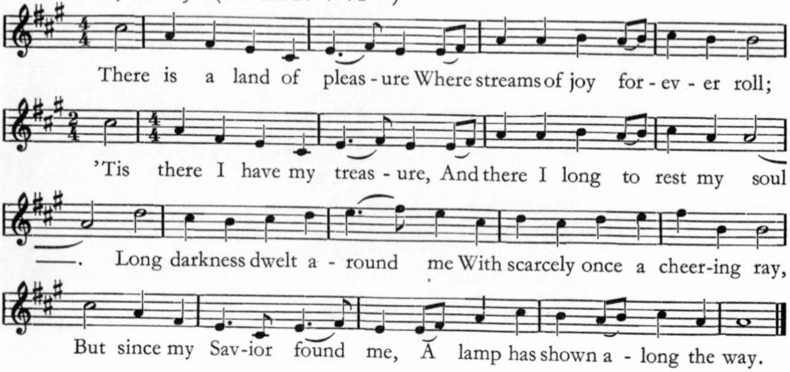
There is a land of pleas - ure Where streams of joy for - ev - er roll;
'Tis there I have my treas - ure, And there I long to rest my soul
—. Long darkness dwelt a - round me With scarcely once a cheer-ing ray,
But since my Sav-ior found me, A lamp has shown a - long the way.

My way is full of danger,
But 'tis the path that leads to God,
And like a faithful soldier
I'll march along the heav'nly road.
Now I must gird my sword on,
My breast plate, helmet and my shield,
And fight the host of Satan,
Until I reach the heav'nly field.

I'm on the way to Zion,
Still guided by my Saviour's hand,
O come along dear sinners
And see Emanuel's happy land.
To all that stay behind me,
I bid a long, a sad farewell.
Come now, or you'll repent it
When you do reach the gates of hell.

Echoes of 'Turkey in the Straw' (see Sandburg, p. 94) are heard in this tune. Compare also 'My Grandma Lived on Yonder Little Green', WS 166. The immediate ancestor of the tune, and the source of its title, is the secular song 'A Rose-Tree in Full Bearing', *The English Musical Repository*, Edinburgh, 1811, p. 127. It appeared in William Shield's ballad opera 'The Poor Soldier', 1783. The 'Rose Tree' air was known in Ireland also as 'Moreen O'Cullenan' and was associated, among other texts, with Moore's 'I'd Mourn the Hopes that Leave Us'. See Joyce, p. 40.

No. 93

CLAMANDA, OSH 42

Heptatonic aeolian, mode 2 A + b (I II 3 IV V 6 7)

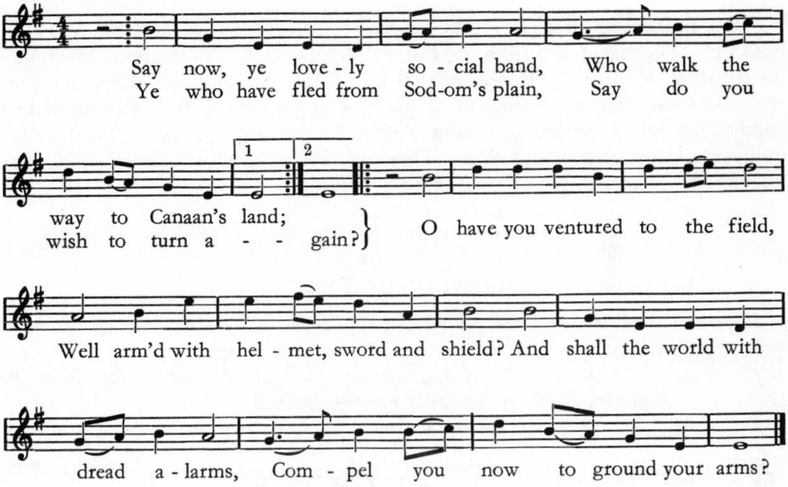
Say now, ye love - ly so - cial band, Who walk the
Ye who have fled from Sod-om's plain, Say do you
1 2
way to Canaan's land;
wish to turn a - - gain?
O have you ventured to the field,
Well arm'd with hel - met, sword and shield? And shall the world with
dread a - larms, Com - pel you now to ground your arms?

Beware of pleasure's siren song,
Alas, it cannot soothe thee long.
It cannot quiet Jordan's wave,
Nor cheer the dark and silent grave.
O what contentment did you find,
While love of pleasure ruled your mind?
No sweet reflection lulled your rest,
Nor conscious virtue calmed your breast.

O, come, young soldiers, count the cost,
And say, what pleasures have you lost?
Or what misfortune does it bring,
To have Jehovah for your king?
Shall sin entice you back again,
And bind you with its iron chain?
Has vice to you such lovely charms,
That you must die within its arms?

Is folly's way the way of peace,
Where fear, and pain, and sorrow cease?
Does pleasure roll its living stream,
And is religion all a dream?
Say, what contentment did you find
When love of pleasure ruled your mind?
No sweet reflection gave you rest,
Nor conscious virtue calm'd your breast.

Tune found also in CHI 12, KNH 109, UH 63, SOC 168, HH 28, SKH 47, GOS 26. The text, taken from the *Dover Selection*, as well as the tune, attributed to 'Chapin', seem to be closely related to a Christmas carol in JFSS, ii., 115. Its first stanza begins: "Come all ye faithful Christians, That dwell within this land. That pass your time in rioting, Remember you are but man." The English folk-song, 'Just as the Tide Was a-Flowing', has an almost identical tune. See Gould and Sharp, *English Folk-Songs for Schools*, p. 52.

No. 94

MECKLINBURG, SKH 30

Heptatonic aeolian, mode 2 A + b (I II 3 IV V 6 7)

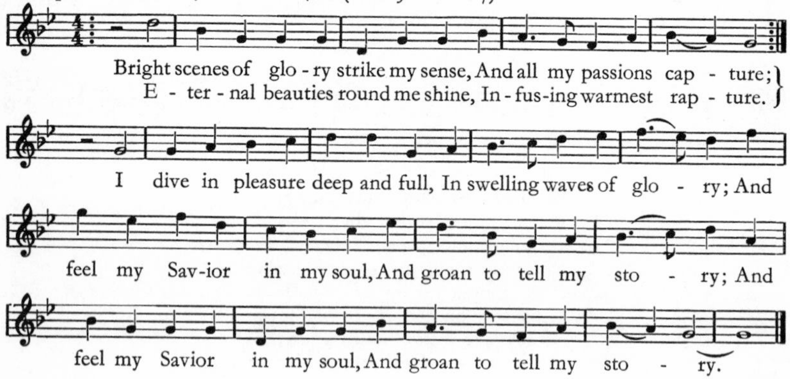
Bright scenes of glo - ry strike my sense, And all my passions cap - ture;
E - ter - nal beauties round me shine, In - fus-ing warmest rap - ture.
I dive in pleasure deep and full, In swelling waves of glo - ry; And
feel my Sav-ior in my soul, And groan to tell my sto - ry; And
feel my Savior in my soul, And groan to tell my sto - ry.

I feast on honey, milk and wine,
I drink perpetual sweetness;
Mount Zion's odours through me shine,
While Christ unfolds his glory.
No mortal tongue can lisp my joys,
Nor can an angel tell them;
Ten thousand times surpassing all
Terrestrial worlds [words?] or emblems.

My captivated spirit flies,
Through shining worlds of beauty;
Dissolv'd in blushes, loud I cry,
In praises loud and mighty;
And here I'll sing and swell the strains
Of harmony delighted,
And with the millions learn the notes
Of saints in Christ united.

The compiler of the SKH attributes the tune to Lowry. See *White Spirituals*, p. 167, for a secular relative of the tune. See also 'St. Patrick was a Gentleman', Petrie, No. 346; and 'I'm Seventeen Come Sunday', JFSS, ii., 269f.

No. 95

SALVATION (B), SOH 84

Heptatonic aeolian, mode 2 A + b (I II 3 IV V 6 7)

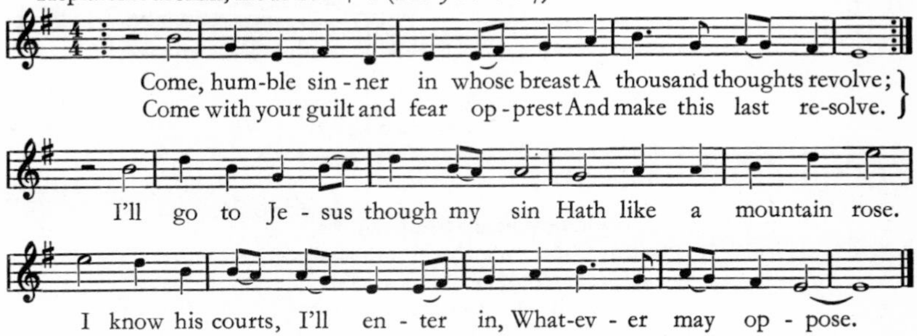
Come, hum-ble sin - ner in whose breast A thousand thoughts revolve;
Come with your guilt and fear op - prest And make this last re-solve.
I'll go to Je - sus though my sin Hath like a mountain rose.
I know his courts, I'll en - ter in, What-ev - er may op - pose.

Prostrate I'll lie before his throne,
And there my guilt confess;
I'll tell him I'm a wretch undone,
Without his sovereign grace.

I'll to the gracious King approach,
Whose sceptre pardon gives;
Perhaps he may command my touch,
And then the suppliant lives.

Of the text which the compiler of the *Southern Harmony* found in "Rippon", three further stanzas are found in Caldwell's *Union Harmony*, p. 35. The tune, ascribed to Robert Boyd, is found also KYH 22, GCM 136, UH 34, KNH 32, HH 71, HOC 24, TZ 101, and GOS 144. A variant tune is 'Come All Ye Worthy Christian Men', Sharp, *One Hundred English Folksongs*, No. 91. Note similarity in the opening words of both songs. See also Sharp's note as to other old related songs. The first melodic sentence is quite similar to that of the tune to 'The Three Ravens' as Motherwell gives it in *Minstrelsy Ancient and Modern*, Edition 1873, Appendix, *Musick*, No. 12:

No. 96

FRENCH BROAD, SOH 265

Hexatonic, mode 2 A (I II 3 IV V — 7)

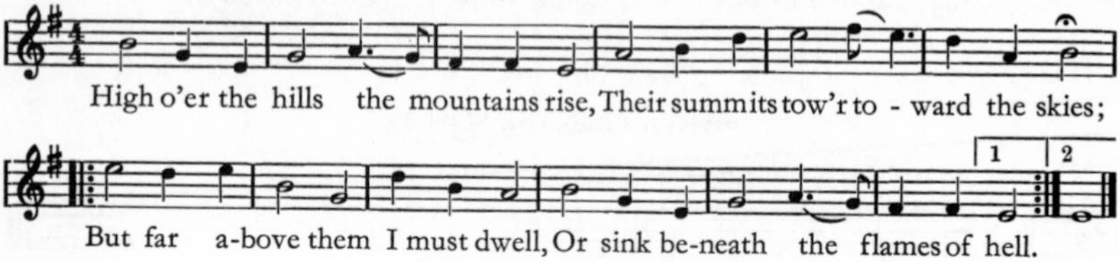
High o'er the hills the mountains rise, Their summits tow'r to - ward the skies;
But far a-bove them I must dwell, Or sink be-neath the flames of hell.
1
2

Although I walk the mountains high,
Ere long my body low must lie,
And in some lonesome place must rot,
And by the living be forgot.

There it must lie till that great day,
When Gabriel's awful trump shall say,
"Arise, the judgment day is come,
When all must hear their final doom."

Four more stanzas in the *Southern Harmony*. Found also GOS 218, CHH 208. William Walker, compiler of the *Southern Harmony*, appends the note: "This song was composed by the author in the fall of 1831, while traveling over the mountains, on French Broad River, in North Carolina and Tennessee". Walker must have been referring simply to the words. He was melodizing, probably unconsciously, in beaten paths. For his tune is almost identical with the older 'Kedron' (this collection) which was attributed to "Dare". Walker declares, in his later song book, *Christian Harmony*, 1866, p. 208, that he "learned the air of this tune from my mother when only five years old." That would have been 1814. Both the Dare and the Walker tunes are closely related to the melody of 'McAfee's Confession', Sharp, ii., 16, lower tune, a western North Carolina recording of 1918; and to the Old World song, 'The Wraggle Taggle Gipsies O', *One Hundred English Folk-Songs*, p. 13.

No. 97

DAVISSON'S RETIREMENT, KNH 117

Pentatonic, mode 4 (I II — IV V — 7)

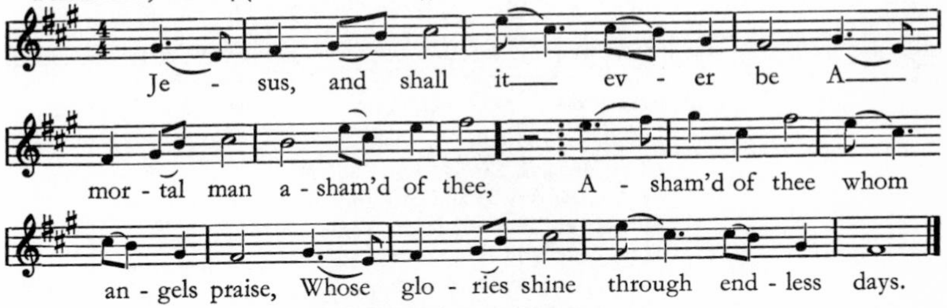
Je - sus, and shall it— ev - er be A—
mor - tal man a - sham'd of thee, A - sham'd of thee whom
an - gels praise, Whose glo - ries shine through end - less days.

Ashamed of Jesus! sooner far
Let evening blush to own a star;
He sheds the beams of light divine
O'er this benighted soul of mine.

Ashamed of Jesus! just as soon
Let midnight be ashamed of noon:
'Tis midnight with my soul till he,
Bright morning star, bid darkness flee.

The poem is by Joseph Grigg (b. 1720). Ananias Davisson of the Valley of Virginia named and claimed the tune in his *Kentucky Harmony* (1815). Annabel Morris Buchanan has found a tune with the title 'Retirement' in a manuscript tune book which she judges to be from the eighteenth century. No text accompanies the tune, and no source is given. It follows:

A comparison of the two tunes indicates rather plainly that Davisson wrote the tune down from oral tradition, and that his noting was indicative of the manner in which it was actually sung.

No. 98

PILGRIM, OSH 201

Hexatonic, mode 2 b (I—3 IV V 6 7)

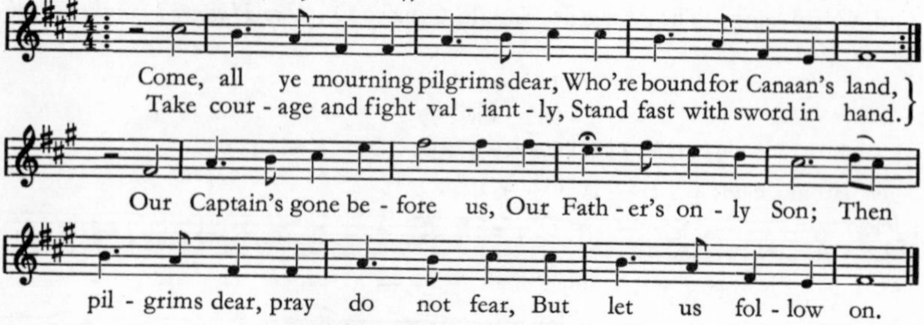
Come, all ye mourning pilgrims dear, Who're bound for Canaan's land,
Take cour - age and fight val - iant - ly, Stand fast with sword in hand.
Our Captain's gone be - fore us, Our Fath - er's on - ly Son; Then
pil - grims dear, pray do not fear, But let us fol - low on.

We have a howling wilderness
To Canaan's happy shore,
A land of dearth and pits and snares,
Where chilling winds do roar.
But Jesus will be with us
And guard us by the way,
Though enemies examine us,
He'll teach us what to say.

Come all you pilgrim travelers,
Fresh courage take with me;
Meantime I'll tell you how I came
This happy land to see:
Through faith, the glorious telescope,
I view'd the worlds above,
And God the Father reconciled,
Which fills my heart with love.

The tune is found also CHI 54, MOH 147, KNH 57, HH 392, SOC 117, and WP 46. Among the many secular songs using this tune are 'Daniel Monroe', dating from around 1785, Rickaby, pp. 184 and 229; 'Lady and the Dragoon', Sharp, i., 337, recorded in North Carolina in 1918; 'Sheffield Apprentice', Sharp, ii., 66; 'Loving Reilly', Sharp, ii., 81 and 82; 'Rebel Soldier', or 'Poor Stranger' Sharp, ii., 215; 'Sons of Liberty', Sharp, ii., 225; 'John Barleycorn', noted by Sharp in England in 1909; 'Gallant Poachers' or 'Van Diemen's Land', also in England, see JFSS, vii., 42, for references; 'I Wish I Was in Dublin Town', or 'The Irish Girl', JFSS, viii., 263; and 'Barley and the Rye', JFSS, viii., 273; 'High Germany' and 'Erin's Lovely Home', *One Hundred English Folk-Songs*, pp. 124 and 127; 'King's Lynn', *Christian Science Hymnal*; and 'Rise Up Young William Reilly', Petrie, No. 510. Stephen Foster's tune 'Way Down in Ca-i-ro' shows influence from this tune formula. See *The Musical Quarterly*, vol. xxii., No. 2.

No. 99
MISSISSIPPI, SKH 34

Heptatonic aeolian, mode A + b (I II 3 IV V 6 7)

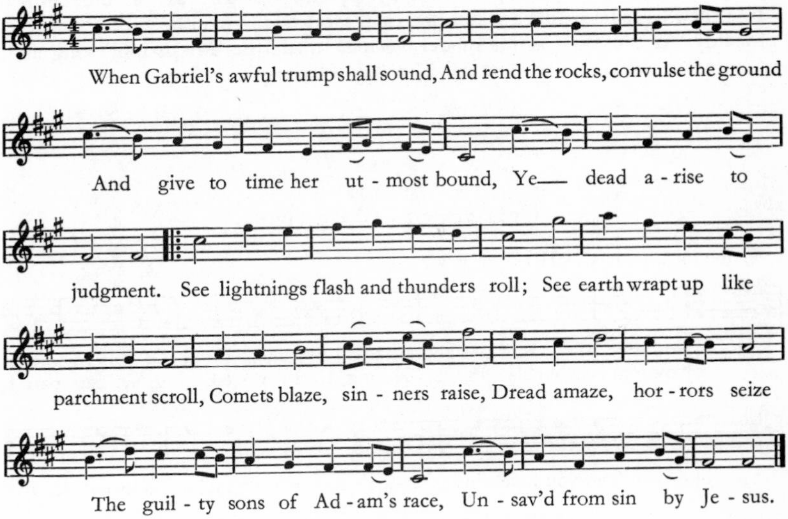
When Gabriel's awful trump shall sound, And rend the rocks, convulse the ground
And give to time her ut - most bound, Ye— dead a - rise to
judgment. See lightnings flash and thunders roll; See earth wrapt up like
parchment scroll, Comets blaze, sin - ners raise, Dread amaze, hor - rors seize
The guil - ty sons of Ad - am's race, Un - sav'd from sin by Je - sus.

The Christian, fill'd with rapturous joy,
Midst flaming worlds he mounts on high,
To meet his Savior in the sky
And see the face of Jesus.
The soul and body reunite,
And fill with glory infinite.
Blessed day, Christians say,
Will you pray that we may
All join that happy company
To praise the name of Jesus.

The compiler of the *Supplement to the Kentucky Harmony* attributed the song to "Bradshaw". I find distinct ancestral traces of its tune in 'Princess Royal' given in a number of traditional forms as a morris dance tune in Sharp, *The Morris Dance Book*. Assuming these to be the oldest forms of the tune, the next younger form seems to have been what was called in Walsh's *Compleat Dancing Master (ca.* 1730), "The Princess Royal, the new way". In 1796 Shield adapted the air to the words of 'The Saucy Arethusa' in the ballad opera *The Lock and Key*.

It may be found entitled 'The Arethusa' in *The English Musical Repository*, p. 32. At about the same time — around the end of the eighteenth century — the tune was used also for 'Bold Nelson's Praise' a version of which was recently recorded by Sharp, *One Hundred English Folk-Songs*, No. 88. The as yet unidentified "Bradshaw" seems to have taken one of these late-eighteenth-century tunes — probably 'Arethusa' — as his model when he made the 'Mississippi' song as it appeared in the *Supplement to the Kentucky Harmony* in 1820.

No. 100
PLEADING SAVIOR, OSH 234

Pentatonic, mode 3 (I II III — V VI —)

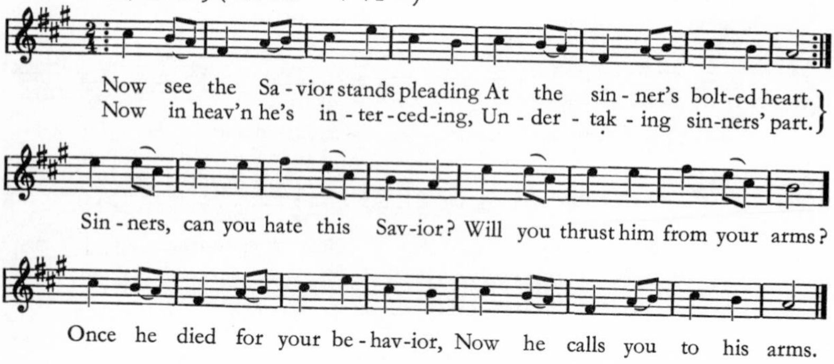
Now see the Sa - vior stands pleading At the sin - ner's bolt-ed heart.
Now in heav'n he's in - ter - ced-ing, Un - der - tak - ing sin-ners' part.
Sin - ners, can you hate this Sav-ior? Will you thrust him from your arms?
Once he died for your be - hav-ior, Now he calls you to his arms.

Sinners, hear your God and Savior,
Hear his gracious voice today;
Turn from all your vain behavior,
Oh repent, return, and pray.
Sinners, can you hate this Savior?
Will you thrust him from your arms?
Once he died for your behavior,
Now he calls you to his arms.

The first line of the text above should probably read

Now the Savior stands a-pleading.

The Methodist Hymn Book of England, London, 1933, has the above tune under the title 'Saltash', and its source is given as the *Plymouth Collection*, 1855.

No. 101

NETTLETON or SINNER'S CALL, PB 4

Hexatonic, mode 3 A (I II III — V VI VII)

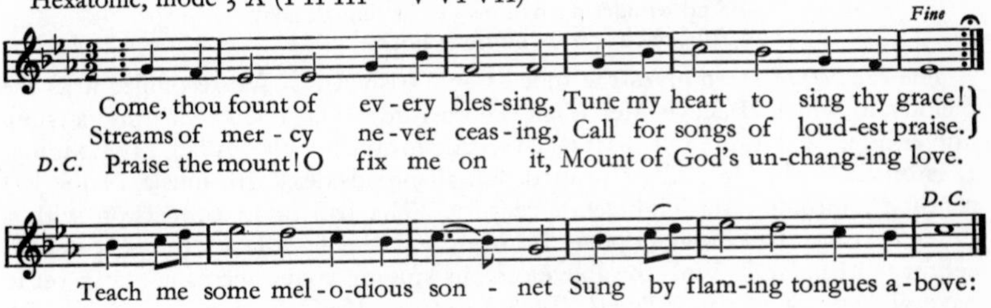
Fine
Come, thou fount of ev-ery bles-sing, Tune my heart to sing thy grace!
Streams of mer-cy ne-ver ceas-ing, Call for songs of loud-est praise.
D.C. Praise the mount! O fix me on it, Mount of God's un-chang-ing love.
D. C.
Teach me some mel-o-dious son-net Sung by flam-ing tongues a-bove:

Here I raise my Ebenezer;
Hither by thy help I'm come;
And I hope, by thy good pleasure,
Safely to arrive at home.
Jesus sought me, when a stranger,
Wandering from the fold of God;
He, to save my soul from danger,
Interposed his precious blood!

The words are the widely sung ones of Robinson. Metcalf (Frank J., *Stories of Hymn Tunes*, p. 141) thinks the tune belongs to John Wyeth (1770—1858). It is the tune that has been used for the Parody 'Tell Aunt Rhody. "And its close relative 'Sweet Affliction' or 'Greenville', in this collection, has been used for the '*Go* Tell Aunt Rhody' parody.

No. 102

CHARIOT OF MERCY, HH 290

Heptatonic ionian, mode 3 A + b (I II III IV V VI VII)

The char-iot of mer-cy is speed-ing its way, Far,
far through the sha-dow-y gloom, Where the lands that in death's
dark ob-scu-ri-ty lay, Are burst-ing the bars of their tomb.
etc.

This familiar tune continues with the words:

> I see where 'tis shedding its luminous ray,
> Dispersing the shadows of night;
> And wondering nations are hailing the day,
> And rejoice in its glorious light.

The *Hesperian Harp* gives the tune as an "Irish Air". We recognize it as the melody to which 'Believe Me, If all Those Endearing Young Charms' is sung universally. Woolridge tells us it is the setting for the popular ballad 'My Lodging, It is on the Cold Ground' as printed "on all broadsides, with music, of the last century", meaning the eighteenth century. The ballad, in connection with a different tune, had been popular from around the middle of the seventeenth century in England. With the above tune its singing vogue seems not even yet to have abated. See Chappell's *Old English Popular Music*, ii., 137ff. An old Irish version of the tune is 'Oh Shrive me Father', Petrie, No. 632. Stephen Foster undoubtedly had this popular tune formula in mind when he composed 'Old Folks at Home'. See *Musical Quarterly*, vol. xxii., No. 2, pp. 158—160.

No. 103

STOCKWOOD or SISTER THOU WAST MILD, OSH 118

Hexatonic, mode 2 A (I II 3 IV V — 7)

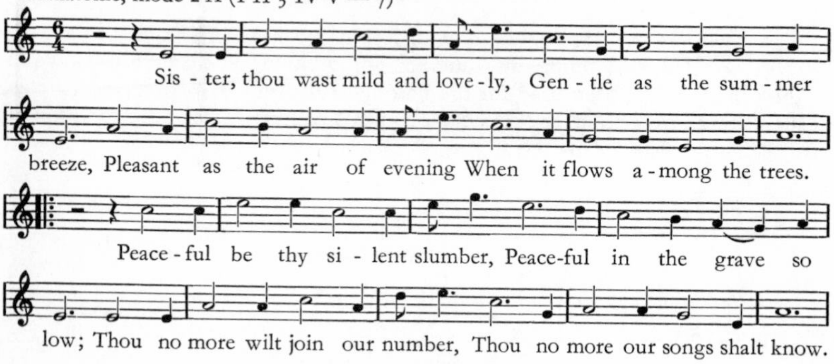
Sis - ter, thou wast mild and love - ly, Gen - tle as the sum - mer
breeze, Pleasant as the air of evening When it flows a - mong the trees.
Peace - ful be thy si - lent slumber, Peace-ful in the grave so
low; Thou no more wilt join our number, Thou no more our songs shalt know.

> Dearest sister, thou hast left us,
> Here thy loss we deeply feel;
> But 'tis God that hast bereft us,
> He can all our sorrows heal.
> Yet again we hope to meet thee,
> When the day of life is fled,
> Then in heaven with joy to greet thee,
> Where no farewell tear is shed.

The words are attributed in the *Sacred Harp* to Samuel Francis Smith, author of 'My Country, 'Tis of Thee'.

No. 104

ROSE, REV 332

Heptatonic aeolian or dorian minorized, cannot be classified (I II 3 IV V [VI] 6 [VII] 7)

O—— tell me no more Of—— this world's vain store, The
A—— coun-try I've found Where true joys a - bound, To
time for such tri - fles With—— me now is—— o'er.
dwell I'm de - ter - mined On—— that hap - py—— ground.

The souls that believe, in paradise live,
And me in that number will Jesus receive;
My soul, don't delay, he calls thee away;
Rise, follow the Savior, and bless the glad day.

Four more stanzas of the text are given in the *Revivalist*. The tune was recorded "as sung by Rev. A. C. Rose" from whom it got its title. The oldest recording of the melody known to me is on page 38 of Ingalls' *Christian Harmony*, 1805. The Reverend Rose's song appears in this collection also as 'O Tell Me No More', in its standardized tune-book form, whereas the recorder of the above variant has caught much of the folk-singing manner. Both of the tunes in question are related to the 'Lord Randal' melodies which are found in Sharp, i., 43, G.

No. 105

SUPPLICATION, OSH 45

Hexatonic, mode 2 A (I II 3 IV V — 7)

O thou who hear'st when sinners cry, Tho' all my crimes be-fore thee lie,
Behold them not with ang - ry look, But blot their mem'ry from thy book.

Create my nature pure within,
And form my soul averse to sin;
Let thy good spirit ne'er depart,
Nor hide thy presence from my heart.

I cannot live without thy light,
Cast out and banished from thy sight;
Thy holy joys, my God, restore,
And guard me that I fall no more.

Words attributed to Watts; tune to Chapin. Found also, *Choral-Music*, p. 48, KYH 20, MOH 26, GCM 110, SOH 5, GOS 589, UH 14. See WS 190 for the tune's use with the 'Wicked Polly' ballad which is also to be found in this collection. It is a variant also of 'Lord Bateman', Sharp, *One Hundred English Folk-songs*, No. 6; and of 'Hind Horn', *British Ballads from Maine*, pp. 73 and 78. *The Singer's Companion* (New York, 1854) has a strikingly similar tune under the title 'Hame, Hame, Hame', a Jacobite song whose words tell of a Scotch exile and his longing for home. The editor of that collection found it in the *Garland of Scotia*. The old Scotch tune is doubtless the source of 'Supplication'.

No. 106

PRAISE GOD, OSH 528

Hexatonic, mode 2 A (I II 3 IV V — 7)

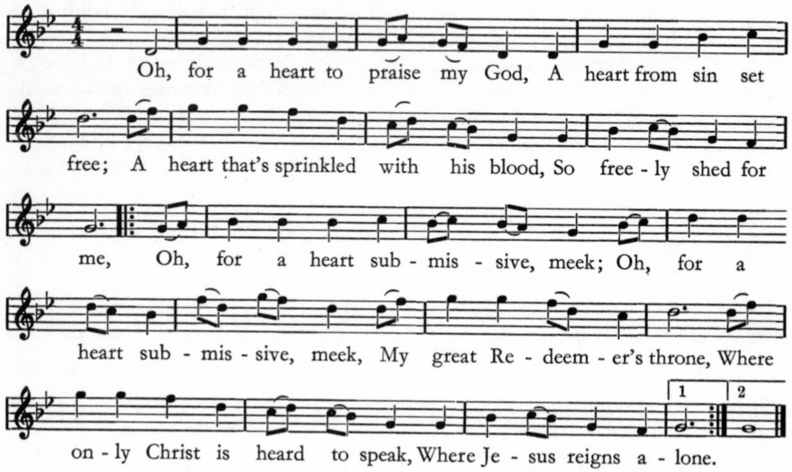
Oh, for a heart to praise my God, A heart from sin set
free; A heart that's sprinkled with his blood, So free - ly shed for
me, Oh, for a heart sub - mis - sive, meek; Oh, for a
heart sub - mis - sive, meek, My great Re - deem - er's throne, Where
on - ly Christ is heard to speak, Where Je - sus reigns a - lone.
1
2

Oh, for an humble, contrite heart, believing, true and clean,
Which neither life nor death can part from him that dwells within.
A heart in every thought renewed, and full of love divine;
Perfect, and right, and pure, and good, a copy, Lord, of thine.

Seaborn M. Denson composed this tune as a setting to Charles Wesley's text and inserted it, in a fuguing-tune setting, in the *Original Sacred Harp* of 1911. The tune is testimony to the fact that its composer was steeped in the traditional Anglo-American folk-melodism and in that particular direction which it took in the hands of the eighteenth century fuguing-song makers. Compare for melodie similarities 'Geordie', JFSS, iii., 191. *White Spirituals* tells more about Mr. Denson who died in 1936.

No. 107

LEANDER, SOH 128

Heptatonic aeolian, mode 2 A+b (I II 3 IV V 6 7)

There's nothing round this spacious earth
That suits my soul's desire;
To boundless joy and solid mirth
My nobler thoughts aspire.
O for the pinions of a dove
To mount the heav'nly road;
There shall I share my Savior's love,
There shall I dwell with God.

The tune is ascribed to "Austin", and the words to Watts. Found also, UH 66, OSH 71, HOC 61, WP 52, TZ 100, MOH 129. The second part of the tune reminds of the second part of 'When Johnny Comes Marching Home'. Variants of the melody are 'Jubilee, CHI 62 and REV 355; and 'This Is the Jubilee'. OL 113.

No. 108
THERE IS A REST REMAINS, REV 135

Hexatonic, minorized, cannot be classified (I II 3 IV [IV'] V — 7 [VII])

Lord, I be-lieve a rest re-mains To all thy peo-ple
A rest where pure en-joy-ment reigns, And thou art loved a-
known; lone. There is a rest re-mains, There is a rest re-mains,
rit.
There is a rest re-mains For all the peo-ple of God.

A rest where all our soul's desire
Is fixed on things above;
Where fear, and sin, and grief expire,
Cast out by perfect love.

O that I now the rest might know,
Believe and enter in;
Now, Savior, now the power bestow,
And let me cease from sin.

Remove this hardness from my heart,
This unbelief remove;
To me the rest of faith impart —
The Sabbath of thy love.

A remarkably close remake of this peculiar song by the negroes is given in Dett, p. 108, under the title 'Go Down, Moses', where we see the melodic setting of the above words "To all thy people known" and "For all the people of God" fitted note for note to "Let thy people go". The tunes of 'Rejected Lover', Sharp, ii., 96ff., show similarities.

No. 109
BOURBON, COH 67

Pentatonic, mode 2 (I — 3 IV V — 7)

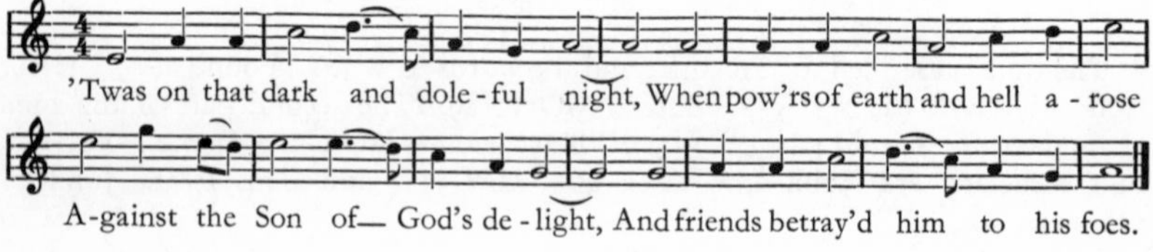
'Twas on that dark and dole-ful night, When pow'rs of earth and hell a-rose
A-gainst the Son of— God's de-light, And friends betray'd him to his foes.

Before the mournful scene began,
He took the bread and blest and brake;
What love through all his actions ran,
What wondrous words of love he spake.

"This is my body, broke for sin,
Receive and eat the living food;"
Then took the cup and bless'd the wine —
"'Tis the new cov'nant in my blood."

"Do this," he cried, "till time shall end,
In mem'ry of your dying Friend;
Meet at my table and record
The love of your departed Lord."

Jesus, thy feast we celebrate,
We show thy death, we sing thy name.
Till thou return, and we shall eat
The marriage supper of the Lamb.

Words attributed sometimes to Watts. Tune attributed to Freeman Lewis. Found also, HH 8, GCM 159, SKY 61, MOH 60 and 143, UH 17, GOS 575. This is the same tune which is used for 'McFee's Confession', Cox, p. 525; 'Samuel Young', Sharp, ii., 271; 'Come, Father Build Me' (as sung in England), JFSS, viii., 212; and it is similar to 'Lord Bateman', *One Hundred English Folksongs*, No. 6. For further tune relationship see 'Kedron' in this collection.

No. 110

GLORIOUS PROSPECT, OL 363

Hexatonic, mode 3 b (I II III IV V VI —)

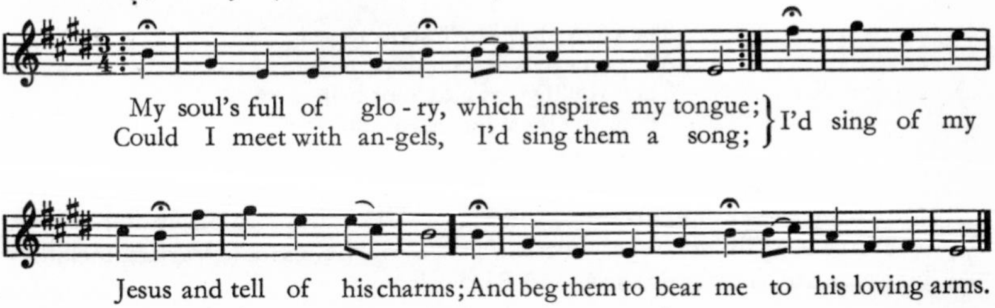
My soul's full of glo - ry, which inspires my tongue;
Could I meet with an-gels, I'd sing them a song;
I'd sing of my
Jesus and tell of his charms; And beg them to bear me to his loving arms.

Methinks they're descending to hear while I sing;
Well pleased to hear mortals sing praise to their King.
O angels! O angels! my soul's in a flame!
I sink in sweet raptures at Jesus' dear name.

O Jesus! O Jesus! thou balm of my soul!
'Twas thou, my dear Savior, that made my heart whole;
Oh bring me to view thee, thou precious, sweet King,
In oceans of glory thy praises to sing!

The author of the *Olive Leaf* tells us: "This is the first tune I ever harmonized; about 1833. I had learned the air—which I suspect [John Adam] Granade originated, before I was born — when a boy, to these words." That the tune went earlier with some secular ballad, seems evident from the resemblances found, for example, in 'Pretty Nancy of Yarmouth', Sharp, i., 379; 'Lamkin', Sharp, i., 201 ff.; 'The Silk Merchant's Daughter', Sharp, i., 383 f.; and 'Green Grows the Laurel', Sharp ii., 211.

No. 111
O YE YOUNG AND GAY AND PROUD or ETERNITY

Pentachordal, cannot be classified (I II III IV V — —)

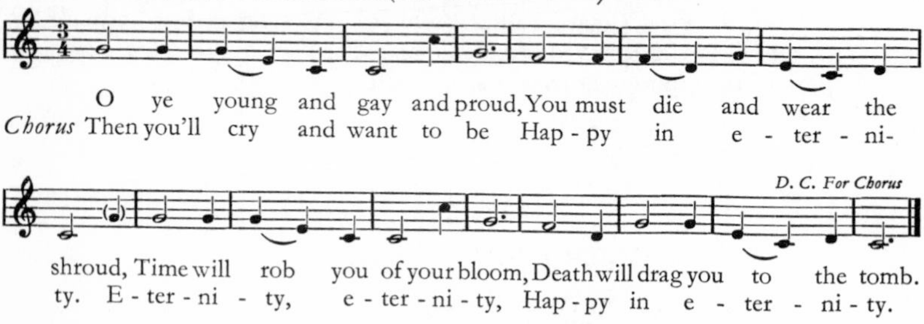
O ye young and gay and proud, You must die and wear the
Chorus Then you'll cry and want to be Hap - py in e - ter - ni-
D. C. For Chorus
shroud, Time will rob you of your bloom, Death will drag you to the tomb.
ty. E - ter - ni - ty, e - ter - ni - ty, Hap - py in e - ter - ni - ty.

The white throne will soon appear,
All the dead will then draw near.
Then you'll go to heav'n or hell.
There you must forever dwell.
Chorus

Recorded by the author from the singing of Mrs. Elizabeth Showalter-Miller, Dayton, Virginia, Jan. 20, 1930. Further stanzas of the text and variant melodies may be found in Thomas, p. 118, and Richardson, p. 73.

No. 112
FRIENDS OF FREEDOM, CH 285

Heptatonic, mode 1 b(I II — IV V VI 7)

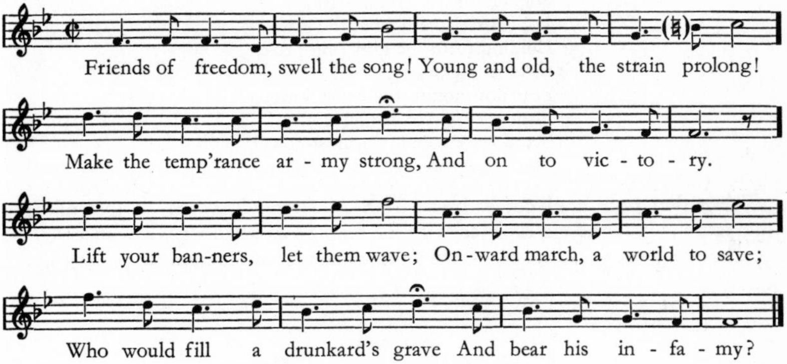
Friends of freedom, swell the song! Young and old, the strain prolong!
Make the temp'rance ar - my strong, And on to vic - to - ry.
Lift your ban-ners, let them wave; On-ward march, a world to save;
Who would fill a drunkard's grave And bear his in - fa - my?

Shrink not when the foe appears;
Spurn the coward's guilty fears;
Hear the shrieks, behold the tears
Of ruined families!
Raise the cry in every spot:
"Touch not, taste not, handle not!"
Who would be a drunken sot,
The worst of miseries.

Give the aching bosom rest;
Carry joy to every breast;
Make the wretched dunkard blest,
By living soberly.
Raise the glorious watchword high:
"Touch not, taste not till you die"
Let the echo reach the sky,
And earth keep jubilee.

God of mercy, hear us plead,
For thy help we intercede;
See how many bosoms bleed!
And heal them speedily.
Hasten, Lord, the happy day,
When, beneath thy gentle ray,
Temp'rance all the world shall sway,
And reign triumphantly.

Evidently the time should be six-eight. It is found, measured thus, in the 1859 edition of the *Sacred Harp*, p. 152, under the title 'Bruce's Address, Spiritualized', and begins,

Soldiers of the cross, arise!
Lo, your Captain from the skies,
Holding forth the glitt'ring prize,
Calls to victory.
Fear not though the battle lower,
Firmly stand the trying hour,
Stand the tempter's utmost power,
Spurn his slavery.

The earlier tune is given, in *Lyric Gems of Scotland*, p. 242, as that of 'Hey tutti tattie'. It is there associated with the text 'Scots wha ha'e wi' Wallace bled', the same as 'Bruce's Address', of which both the texts cited here are parodies.

No. 113

PILGRIM'S SONG, REV 369

Heptatonic mixolydian, mode 1 A+b (I II III IV V VI 7)

Oh, brethren I have found a land that doth a-bound With fruit as sweet as
The more I eat, I find, the more I am in-clined To shout and sing ho-
D. C. And as I pass a - long I'll sing the Christian's song, I'm go-ing to live for-

D. C.

honey; } My soul doth long to go where I may ful-ly know The glo-ries of my Sav-ior;
san-na.
ev-er.

Perhaps you think me wild, or simple as a child;
I am a child of glory;
I am born from above, my soul is filled with love;
I love to tell the story.

My soul now sits and sings, and practices her wings,
And contemplates the hour
When the messenger shall say: "Come quit this house of clay,
And with bright angels tower."

The tune is a variant of 'The Winter it is Past', Petrie, No. 439.

No. 114

HOLY MANNA, HOC 122

Pentatonic, mode 3 (I II III — V VI —)

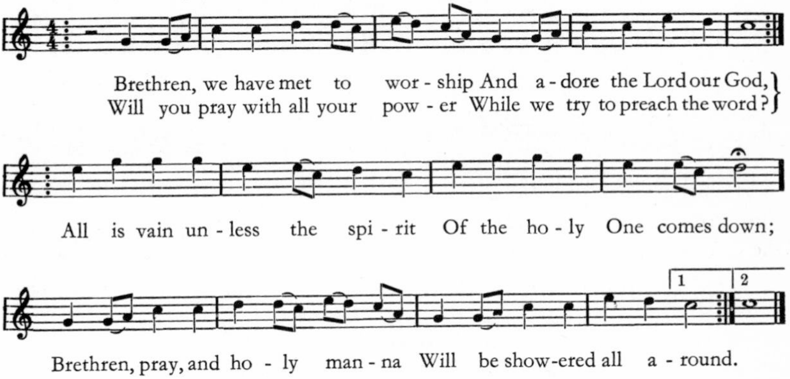
Brethren, we have met to wor - ship And a - dore the Lord our God,
Will you pray with all your pow - er While we try to preach the word?
All is vain un - less the spi - rit Of the ho - ly One comes down;
1
2
Brethren, pray, and ho - ly man - na Will be show-ered all a - round.

Brethren, see poor sinners round you,
Trembling on the brink of wo;
Death is coming, hell is moving,
Can you bear to let them go?
See our fathers, see our mothers
And our children sinking down;
Brethren, pray, and holy manna
Will be showered all around.

Is there here a trembling jailor
Seeking grace and fill'd with fears?
Is there here a weeping Mary,
Pouring forth a flood of tears?
Brethren, join your cries to help them;
Sisters, let your prayers abound;
Pray, O pray that holy manna
May be scatter'd all around.

Two more stanzas are in SOH 103. This rousing song, still immensely popular, was claimed (probably first recorded) by William Moore, compiler of the *Columbian Harmony*, in 1825. Subsequent compilers have allowed his claim to stand. Found also, KNH 88, OSH 59, HH 244, SOC 191, HOC 107, WP 89, TZ 301, GOS 340, PB 291. The numerous imitations which flattered this tune are exemplified by GOS 243 and 633, and REV 148. For negro adoptions see WS 268.

No. 115

WAR DEPARTMENT, SOH 94

Chinese pentatonic, cannot be classified (I II — IV V 6 —)

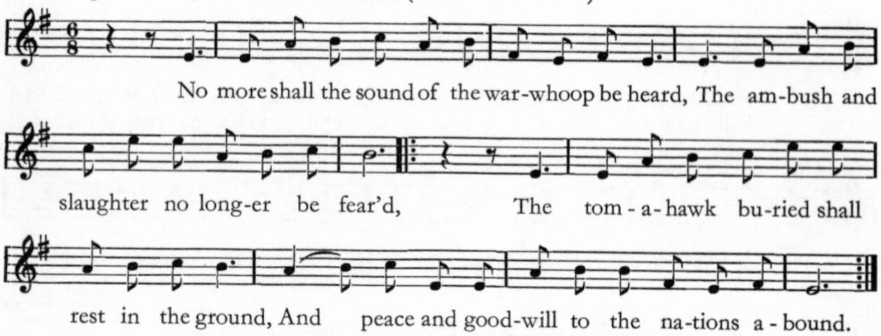
No more shall the sound of the war-whoop be heard, The am-bush and
slaughter no long-er be fear'd, The tom-a-hawk bu-ried shall
rest in the ground, And peace and good-will to the na-tions a-bound.

All spirit of war to the gospel shall bow,
The bow lie unstrung at the foot of the plow;
To prune the young orchard the spear shall be bent,
And love greet the world with a smile of content.

The words were found by the *Southern Harmony* compiler in *Mercer's Cluster*. The tune is found also HH 277, OSH 160, SOC 167. It is possibly related to Petrie, Nos. 1030 and 1285.

No. 116

DROOPING SOULS, OL 184

Hexatonic, mode 3 A (I II III — V VI VII)

Droop-ing souls, no long-er grieve, Heav-en is pro-pi-tious;
If on Je-sus you be-lieve, You will find him pre-cious.
Je-sus now is pass-ing by, Call-ing mourners to him;
Droop-ing souls, you need not die; Now look up and view him.

For complete text see 'Lebanon'. The song is inscribed "Wm. Hauser, M. D., May 29th, and July 18th, 1874."

No. 117
BE GONE UNBELIEF, OL 187

Pentatonic, mode 2 (I — 3 IV V — 7)

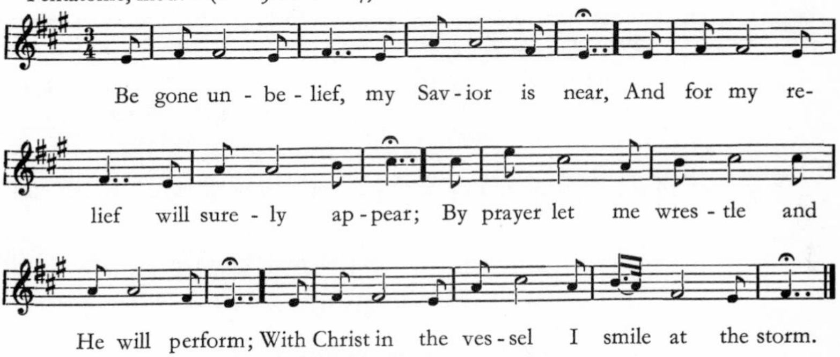
Be gone un - be - lief, my Sav - ior is near, And for my re-
lief will sure - ly ap - pear; By prayer let me wres - tle and
He will perform; With Christ in the ves - sel I smile at the storm.

Tho' dark be my way, since He is my guide,
'Tis mine to obey, 'Tis His to provide;
Tho' cisterns be broken, and creatures all fail,
The word He has spoken will surely prevail.

His life in time past forbids me to think
He'll leave me at last, in trouble to sink;
Each sweet Ebenezer, I have in review,
Confirms His good pleasure to bring me quite thro'.

Since all that I meet shall work for my good;
The bitter, the sweet; the medicine, food;
Tho' painful at present 'twill cease before long,
And then, O how pleasant the conqueror's song!

William Hauser, compiler of the *Olive Leaf* tells that this "air [was] learned of Reverend Samuel Anthony, of Georgia, in 1841." The tune of a Virginia version of the 'Brown Girl' (Sharp, i., 303) is very close to this in note-trend and character. Also 'Pretty Saro', Sharp, ii., 10—12; 'Cuckoo', Sharp, ii., 180; 'Green Bushes', Sharp, ii., 155; 'Farewell, Dear Rosanna', Sharp, ii., 243 and 244, are the same type. Negro adoptions of the tune are Marsh, pp. 144 and 173, and SS, p. 33. A variant in this collection is 'Rest in Heaven'. For its relationship to the 'I Will Arise' tune family, see the song with that title in this collection. The errors in Hauser's notation of the tune (second, fourth, sixth measures etc.) have been left uncorrected.

No. 118

PILGRIM'S TRIUMPH, OL 61

Heptatonic ionian, mode 3 A + b (I II'III IV V VI VII)

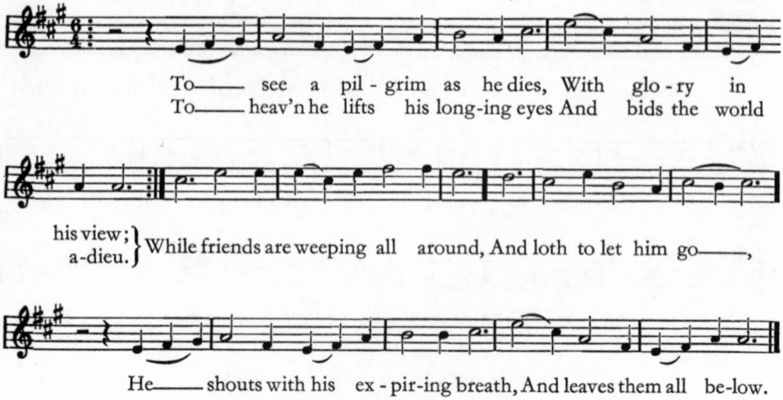
To—— see a pil - grim as he dies, With glo - ry in
To—— heav'n he lifts his long-ing eyes And bids the world
his view; a-dieu. While friends are weeping all around, And loth to let him go——,
He—— shouts with his ex - pir-ing breath, And leaves them all be-low.

O Christians, are you ready now,
To cross the rolling flood?
On Canaan's happy shore to stand,
And see your smiling God?
The dazzling charms of that bright world
Attract my soul above;
My tongue shall shout redeeming grace,
When perfected in love.

Come on, my brethren in the Lord,
Whose hearts are join'd in one;
Hold up your heads with courage bold,
Your race is almost run:
Above the clouds behold Him stand,
And smiling bid you come;
And angels whisper you away,
To your eternal home.

"This enrapturing song [the text] was written by Rev. Jno. Adam Granade, about 1802", the compiler of the *Olive Leaf* says. And he adds, "Structure of this air learned of a negro, Mark Hull, 1843." The tune belongs to the 'Hallelujah' group, which see for many related tunes.

No. 119

TO BE WITH CHRIST, REV 14

Hexatonic, mode 2 b (I — 3 IV V 6 7)

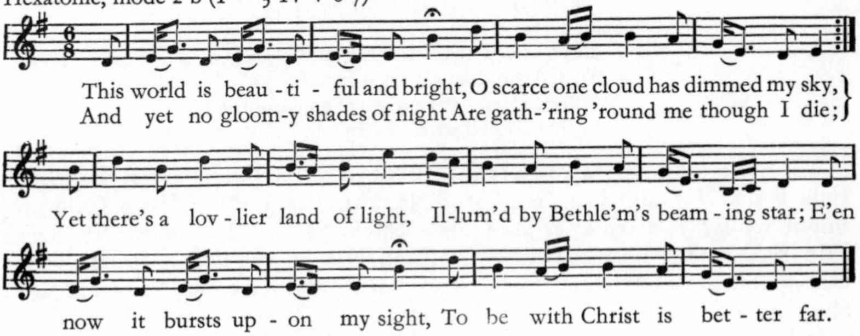
This world is beau - ti - ful and bright, O scarce one cloud has dimmed my sky,
And yet no gloom-y shades of night Are gath-'ring 'round me though I die;
Yet there's a lov - lier land of light, Il-lum'd by Bethle'm's beam - ing star; E'en
now it bursts up - on my sight, To be with Christ is bet - ter far.

True, life is sweet and friends are dear,
And youth and health are pleasant things;
Yet, leave I all, without a tear,
No sad regret my bosom wrings.
The ties of earth are broken all,
My chainless soul, above yon star,
Shall wing its way beyond recall,
To be with Christ is better far.

And is this death? My soul is calm,
No sting is here, the strife is done;
Glory to God and to the Lamb!
Sweet triumph! I have won, I've won!
A crown immortal, robes of white,
For me, for me in waiting are;
Arrayed in glory, clothed in light,
To be with Christ is better far.

One more stanza of the text is in the *Revivalist*. The tune is notated "as sung by Rev. B. I. Ives."

No. 120

DEVOTION, OSH 48

Pentatonic, mode 3 (I II III — V VI —)

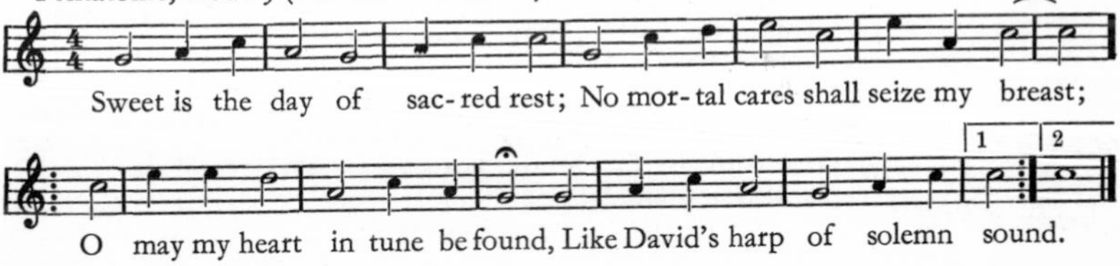
Sweet is the day of sac- red rest; No mor- tal cares shall seize my breast;
1
2
O may my heart in tune be found, Like David's harp of solemn sound.

Then shall I share a glorious part,
When grace hath well refined my heart,
And fresh supplies of joy are shed,
Like holy oil, to cheer my head.

Then shall I see, and hear, and know
All I desired and wished below;
And ev'ry power find sweet employ,
In that eternal world of joy.

Watts wrote the words. The tune is ascribed in the *Sacred Harp* to Americk Hall. Found also, MOH 34, GCM 91, SOH 13, UH 48, WP 17, SKH 9, GOS 548; and in *Social Hymn and Tune Book* (Philadelphia, 1865) under the title 'Penitent'.

In JFSS, viii., 72, Miss Gilchrist calls attention to the likeness of the above tune to Sharp's Appalachian versions of 'Little Musgrave and Lady Barnard'. She also notes Miss Broadwood's discovery of its likeness to two Gaelic tunes, 'Tearlach Og' in the *Gesto Collection*, and 'Muile nam Morbheann' in the *Celtic Lyre*. I append also 'Lost Babe', Sharp, ii., 161, as a further relative.

No. 121

TENDER CARE, GOS 291

Hexatonic, mode 1 b (I II — IV V VI 7)

When all thy mer - cies, O my God, My ris - ing soul sur-veys,
Trans- por- ted with the view, I'm lost In won-der, love and praise.
Un-num-ber'd com-forts on my soul Thy ten - der care be-stow'd,
Be - fore my in - fant soul conceiv'd From whom those comforts flow'd.

When in the slippery paths of youth,
With heedless steps I ran,
Thine arm, unseen, conveyed me safe,
And led me up to man.
Ten thousand thousand precious gifts
My daily thanks employ;
Nor is the least a cheerful heart,
That tastes those gifts with joy.

Through every period of my life,
Thy goodness I'll pursue;
And after death in distant worlds,
The pleasing theme renew.
In all eternity to Thee
A grateful song I'll raise;
But! O eternity's too short
To utter all thy praise.

Ascribed to P. M. Atchley who was a singing-school man in eastern Tennessee in the early part of the nineteenth century. The tune belongs to the 'Hallelujah' family. See the song by that name in this collection for many related melodies.

No. 122

REFLECTION, MOH 444

Hexatonic, mode 1 b (I II — IV V VI 7)

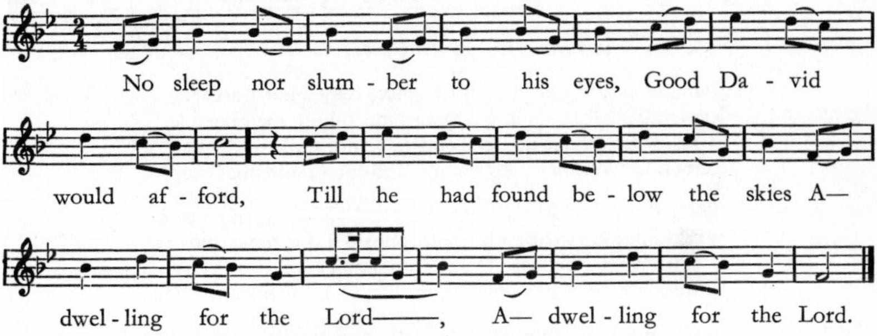
No sleep nor slum - ber to his eyes, Good Da - vid
would af - ford, Till he had found be - low the skies A—
dwel - ling for the Lord———, A— dwel - ling for the Lord.

The Lord in Zion placed his name,
His ark was settled there;
And there th'assembled nation came,
To worship twice a year,
To worship twice a year.

We trace no more those toilsome ways,
Nor wander far abroad;
Where e'er thy people meet for praise,
There is a house for God,
There is a house for God.

The tune is usually attributed to Davisson, and this probably as a result of Davisson's own claim in the *Kentucky Harmony*. Found also, KYH 42, UH 31, KNH 22, HOC 13, WP 36.

No. 123
PISGAH, OSH 58

Hexatonic, mode 3 A (I II III — V VI VII)

Je - sus, thou art the sin - ner's friend, As such I look on
thee———, Now in the bow - els of thy love, O Lord re - mem - ber
me. O Lord re - mem - ber me———, O Lord re-mem-ber me———
———; Now in the bow - els of thy love, O Lord re - mem - ber me.

Remember thy pure words of grace, remember Calvary,
Remember all thy dying groans, and then remember me.
O Lord remember me, O Lord remember me;
Remember all thy dying groans, and then remember me.

Thou wondrous advocate with God, I yield myself to thee,
While thou art sitting on thy throne, O Lord remember me.
O Lord remember me, O Lord remember me;
While thou art sitting on thy throne, O Lord remember me.

And when I close my eyes in death, and creature helps all flee,
Then O my great Redeemer, God, I pray remember me.
I pray remember me, I pray remember me;
Then O my great Redeemer, God, I pray remember me.

The poem is attributed in the *Sacred Harp* to Richard Burnham. The tune there, and generally in the southern books, is credited to J. C. Lowry. Found also, MOH 59, GCM 104, SOH 80, UH 23, KNH 56, HH 112, SOC 205, WP 83, TZ 92, SKH 25, GOS 311. A negro spiritual inspired by this song is 'Lord, Remember Me', SS 12, No. 15. Miss Gilchrist sees in 'Pisgah' a variant of 'Little Musgrave and Lady Barnard' as found in the Appendix of Motherwell, *Minstrelsy*, and later published in Chappell's *Popular Music*. (See JFSS, viii., 61—95.) Despite the apparently English source of 'Pisgah', the *Methodist Hymn Book* of England reproduces the tune under the title 'Covenanters' and calls it "an American Melody."

No. 124

GAINES, HH 122

Hexatonic, mode 3 A (I II III — V VI VII)

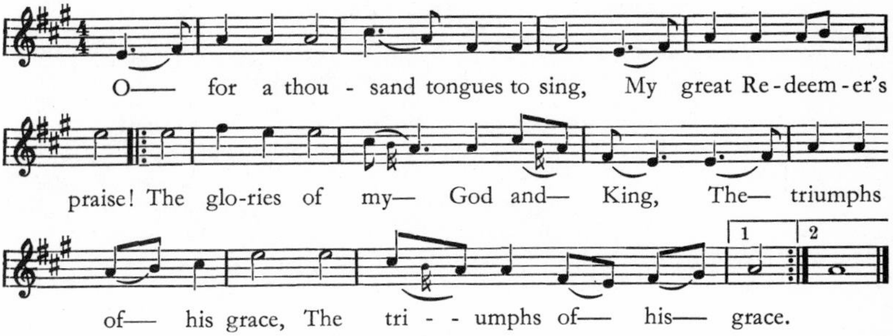
O— for a thou - sand tongues to sing, My great Re-deem-er's
praise! The glo-ries of my— God and— King, The— triumphs
of— his grace, The tri - - umphs of— his— grace.
1
2

My gracious Master and my God,
Assist me to proclaim,
To spread through all the earth abroad
The honors of thy name,
The honors of thy name.

Jesus! the name that charms our fears,
That bids our sorrows cease;
'Tis music in the sinner's ears,
'Tis life and health and peace,
'Tis life and health and peace.

Charles Wesley wrote the words. William Hauser, *Hesperian Harp* compiler, claims the tune. For melodic similarities in other spiritual songs see 'One More River to Cross', in this collection; 'Cherry Tree Carol', Sharp, i., 92 and 93; and 'Geordie', Sharp, i., 240.

No. 125

HUMBLE PENITENT, SKH 14

Hexatonic, mode 3 b (I II III IV V VI —)

Stay, thou in - sul - ted spi - rit, stay! Though
I have done thee such des-pite, Cast not a sin - ner
quite a - way, Nor take thine ev - er - last - ing flight.

Though I have most unfaithul been, of all whoe'er thy grace received;
Ten thousand times thy goodness seen, ten thousand times thy goodness griev'd.

But O, the chief of sinners spare, in honor of my great priest;
Nor in thy righteous anger swear I shall not see thy people rest.

If yet thou canst my sins forgive, e'en now, O Lord, relieve my woes;
Into thy rest of love receive, and bless me with the calm repose.

E'en now my weary soul release, and raise me by thy gracious hand;
Guide me into thy perfect peace, and bring me to the promis'd land.

Davisson, the compiler of the *Supplement to the Kentucky Harmony*, claims this tune. It is similar to 'The Bird Song', Sharp, ii., 215. For other tune relationships see 'I Will Arise' in this collection.

No. 126

CHARMING NAME, CHH 90

Heptatonic ionian, mode 3 A b (I II III IV V VI VII)

Je - sus, I love thy charm - ing name, 'Tis mus - ic
to my ear; Fain would I sound it out so loud
That earth and heav'n should hear, That earth and heav'n should hear.

Yes, thou art precious to my soul,
My transport and my trust;
Jewels, to thee, are gaudy toys,
And gold is sordid dust.

I'll speak the honors of thy name
With my last lab'ring breath;
Then speechless clasp thee in mine arms,
The antidote of death.

The notated form of this tune (the work is claimed by, and is doubtless that of, William Walker) illustrates excellently the manner of singing in rural America in earlier times. See also WS, p. 211f.

No. 127
BALM IN GILEAD, REV 15

Pentatonic, mode 3 (I II III — V VI —)

1
How lost was my con - di - tion Till Je - sus made me whole——
There is but one Phy - si - cian
2
Can cure a sin - sick soul. There's a balm in Gil - ead to make the wound-ed
whole—; There's pow'r e-nough in Je - sus to cure a sin - sick soul.

I have reproduced the notation of the *Revivalist* tune with all its mistakes. A fuller text is given under 'Good Physician' in this collection. A negro version entitled 'There is a Balm in Gilead' is given in Dett, p. 88. Another is in Work, p. 43.

No. 128
PLENARY, SOH 262

Pentatonic, mode 3 (I II III — V VI —)

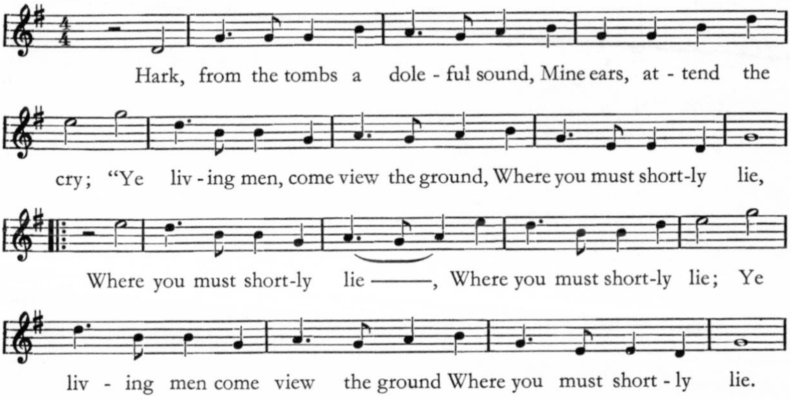
Hark, from the tombs a dole - ful sound, Mine ears, at - tend the
cry; "Ye liv - ing men, come view the ground, Where you must short-ly lie,
Where you must short-ly lie ——, Where you must short-ly lie; Ye
liv - ing men come view the ground Where you must short - ly lie.

"Princes, this clay must be your bed,
In spite of all your towers;
The tall, the wise, the reverend head
Must lie as low as ours."
Grant us the power of quickening grace,
To fit our souls to fly;
Then, when we drop this dying flesh,
We'll rise above the sky.

The tune is the same as the popular 'Old Grimes is Dead' and 'Auld Lang Syne'. It occurs also OSH 162 and CHH 94. The *Methodist Hymnal* (1935) attributes it to William Shield. In the *Southern Harmony* its author is given as A. Clark.

No. 129

SAWYER'S EXIT, OSH 338

Hexatonic, mode 3 A (I II III — V VI VII)

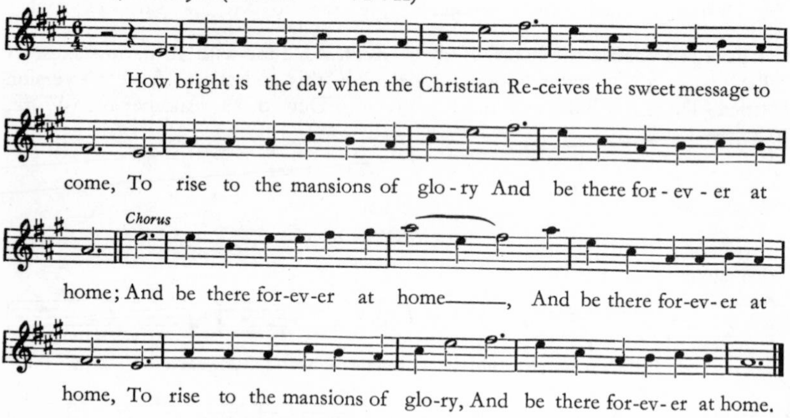
How bright is the day when the Christian Re-ceives the sweet message to
come, To rise to the mansions of glo - ry And be there for - ev - er at
Chorus
home; And be there for-ev-er at home———, And be there for-ev-er at
home, To rise to the mansions of glo-ry, And be there for-ev-er at home.

The angels stand ready and waiting,
The moment the spirit is gone,
To carry it upward to heaven,
And welcome it safely at home.
Chorus

The saints that have gone up before us,
All raise a new shout as we come,
And sing hallelujah the louder,
To welcome the travelers home.
Chorus

For source of tune and words see WS, p. 167. The tune is borrowed from 'Old Rosin the Bow', see Sandburg, p. 167. See also 'My Sister She Works in a Laundry' Sandburg, 381; 'When Sherman Marched Down to the Sea', Dolph, 347; 'Washington Badge', HH 536; 'Lord Randal', Sharp, i., 39; and 'I wonder When I'm to Be Married', from Dumphriesshire, England, 1855, see JFSS, viii., 142.

No. 130

O TELL ME NO MORE, OL 301

Pentatonic, mode 3 (I II III — V VI —)

O tell me no more of this world's vain store; The time for such
tri - fles with me now is o'er. A coun - try I've found, where
true joys a - bound, To dwell I'm de - ter-min'd on that hap-py ground.

The souls that believe, in Paradise live;
And me in that number will Jesus receive:
My soul, don't delay, he calls thee away;
Rise, follow thy Savior, and bless the glad day.

No mortal doth know what he can bestow,
What light, strength, and comfort; go after him, go!
Lo! onward I move, to a city above;
None guesses how wondrous my journey will prove.

The text is attributed to "John Gambold, of England." I find the tune to be a relative of a 'Lord Randal' variant which Sharp (i., 43, G) found in eastern Tennessee. The resemblance of the two tunes runs throughout; but in the last four-measure phrase (going with the worldly sentence "I'm sick to the heart and I fain would lie down") they are practically identical. 'Rose' in this collection is a variant of this tune, notated in the folk manner of singing.

No. 131

HEAVENLY DOVE, SOC 23

Pentatonic, mode 3 (I II III — V VI —)

Come, Ho - ly Spi- rit, heav'n-ly dove, With all thy quick'n-ing pow-ers;
Come shed a - broad a Sav-ior's love, And that will kin - dle ours——.

This is quite clearly the 'Barbara Allen' tune as it is seen, for example, in Sharp, i., 183 ff. It is also related to 'Lonesome Grove' in this collection. The "dove" theme in the text of the above song and in the 'Lonesome Grove' song was possibly the magnet which attracted the texts to variant tunes.

No. 132

CEYLON, PB 372

Pentatonic, mode 3 (I II III — V VI VII)

How long, O Lord our Sa - vior, wilt thou re - main a-
way——? Our hearts are grow - ing wea - ry of thy so
long de - lay. O when will come the mo-ment when, brighter far than
morn, The sun-shine of thy glo - ry will on thy peo- ple dawn.

How long, O gracious Saviour, wilt Thou Thy household leave?
So long hast Thou now tarried, few Thy return believe;
Immersed in sloth and folly, Thy servants, Lord, we see;
And few of us stand ready, with joy to welcome Thee.

How long, O heav'nly Bridegroom, how long wilt Thou delay?
And yet how few are grieving, that Thou dost absent stay;
Thy very bride her portion and calling hath forgot,
And seeks for ease and glory, where Thou, her Lord, art not.

The tune is a close relative of 'Love Divine' CHI 63, 'Heavenly Welcome' HH 482, 'Baltimore' SKH 53, 'Garden Hymn' REV 164, and a less close one to 'Heavenward', *Christian Science Hymnal* (1932), No. 136, which is an ancient Irish tune from the Petrie collection. Compare Petrie, No. 993.

No. 133

NEW PROSPECT or O LAND OF REST, OSH 390

Pentatonic, mode 3 (I II III — V VI —)

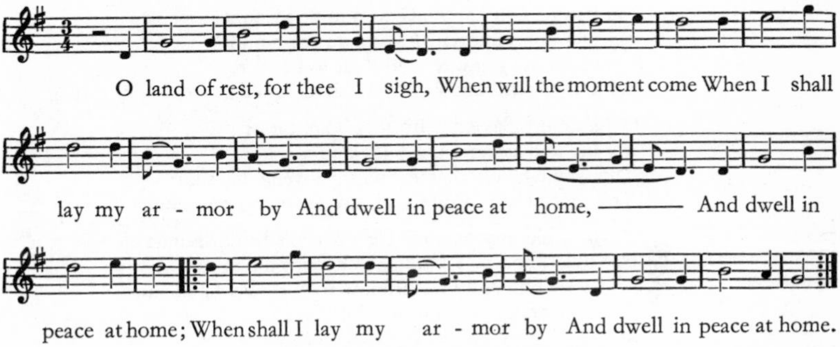
O land of rest, for thee I sigh, When will the moment come When I shall
lay my ar - mor by And dwell in peace at home, ——— And dwell in
peace at home; When shall I lay my ar - mor by And dwell in peace at home.

No tranquil joy on earth I know,
No peaceful, sheltering dome;
This world's a wilderness of woe,
This world is not my home.

Our tears shall all be wiped away
When we have ceased to roam,
And we shall hear our Father say,
"Come, dwell with me at home.

J. S. James, editor of the 1911 *Original Sacred Harp*, attributes tune and words to W. S. Turner of Georgia. It is found also, GOS 390.

Close relatives of this tune are 'Deep Spring' in this collection, 'Lord Thomas and Fair Eleanor', Sharp, i., 118; and 'Little Musgrave and Lady Barnard', Sharp, i., 166.

No. 134
I LOVE THEE, OL 318

Pentatonic, mode 3 (I III II — V VI —)

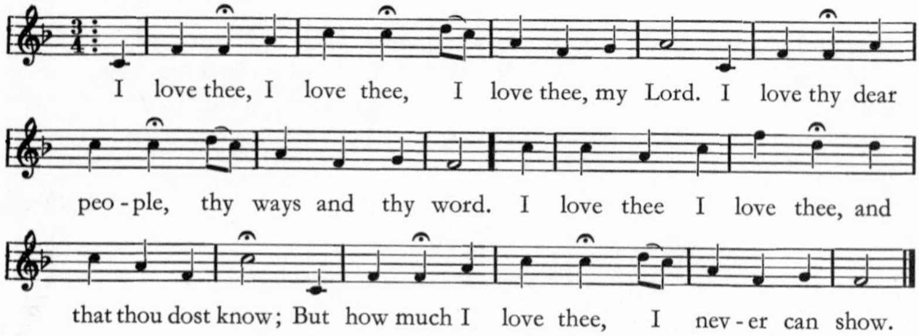
I love thee, I love thee, I love thee, my Lord. I love thy dear
peo-ple, thy ways and thy word. I love thee I love thee, and
that thou dost know; But how much I love thee, I nev-er can show.

I'm happy, I'm happy, O wondrous account!
My joys are immortal, I stand on the mount!
I gaze on my treasure, and long to be there,
With Jesus and angels, my kindred so dear.

O Jesus, my Savior, with thee I am blest!
My life and salvation, my joy and my rest!
Thy Name be my theme, and thy love be my song!
Thy grace shall inspire both my heart and my tongue.

O who's like my Savior? He's Salem's bright King;
He smiles, and he loves me, and helps me to sing:
I'll praise him and bless him, with notes loud and shrill,
While rivers of pleasure my spirit do fill:

O Jesus, my Savior! I know thou art mine;
For thee all the pleasures of sin I resign:
Of objects most pleasing I love thee the best;
Without thee I'm wretched, but with thee I'm blessed.

Tho' weak and despised, by faith I now stand,
Preserv'd and defended by Heaven's kind hand:
By Jesus supported, I'll praise his dear name,
Regardless of danger, of praise, or of blame.

I find him in singing, I find him in prayer;
In sweet meditation he always is near:
My constant companion, Oh may we ne'er part!
All glory to Jesus, who dwells in my heart!

The text is attributed to John Adam Granade, the "Billy Sunday" of the revival movement which reached a high point in its trend at about the beginning of the nineteenth century. Granade was the author of many widely sung texts.

The tune is clearly of the 'Lord Lovel' family. Compare, for example, the melody which Sharp found in North Carolina; see Sharp, i., 38, A. Its earliest appearance in American religious song books seems to have been in Ingalls' *Christian Harmony*, 1805, p. 44.

No. 135

NEW BRITAIN or HARMONY GROVE, SOH 8

Pentatonic, mode 3 (I II III — V VI —)

A - maz - ing grace! (how sweet the sound) That saved a wretch like me!
1
2
I once was lost, but now am found, Was blind, but now I see.

The poem is by Newton. The tune's source is unknown to the southern compilers. It goes also under the names 'Symphony', 'Solon', and 'Redemption'. Found also, WP 27, GCM 105, OSH 45, HH 104, SOC 190, TZ 90, VH 19, *Church Harmony* 91. A close relative of the tune is 'Primrose' in this collection. Further stanzas of the text are given under 'Melody'.

I recorded this tune also as it was sung by F. Fagan Thompson of Vanderbilt University, Nashville, Tennessee, February, 1936. I reproduce here his version, one in which the tune is slowed and many graces are introduced, as an excellent illustration of the widespread southern folk-manner in the singing of hymns of this sort.

very slow

A - - maz - ing— grace! (how sweet the—— sound) That——
saved a—— wretch like— me! I—— once was—— lost,
but now I'm—— found, Was— blind but— now I——— see.

No. 136
SPIRITUAL SAILOR, SOH 41

Heptatonic aeolian, mode 2 A+b (I II 3 IV V 6 7)

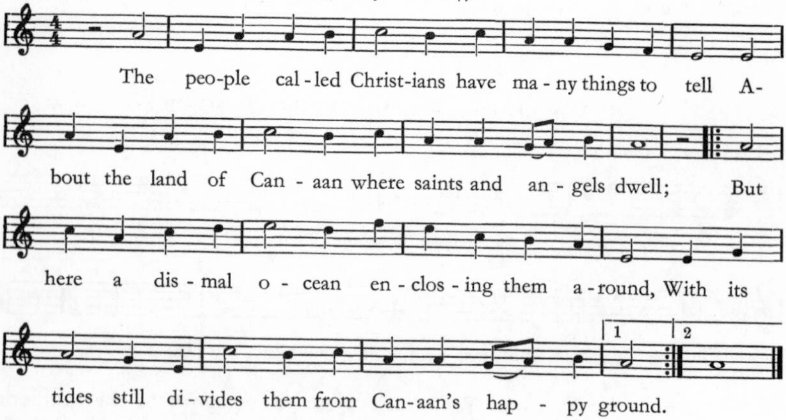
The peo-ple cal-led Christ-ians have ma-ny things to tell A-
bout the land of Can-aan where saints and an-gels dwell; But
here a dis-mal o-cean en-clos-ing them a-round, With its
tides still di-vides them from Can-aan's hap-py ground.
1
2

Many have been impatient to work their passage through,
And with united wisdom have tried what they could do;
But vessels built by human skill have never sailed far,
Till we found them aground on some dreadful, sandy bar.

The everlasting gospel hath launch'd the deep at last;
Behold the sails expanded around the tow'ring mast!
Along the deck in order, the joyful sailors stand,
Crying, "Ho! — here we go to Immanuel's happy land!"

We're now on the wide ocean, we bid the world farewell!
And though where we shall anchor no human tongue can tell;
About our future destiny there need be no debate,
While we ride on the tide, with our Captain and his Mate.

To those who are spectators what anguish must ensue,
To hear their old companions bid them a last adieu!
The pleasures of your paradise no more our hearts invite;
We will sail — you may rail, we shall soon be out of sight.

The passengers united in order, peace, and love;
The wind is in our favour, how swiftly do we move!
Though tempests may assail us, and raging billows roar,
We will sweep through the deep, till we reach fair Canaan's shore.

The *Southern Harmony* gives the maker of this song as I. Neighbours, who may indeed have been the author of the text. This text is clearly a parody, and the tune a close variant, of 'When the Stormy Winds do Blow' or 'You Gentlemen of England', a song of seafaring which appears to have been widely sung in England over a long period. References to a 'Stormy Winds' ballad reach back to 1660. The tune with different texts appeared as 'Saylers for my Money', 'The Bride-groom's Salutation', 'You Calvinists of England' and 'England's Valour and Holland's Terrour'. See Vincent Jackson, *English Melodies from the 13th to the 18th Century*, p. 114.

Other melodic relatives which have come to my notice are 'The Trees do Grow High', Sharp, *One Hundred English Folk-Songs*, No. 25; and 'John Anderson My Jo John', *The Singer's Companion*, p. 72, and SMM, No. 146.

No. 137

IDUMEA, OSH 47

Pentatonic, mode 2 (I — 3 IV V — 7)

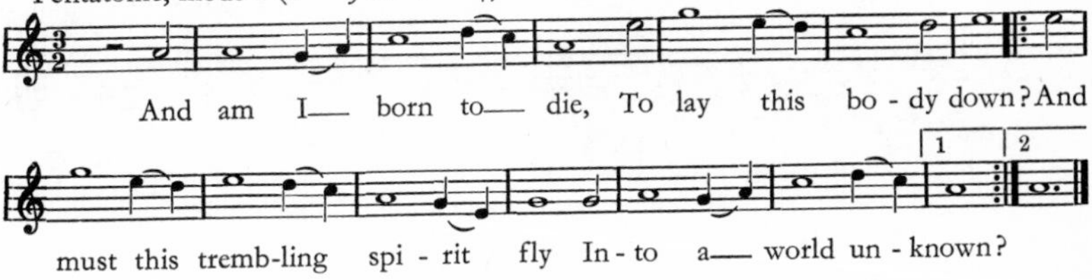
And am I— born to— die, To lay this bo - dy down? And
must this tremb-ling spi - rit fly In - to a— world un - known?
1
2

Waked by the trumpet's sound,
I from the grave shall rise,
To see the Judge with glory crowned,
And view the flaming skies.

How shall I leave the tomb?
With triumph or regret?
A fearful or a joyful doom?
A curse or blessing meet?

I must from God be driv'n,
Or with my Saviour dwell;
Must come at His command to heav'n,
Or else depart — to hell.

The words are by Charles Wesley. The tune is claimed by Ananias Davisson in his *Kentucky Harmony* (1815) whence it was borrowed by practically all the subsequent book compilers in the South. The tune was used for the secular ballad 'Lord Lovel'; see *White Spirituals*, p. 177. Also found KYH 33, GCM 36, SOH 31,

UH 19, KNH 36, HH 224, SOC 55, HOC 44, TZ 122, MOH 38, *Church Harmony*, p. 35, GOS 184, PB 246. An imitation of this tune is GOS 325. 'Lord Thomas and Fair Eleanor', Davis, p. 570, shows the same trend, as does also 'Young Hunting', Sharp, i., 112.

No. 138

BOZRAH, GOS 59

Hexatonic, mode 2 b (I — 3 IV V 6 7)

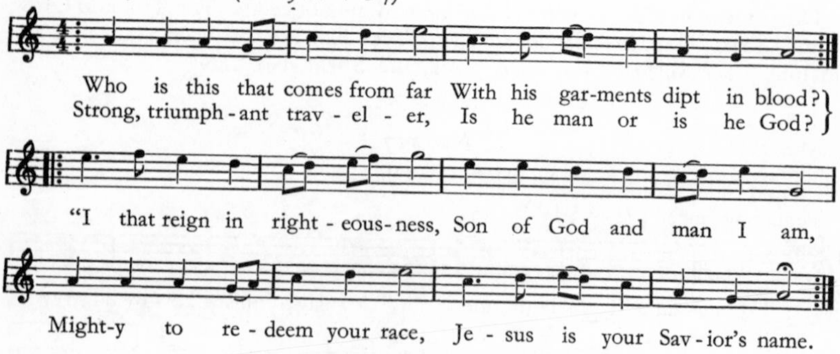
Who is this that comes from far With his gar-ments dipt in blood?
Strong, triumph-ant trav-el-er, Is he man or is he God?
"I that reign in right-eous-ness, Son of God and man I am,
Might-y to re-deem your race, Je-sus is your Sav-ior's name.

"Wide, ye heavenly gates, unfold,
Closed no more by death and sin;
Lo, the conquering Lord behold;
Let the King of glory in."
Hark, th'angelic host inquire,
"Who is He, th'almighty King?"
Hark again, the answering choir
Thus in strains of triumph sing:

"He whose powerful arm, alone,
On His foes destruction hurled;
He who hath the victory won;
He who saved you by His blood;
He who God's pure law fulfilled;
Jesus, the incarnate Word;
He whose truth with blood was sealed;
He is heaven's all-glorious Lord."

The melodic sentence at the beginning and at the end is a favorite. It may be found, for example, also in 'Greenwood Siding', Cox, p. 522. A variant of the tune is 'When I First Left Old Ireland', Petrie, No. 863. See 'I Will Arise' in this collection for further tune relationships.

No. 139

NEW ORLEANS, PB 255

Heptatonic aeolian, mode 2 A+b (I II 3 IV V 6 7)

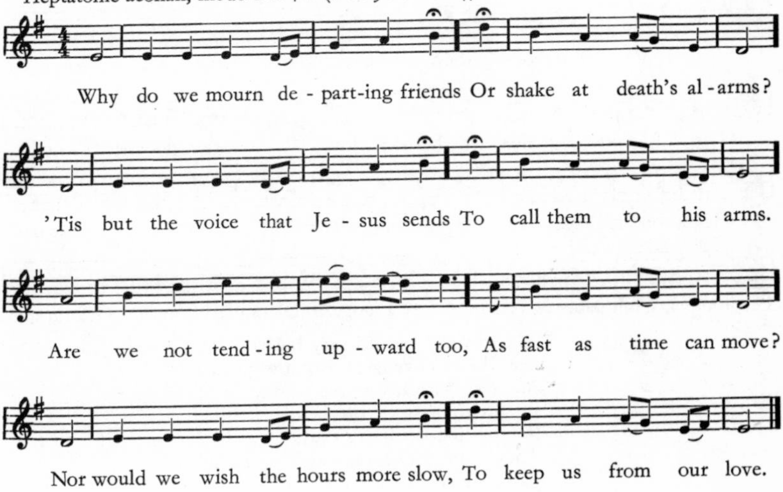
Why do we mourn de - part-ing friends Or shake at death's al - arms?
'Tis but the voice that Je - sus sends To call them to his arms.
Are we not tend - ing up - ward too, As fast as time can move?
Nor would we wish the hours more slow, To keep us from our love.

For variant forms of the tune see 'Marion' and 'I Will Arise' in this collection. Among its related secular tunes are 'Greenwood Siding' ('Cruel Mother'), Cox, p. 522; an unnamed tune in Petrie, No. 193; 'Oh Love it is a Killing Thing', Petrie, No. 469; and 'When First I left Old Ireland', Petrie, No. 863. A remarkable tune resemblance and one which opens to the imagination surprising vistas as to the possible age of the 'New Orleans' tune, is to be seen in the Whitsuntide church melody 'Iam Christus astra ascenderat' from the eleventh century:

Iam Christus as - tra as - cen - de - rat re - gres - sus un - de ve - ne - rat.

The same melodic trend is seen also in the German tune set to 'Christ der du bist der helle Tag' from the year 1568. See *Hymns Ancient and Modern*, Nos. 178 and 604.

No. 140

HOLY SON OF GOD, REV 365

Hexatonic, mode 2 A (I II 3 IV V — 7)

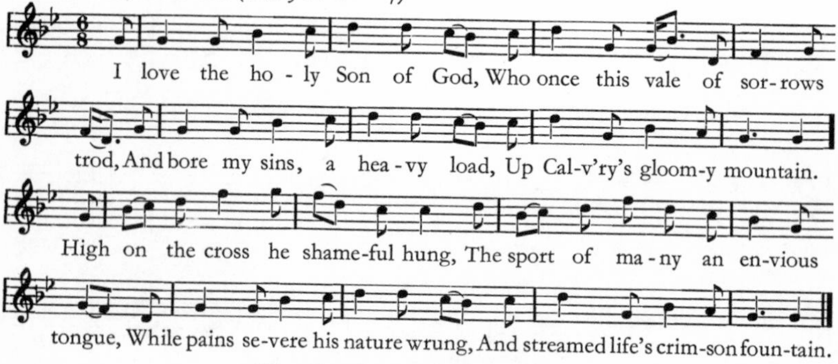
I love the ho - ly Son of God, Who once this vale of sor - rows
trod, And bore my sins, a hea - vy load, Up Cal-v'ry's gloom-y mountain.
High on the cross he shame-ful hung, The sport of ma - ny an en-vious
tongue, While pains se-vere his nature wrung, And streamed life's crim-son foun-tain.

Oh, why did not his fury burn,
And floods of vengeance on them turn?
Amazing! See his bowels yearn
In soft compassion on them.
No fury kindles in his eyes;
They beam with love, and when he dies,
Father, forgive, the sufferer cries,
They know not — Oh, forgive them.

No. 141

WORTHY THE LAMB, SWP 92

Heptatonic aeolian, mode 2 A + b (I II 3 IV 6 7)

Glo - ry to God on high——; Let earth and skies re-
ply, Praise ye his name, praise ye his name; His— love and
grace a - dore———, Who all our sor - rows bore, Sing a - loud
ev - er - more———, Worth - y the Lamb, worth - y the Lamb.

Jesus, our Lord and God,
Bore sin's tremendous load,
Praise ye his name, praise ye his name;
Tell what his arm has done,
What spoils from death he won;
Sing his great name alone;
Worthy the Lamb.

While they around the throne
Cheerfully join as one,
Praising his name, praising his name,
Those who have felt his blood
Sealing their peace with God,
Sound his dear fame abroad,
Worthy the Lamb.

Three more stanzas of the text are in the *Southern and Western Pocket Harmonist*. The tune is attributed to Bradshaw.

No. 142
CAPTAIN KIDD, COH 73

Hexatonic, mode 4 b (I II 3 IV V — 7)

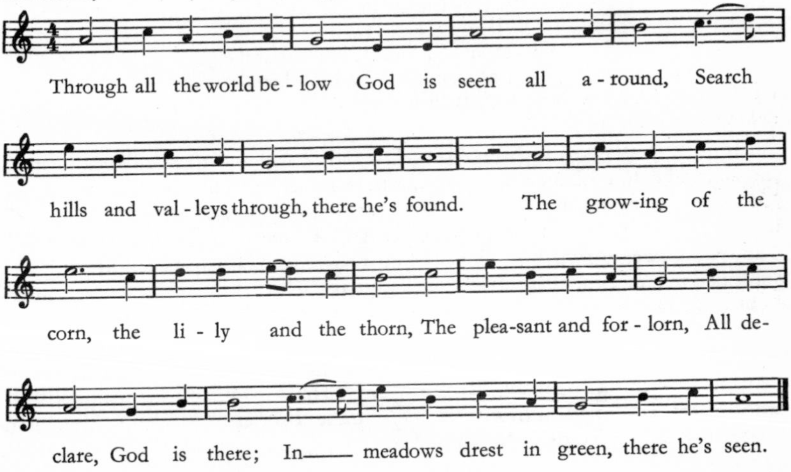
Through all the world be - low God is seen all a - round, Search
hills and val - leys through, there he's found. The grow-ing of the
corn, the li - ly and the thorn, The plea-sant and for - lorn, All de-
clare, God is there; In—— meadows drest in green, there he's seen.

See springing waters rise,
Fountains flow, rivers run;
The mist that veils the sky
  Hides the sun;
Then down the rain doth pour,
The ocean it doth roar,
And beat upon the shore;
And all praise in their ways
The God who ne'er declines
  His designs.

The sun with all his rays
Speaks of God as he flies;
The comet in her blaze,
  God she cries.
The shining of the stars,
The moon when she appears,
His awful name declares;
See them fly through the sky,
And join the solemn sound
  All round.

Not India's hills of gold,
Where the wonders are told,
Nor zephyrs strong and bold
  Can unfold
The mountain Calvary,
Where Christ our Lord did die.
Hark, hear the Savior cry,
Mountains quake, heavens shake,
Christ, call'd to heaven's host,
  Left their coast.

The tune is ascribed to Nicholson. The oldest American recording known to me is in the four-shape-note manuscript song collection made by Catherine Alderice in or near Emmittsburg, Md., 1800—1830, p. 37. Miss Gilchrist calls attention to the secular 'Captain Kidd' ballad, of which the above is a parody, as it appeared, twenty-five verses long, in *Our Familiar Songs and Who Made Them*, published in America, 1889. She describes it as "a sort of dying speech and testament probably dating from about 1701 in which year Kidd and nine of his associates were hanged in Execution Dock.... There were many other eighteenth century songs, built on this peculiar stanzaic plan, celebrating other notorious characters, 'Admiral Benbow,' 'Jack (or Sam) Hall.'" Other American spiritual songs in this collection having the same stanzaic form are 'Wondrous Love' and 'Remember Sinful Youth'.

No. 143

JERUSALEM, SOH (1835) 60

Heptatonic aeolian, mode 2 A+b (I II 3 IV V 6 VII).

Je - ru - sa - lem, my hap - py— home, O how I long for
When will my sor-rows have an— end, Thy joys when shall I
thee!
see?
But O, the hap-py, hap-py place, The place where Je - sus reigns;
The place where Christians all shall meet, Ne-ver to part a - gain.

Further stanzas of the text are given under 'Long-Sought Home' in this collection. The song is attributed to Benjamin White. This is Benjamin Franklin White, brother-in-law of, and co-worker with, William Walker (compiler of the *Southern Harmony)* and author subsequently of the *Sacred Harp*. See *White Spirituals*, p. 84.

No. 144

ROBY, OL 273

Heptatonic dorian, mode 2 A+B with altered 3rd (I II 3 [III] IV V VI 7)

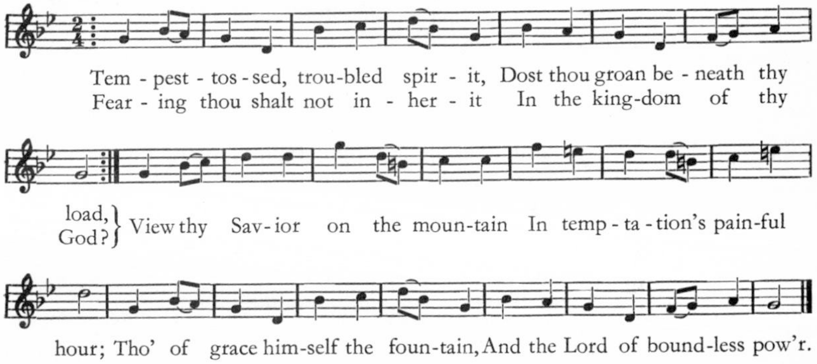
Tem - pest - tos - sed, trou-bled spir - it, Dost thou groan be - neath thy
Fear - ing thou shalt not in - her - it In the king-dom of thy
load,
God?
View thy Sav-ior on the moun-tain In temp - ta - tion's pain-ful
hour; Tho' of grace him-self the foun-tain, And the Lord of bound-less pow'r.

Do thy blooming prospects languish?
Sayest thou still, "I'm not his child?"
View thy Savior's dreadful anguish,
Famished in the gloomy wild.
Not a step in all thy journey,
Thro' this gloomy vale of tears,
But thy Lord hath trod before thee;
He thy way to glory clears.

The *OliveLeaf* compiler informs us that this song which was a favorite with the late Rev. Wesley P. Arnold, of Georgia, was "learned of some dear Baptist friends in Iridell Co., N. C., in 1839, and called 'Roby', their name."

No. 145

REMEMBER SINFUL YOUTH or SOLEMN THOUGHT, SOH 29

Pentatonic, mode 2 (I — 3 IV V — 7)

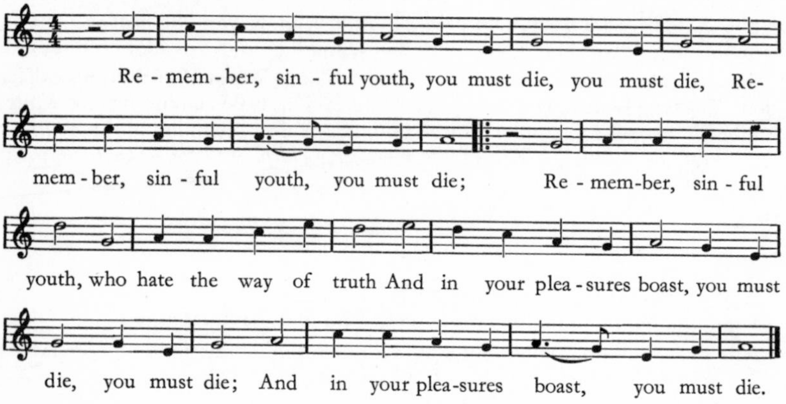
Re - mem - ber, sin - ful youth, you must die, you must die, Re-
mem - ber, sin - ful youth, you must die; Re - mem-ber, sin - ful
youth, who hate the way of truth And in your plea - sures boast, you must
die, you must die; And in your plea-sures boast, you must die.

Uncertain are your days here below, here below,
Uncertain are your days here below,
Uncertain are your days, for God hath many ways
To bring you to your graves here below, here below,
To bring you to your graves here below.

The God that built the sky, great I AM, great I AM,
The God that built the sky, great I AM,
The God that built the sky, hath said, (and cannot lie),
Impenitents shall die, and be damn'd, and be damn'd,
Impenitents shall die, and be damn'd.

And, O my friends, don't you, I entreat, I entreat,
And, O my friends, don't you, I entreat,
And, O my friends, don't you your carnal mirth pursue,
Your guilty souls undo, I entreat, I entreat,
Your guilty souls undo, I entreat.

Unto the Saviour flee, 'scape for life! 'scape for life!
Unto the Saviour flee, 'scape for life!
Unto the Saviour flee, lest death eternal be
Your final destiny, 'scape for life! 'scape for life!
Your final destiny, 'scape for life!

The mood of the poem indicates a considerable age for it. That the song as a whole was decidedly among the stock of orally transmitted ones is indicated by the many claimants to its authorship. Such claimants in the southern books are F. Price, William Caldwell, James Carrell and Ananias Davisson. Found also, UH 56, KNH 108, HH 225, SKH 66, CHH 361. The stanzaic form is that of 'Captain Kidd' in this collection. In his *Christian Harmony*, William Walker adds the note that "I learned it [the tune] from my dear mother (who now sings in heaven) when I was only three years old, — the first tune I ever learned." That was in 1812. That the song was even older, however, is shown by its appearance in Ingalls' *Christian Harmony* of 1805, p. 39.

No. 146

WEEPING SAVIOR, OSH 33

Hexatonic, mode 2 A (I II 3 IV V — 7)

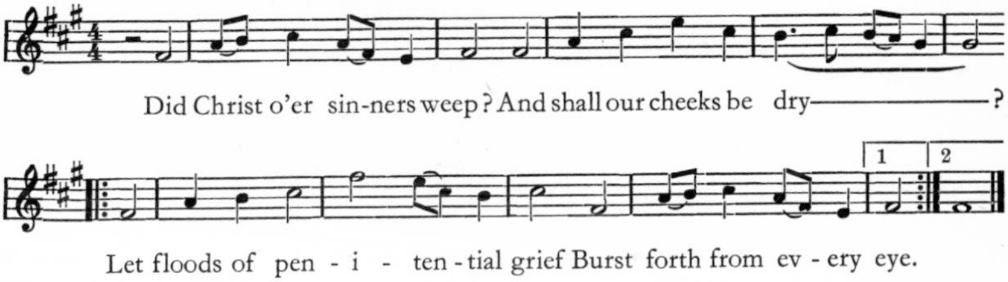
Did Christ o'er sin-ners weep? And shall our cheeks be dry——————?
1
2
Let floods of pen - i - ten - tial grief Burst forth from ev - ery eye.

The Son of God in tears,
Angels with wonder see;
Be thou astonished, O my soul;
He shed those tears for thee.

He wept that we might weep;
Each sin demands a tear;
In heav'n alone no sin is found,
And there's no weeping there.

The text is attributed to Benjamin Beddome, and the tune to Joseph Barnby, and to E. J. King. The first, sixth, and seventh measures had only quarter notes in the *Sacred Harp*. The slurred eighth notes are inserted from a variant of the tune found in the *Olive Leaf*. They represent probably an effort on the part of the editor of that song book to present the tune as really sung.

No. 147

DETROIT, SOH 40

Hexatonic, mode 2, b (I — 3 IV V 6 7)

Do I not love thee, O my Lord? Be - hold my heart and see;
And turn each curs - ed i - dol out, That dares to ri - val thee.

Hast thou a lamb in all thy flock
I would disdain to feed?
Hast thou a foe before whose face
I fear thy cause to plead?

Would not my ardent spirit vie
With angels 'round thy throne,
To execute thy sacred will,
And make thy glory known?

Thou know'st I love thee, dearest Lord,
But Oh! I long to soar
Far from the sphere of mortal joys,
That I may love thee more.

Philip Doddridge is credited with the words. The tune is attributed to 'Bradshaw' in the *Southern Harmony*. Found also, UH 33, KNH 23, OSH 39, HH 158, SOC 175, HOC 22, WP 24, SKH 85, GOS 282. The melody is similar to a number of those given by Sharp (i., 150ff.) with 'The Wife of Usher's Well'.

No. 148

I SHALL BE SATISFIED, REV 62

Hexatonic, mode 4 b minorized (I II 3 IV V — 7 [VII])

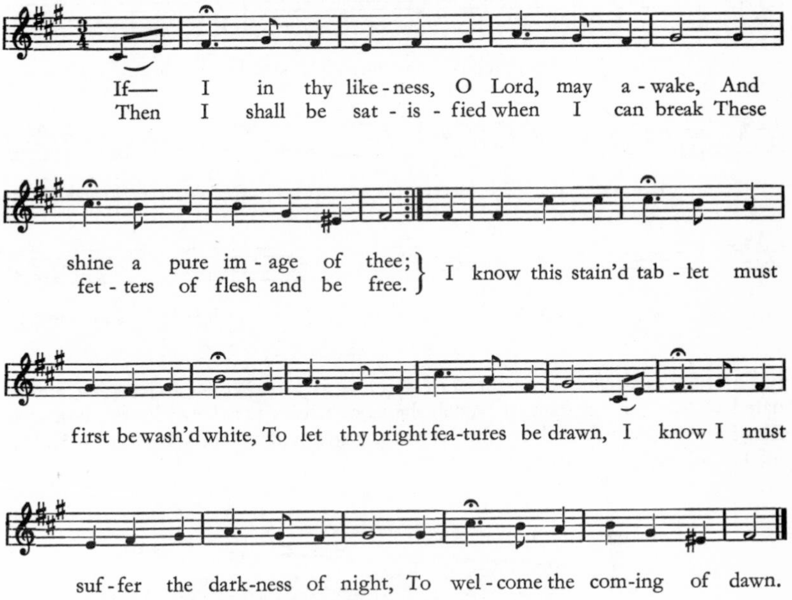
If— I in thy like-ness, O Lord, may a-wake, And
Then I shall be sat-is-fied when I can break These
shine a pure im-age of thee;
fet-ters of flesh and be free.
I know this stain'd tab-let must
first be wash'd white, To let thy bright fea-tures be drawn, I know I must
suf-fer the dark-ness of night, To wel-come the com-ing of dawn.

Then I shall be satisfied when I can cast
The shadows of nature all by,
When this cold dreary world from my vision is past,
And let this soul open her eye.
I gladly shall feel the blest morn drawing near,
When time's dreary fancy shall fade,
If then in thy likeness I may but appear,
I rise with thy beauty arrayed.

One more stanza of text in the *Revivalist*. The song is used "as sung by Rev. G. C. Wells." It is reminiscent of the 'Henry Martin' tune; see Gould and Sharp, *English Folk-Songs for Schools*, p. 22.

No. 149
EDGEFIELD, OSH 82

Heptatonic aeolian, mode 2 A+b (I II 3 IV V 6 7)

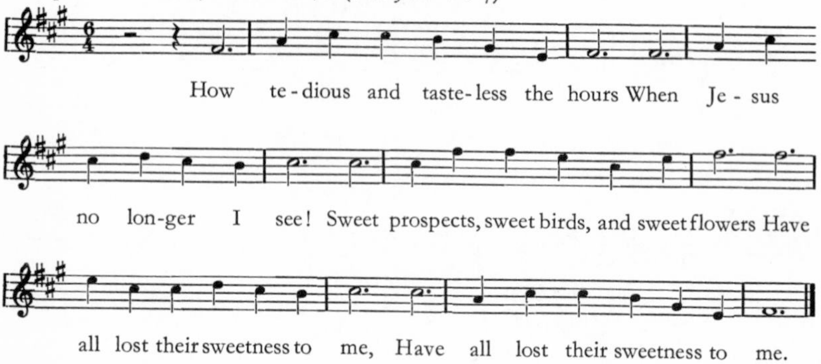
How te-dious and taste-less the hours When Je-sus
no lon-ger I see! Sweet prospects, sweet birds, and sweet flowers Have
all lost their sweetness to me, Have all lost their sweetness to me.

The tune is attributed, in the *Sacred Harp*, to J. T. White, a Georgian, and is dated 1844. It is a variant of 'When the Cock Crows it is Day', Petrie, No. 478. The fuller text, attributed to John Newton, is given under the song 'Green Fields' in this collection.

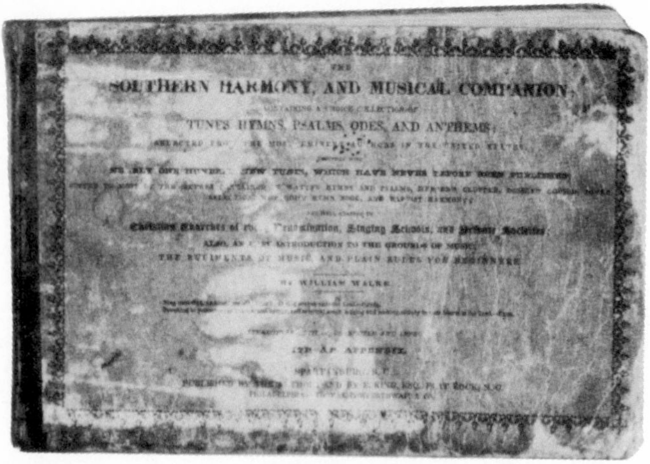
SOUTHERN HARMONY, AND MUSICAL COMPANION
TUNES HYMNS, PSALMS, ODES, AND ANTHEMS

FROM ITS FIRST APPEARANCE IN 1835 UP TO THE TIME OF THE CIVIL WAR, 600,000 copies of *The Southern Harmony* went into southern homes. Twenty-four songs from this book are in the present collection.

One Hundred and one
Revival Spiritual Songs

WILLIAM (SINGIN' BILLY) WALKER, OF SPARTANBURG, SOUTH CAROLINA, was perhaps the foremost among those singing masters who welded folk to folk-song. In all his singing schools throughout the southeastern states his handbook was his own excellent collection of spiritual folk-tunes, *The Southern Harmony.*

IN THE NEGLECTED MAGNOLIA CEMETERY IN SPARTANBURG this grave stone was recently found lying flat on the ground. The wording below the representation of Walker's last song book, *The Christian Harmony*, reads:

IN

Memory of

Wm. WALKER, A. S. H.*

Died Sept. 24th, 1875, in the 67th year of his age. He was a devoted Husband & kind Father. A consistent Baptist 47 years, Taught music. 45 yrs. The Author of 4 Books of sacred music. He rests from his labors. He died in the triumphs of faith.

Sing praises unto the Lord.

* Author of Southern Harmony.

No. 150

JESUS IS MY FRIEND (A), OSH 345

Hexatonic, mode 3 A (I II III — V VI VII)

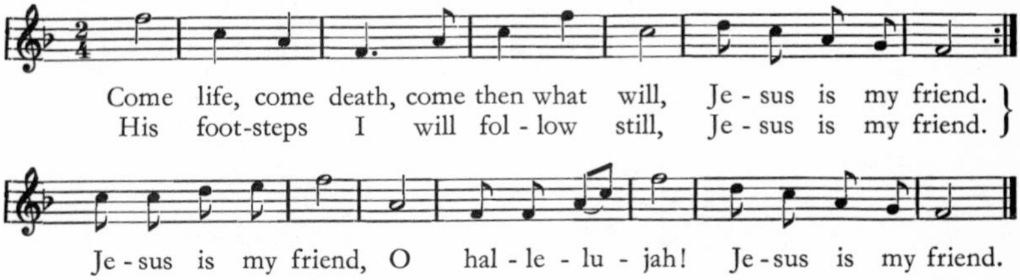
Come life, come death, come then what will, Je - sus is my friend.
His foot-steps I will fol - low still, Je - sus is my friend.
Je - sus is my friend, O hal - le - lu - jah! Je - sus is my friend.

In the *Sacred Harp* of 1859 this song, tune and words, is attributed to the Georgian, J. P. Rees. I have heard my negro servant, Annie Ware, singing it, or fragments of it including the final phrase, "Jesus is my friend," in Nashville, Tennessee, 1932. It is found also GOS 652.

No. 151

LOST CITY or TO GLORY I WILL GO, OSH 320

Heptatonic ionian, mode 3 A + b (I II III IV V VI VII)

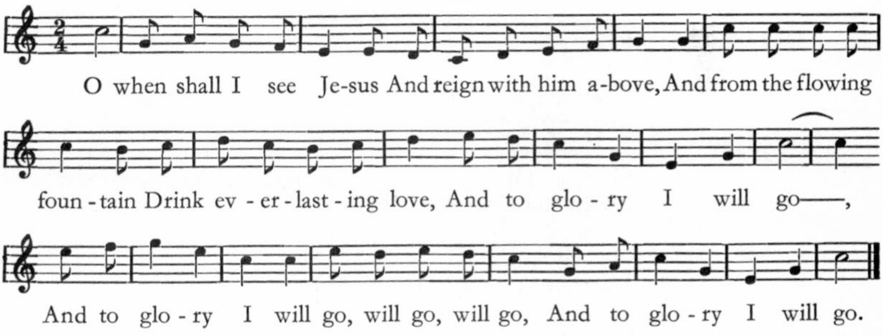
O when shall I see Je-sus And reign with him a-bove, And from the flowing
foun - tain Drink ev - er - last - ing love, And to glo - ry I will go——,
And to glo - ry I will go, will go, will go, And to glo - ry I will go.

The words are by John Leland. The old tune seems to have been wedded to the above text by E. L. King, about 1844, according to the *Original Sacred Harp*. John G. McCurry applied the same tune to a text beginning:

> I'd rather live a beggar
> While here on earth I stay

and ending with the refrain

> And to begging I will go.

See 'Beggar' in this collection where there are references to the seventeenth century prototype of the above song. Further stanzas of the above spiritual text are given under 'Faithful Soldier'.

No. 152

GOLDEN HARP or TO PLAY ON THE GOLDEN HARP, OSH 274

Pentatonic, mode 2 (I — 3 IV V — 7)

Fare-well, vain world, I'm go - ing home, To play on the gold-en harp;
My Sav - ior smiles and bids me come, To play on the gold-en harp.
Chorus I want to be where Je - sus is, To play on the gold-en harp.

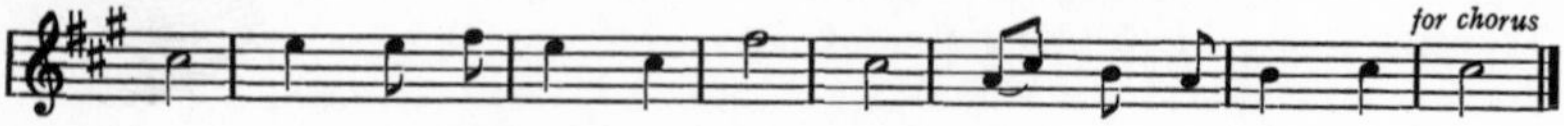

To play on the gold - en harp, To play on the gold - en harp;

Sweet angels beckon me away
To sing God's praise in endless day.

I'm glad that I am born to die,
From grief and woe my soul shall fly.

Bright angels shall convey me home,
Away to New Jerusalem.

I'll praise my Master while I've breath,
I hope to praise him after death.

I hope to praise him when I die,
And shout salvation as I fly.

I soon shall pass this vale of death,
And in his arms I'll lose my breath.

And then my happy soul shall tell
My Jesus hath done all things well.

Recorded in 1869 for the edition of the *Sacred Harp* which appeared in that year. The tune stems from some variants of 'Come all ye Faithful Christians', cf. JFSS, ii., 115 ff.

No. 153
I CAN'T STAY AWAY, CSH 95

Heptatonic aeolian, mode 2 A+b (I II 3 IV V 6 7)

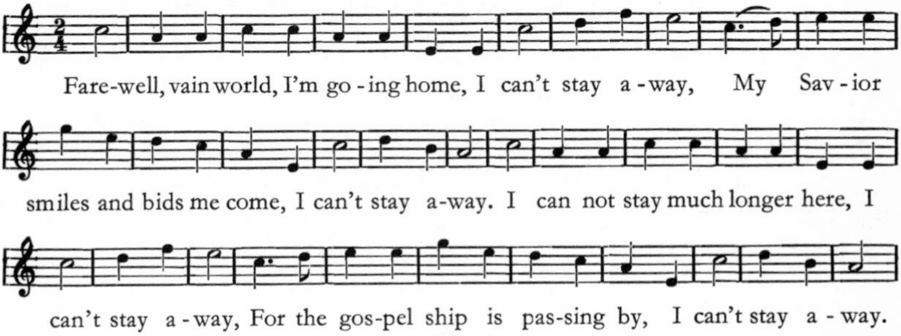
Fare-well, vain world, I'm go - ing home, I can't stay a - way, My Sav - ior
smiles and bids me come, I can't stay a-way. I can not stay much longer here, I
can't stay a - way, For the gos-pel ship is pas-sing by, I can't stay a - way.

Further stanzas of the text are given under 'Golden Harp'. Compare, for melodic similarities 'Little Musgrave and Lady Barnard', Sharp, i., 161, 162, 164, 168, and 170.

No. 154
MY HOME IS OVER JORDAN, REV 390

Pentachordal, cannot be classified (I II 3 IV V — —)

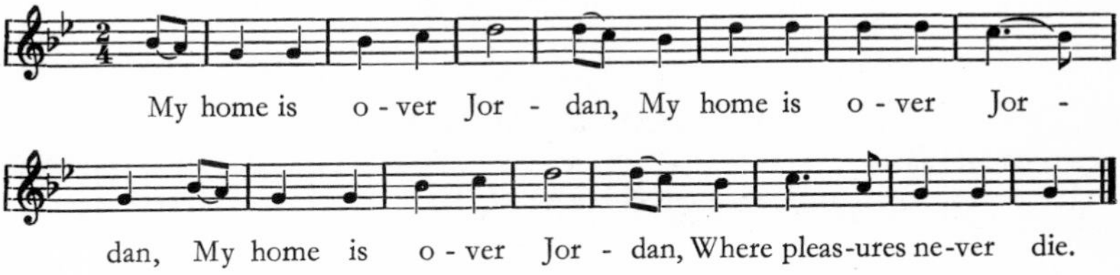
My home is o - ver Jor - dan, My home is o - ver Jor -
dan, My home is o - ver Jor - dan, Where pleas-ures ne-ver die.

Where the wicked cease from troubling, *etc.*
And the weary are at rest.

Farewell to sin and sorrow, *etc.*
I bid you all adieu.

And you, my friends, prove faithful, *etc.*
And on your way pursue.

This spiritual tune has been widely used as a chorus to other songs. An example is 'Wings of the Morning' in this collection.

No. 155

O I'M SO HAPPY

Pentatonic, mode 1 (I II — IV V VI —)

O I am so hap-py in Je - sus, His blood has re-
I shout and I sing in my glad - ness, To know he is
deem'd me from sin;
dwelling with - in.
O I am so hap - py in Je - sus, His
rit.
blood has redeem'd me from sin——, So hap - py that
he is my Sav - ior, So hap - py he's dwelling with - in.

Recorded by the author, September 21, 1932, in Nashville, Tennessee, from the singing of Samuel E. Asbury who learned it from hearing it sung at camp meetings in western North Carolina in the 1880's. The tune is quite evidently an orally transmitted version of that of 'Faithful Soldier', in this collection, which first appeared in the *Southern Harmony* (1835) and was claimed by William Walker, the compiler of that collection. See also 'Hallelujah' in this collection, a type tune to which the above melody is organically related, for further data as to kindred tunes.

No. 156

CUBA or GO PREACHERS or POOR MOURNER'S FOUND A HOME, OSH 401

Hexatonic, mode 3 A (I II III — V VI VII)

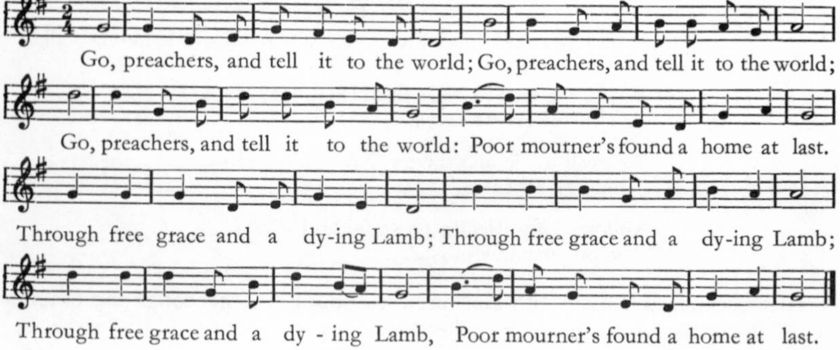
Go, preachers, and tell it to the world; Go, preachers, and tell it to the world;
Go, preachers, and tell it to the world: Poor mourner's found a home at last.
Through free grace and a dy-ing Lamb; Through free grace and a dy-ing Lamb;
Through free grace and a dy - ing Lamb, Poor mourner's found a home at last.

This typical spiritual was taken into the 1859 edition of the *Sacred Harp*. Other stanzas were added by simply substituting in the place of "preachers," the words "fathers," "mothers," etc. A negro version of tune and words is in *Slave Songs*, No. 24.

No. 157

SINNERS TURN, OL 266

Heptatonic, essentially aeolian, mode 2 A+b (I II 3 [III] IV V 6 [VI] 7)

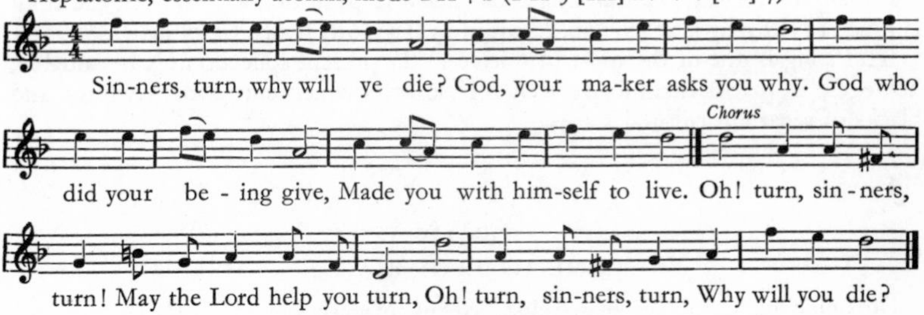
Sin-ners, turn, why will ye die? God, your ma-ker asks you why. God who
Chorus
did your be - ing give, Made you with him-self to live. Oh! turn, sin-ners,
turn! May the Lord help you turn, Oh! turn, sin-ners, turn, Why will you die?

He the fatal cause demands,
Asks the work of his own hands,
Why, ye thankless creatures, why
Will you cross his love and die?
Chorus

Sinners, turn, why will ye die?
God, your Savior, asks you why!
God, who did your souls retrieve,
Died himself that ye might live.
Chorus

This tune is closely related to 'Animation' and, like it, to the worldly tune 'Ropesman' in Thomas, p. 164. The melody of the above chorus seems to have been derived from 'Willy Taylor', Petrie, No. 745. Compare for similarities 'Run Nigger Run', SS 89.

No. 158

DEATH AIN'T YOU GOT NO SHAME

Pentachordal, cannot be classified (I II III IV V — —)

Death, ain't you got no shame, shame? Death, ain't you got no shame,
shame? Death, ain't you got no shame, shame? Death, ain't you got no shame?

Recorded by the compiler of this collection from the singing of Francis Arthur Robinson, Nashville, Tennessee, as he had heard it in the backwoods of Wayne County, Tennessee, in 1926. Mr. Robinson called it a "barefoot white" song. The tied notes are sung in a skid or scoop. Subsequent stanzas:

Left his pappy to moan, moan, *etc.*
Left his widder a-lone, lone, *etc.*
Left his mammy to weep, weep, *etc.*

and many more. In *The Carolina Low-Country*, page 249, a version of the song is given as sung by a negro congregation in Beaufort, South Carolina.

This song is one of the most primitive in the present collection. It is valuable, however, in that it exemplifies well a lyric level which suited both whites and blacks of a certain cultural status.

No. 159
COME TO JESUS, REV 142

Hexatonic, 6th missing, cannot be classified but obviously ionian (I II III IV V — VII)

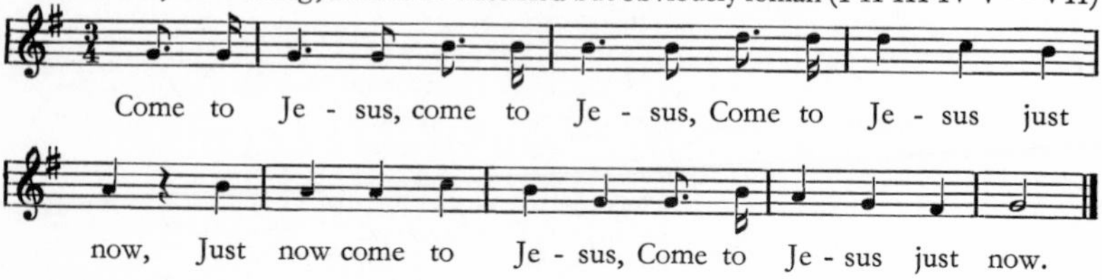

Subsequent verses are built up on: He will save you; O, believe him; He is able; He is willing; He'll receive you; Call upon him; He will hear you; Look unto him; He'll forgive you; He will cleanse you; He will clothe you; Jesus loves you; Don't reject him; and, Only trust him. A negro version of tune and text is in *Slave Songs*, No. 85.

Was 'Come to Jesus' a tune importation from Germany? Erk and Böhme (*Deutscher Liederhort*, vol. iii., p. 735) bring several variants of what is called an "altes Fastenlied." I reproduce one of them:

The first part of the German tune is almost identical with the corresponding part of the one, heard widely among American students, with such texts as 'O My Darling Clementine' and 'Found a Horseshoe Just Now' — evident parodies on the 'Come to Jesus' tune and words. The second part of the German melody is strikingly like that of the above mentioned negro version in *Slave Songs*.

No. 160

GLAD NEWS or WE'LL LAND ON SHORE, SOC 18

Hexatonic, mode 3 A (I II III — V VI VII)

Come, Thou fount of ev - ery bless - ing, Tune my heart to sing Thy grace;
Streams of mer - cy nev - er ceas - ing, Call for songs of loud - est praise.
And we'll land on shore, Yes, we'll land on shore, And we'll land on shore And be safe for ev - er - more.

A variant of the above text and tune is 'when we pass over Jordan', Mason's, *Harp of the South*, p. 295.

No. 161

CHRISTIAN PROSPECT or THERE'S A BETTER DAY, SOH 323

Heptatonic ionian, mode 3 A+b (I II III IV V VI VII)

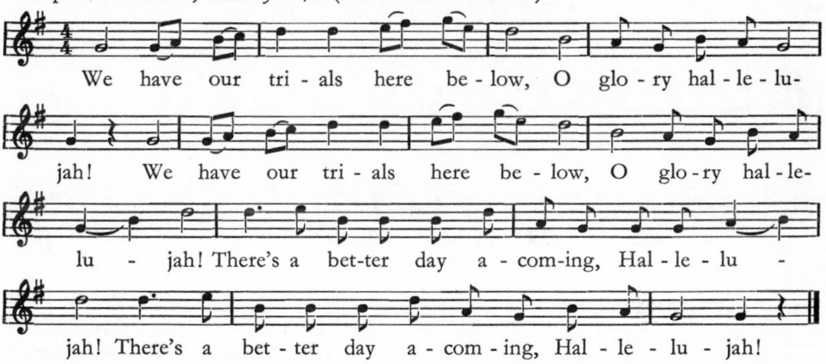
We have our tri - als here be - low, O glo - ry hal - le - lu- jah!
We have our tri - als here be - low, O glo - ry hal - le- lu - jah!
There's a bet-ter day a - com-ing, Hal - le - lu - jah!
There's a bet - ter day a - com - ing, Hal - le - lu - jah!

A few more beating winds and rains,
O glory hallelujah!
A few more beating winds and rains,
O glory hallelujah!
And the winter will be over,
Hallelujah!
And the winter will be over,
Hallelujah!

A few more rising and setting suns
And we'll all cross over Jordan.

I feel no ways like getting tired,
I am making for the harbor.

I hope to get there by and by,
My home is over Jordan.

There are four more stanzas. The song is found also in KNH 52. Both Walker, compiler of the *Southern Harmony*, and Davisson, compiler of the *Kentucky Harmony*, laid claim to its authorship.

They were doubtlessly both recorders of this same piece of unwritten music. That was in the 1830's. See the first phrase of 'Glorishears' (Sharp, *Morris Dances* Set 5, No. 6) for melodic similarities. The above song, both tune and words, inspired the composition of 'Christian's Hope' in this collection. A negro remake of tune and words is in Dett, p. 36.

No. 162

CHRISTIAN'S HOPE or WHERE ALL IS PEACE AND LOVE, OSH 506

Heptatonic ionian, mode 3 A+b (I II III IV V VI VII)

We have our troubles here be - low, We're trav'ling
through this world of woe, To that bright world where loved ones
go, Where all is peace and love. Where all is peace and love, To
that bright world where loved ones go, Where all is peace and love.
1
2

We're fettered and chained up in clay,
While in this body here we stay;
By faith we know a world above,
Where all is peace and love.

I feel no way like getting tired,
I'm trusting in his holy word,
To guide my weary feet above,
Where all is peace and love.

The *Sacred Harp*, edition of 1911, has the following note: "H. A. Parris, who composed the words and music to the 'Christian's Hope', resides at this time, 1911, at Helicon, Alabama. He is a great lover of the old *Sacred Harp* tunes." Mr. Parris composed the song by assembling, happily withal, wandering distichs and melodic phrases from songs of much older times. His chief source, both tonally and textually, was 'Christian Prospect' in this collection. I have been told that this spiritual grips the *Sacred Harp* singers' emotions so deeply that they can hardly get to the third verse before many burst into tears.

No. 163

DULCIMER or BELOVED, PB 309

Heptatonic ionian, mode 3 A+b (I II III IV V VI VII)

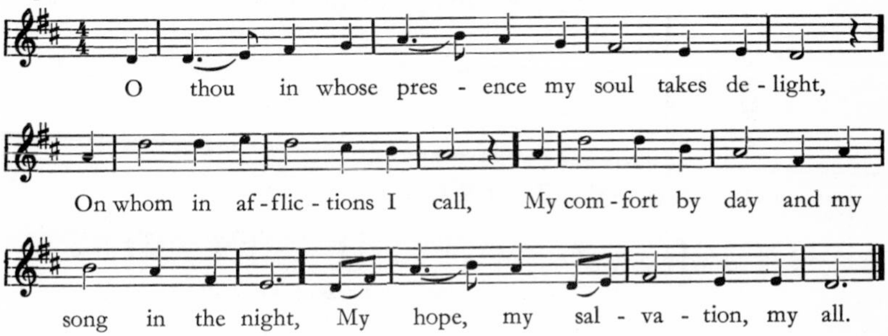
O thou in whose pres - ence my soul takes de - light,
On whom in af - flic - tions I call, My com - fort by day and my
song in the night, My hope, my sal - va - tion, my all.

The poem is by Joseph Swain of England (1762—1796). The tune is attributed to Freeman Lewis whom Tillett calls merely "an American musican." His dates are 1780—1859. Found also GCM 65, *Baptist Hymnal* (1902), No. 389. *Methodist Hymnal* (1905), No. 530; GOS 102, SOH 15. Miss Gilchrist *(op. cit.)* compares this tune with 'Fair Rosie Ann' in Greig's *Last Leaves of Traditional Ballads*, p. 771. The chorus of 'The Sinking of the Titanic' a phonograph-recorded song of wide popularity in America during the 1920's, is practically the same melodic trend as that of 'Dulcimer'. Its text is:

It was bad when that great ship went down,
It was bad when that great ship went down,
There was husbands and wives,
Little child'en lost their lives,
It was bad when that great ship went down.

A song curiously similar to the 'Titanic' song is in *The Carolina Low-Country*, page 296, as sung by the negroes on the Santee River in South Carolina. The tune is changed but little. The words are:

It was sad w'en duh grabe sinkin' down,
It was sad w'en duh grabe sinkin' down,
Ain' dat uh awful time,
People keep awake all night,
It was sad w'en duh grabe sinkin' down.

The tune of 'Dulcimer' is of the 'Lord Lovel' type mentioned in the Introduction, p. 14. Other songs in this collection belonging to this type are 'Yongst', 'Dunlap's Creek', 'Liverpool', 'Ester', 'Lonesome Grove', and 'Land of Rest'. Other spiritual folk-tunes of the same type are 'Eden', GOS 558; 'Thy Way O God', PB 29; 'Charlestown', GOS 255; 'Lord of Glory', PB 374; 'New Hope', PB 373; 'Golden Hill', HH 211; 'Webster', OSH 31; 'Hollis', GOS 73; 'Edneyville' HH 193; 'Blissful Hope', REV 140; and 'Tedious Hours', SOC 69. Further secular tunes of the type are 'Lord Lovel', Sharp, i., 148; 'The Two Brothers', Davis, 563; 'The Mermaid', Sharp, i., 293; 'Every Night When the Sun Goes In', Sharp, ii., 269; 'Three Little Babes', Davis, 576; 'Come All You Fair and Tender Ladies', Sharp, ii., 135; 'Barbara Allen', Sharp, i., 195; 'Gypsy Laddie', Sharp, i., 237; 'Horn Fair', JFSS, ii., 204; and 'The Cuckoo', Sharp, ii., 177.

No. 164

WEEPING MARY (A), SOC 98

Heptatonic aeolian, mode 2 A+b (I II 3 IV V 6 7)

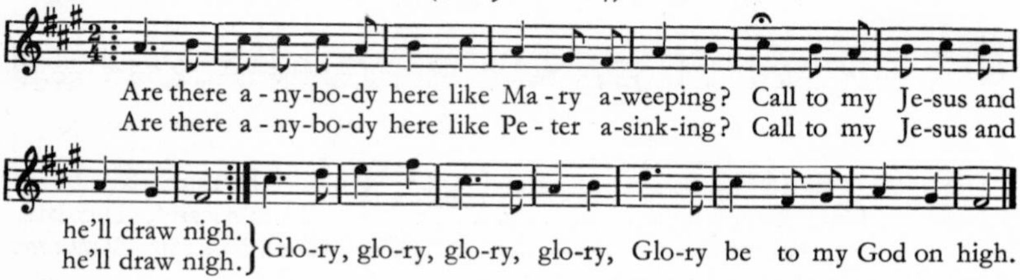
Are there a-ny-bo-dy here like Ma-ry a-weeping? Call to my Je-sus and
Are there a-ny-bo-dy here like Pe-ter a-sink-ing? Call to my Je-sus and
he'll draw nigh.
he'll draw nigh.
Glo-ry, glo-ry, glo-ry, glo-ry, Glo-ry be to my God on high.

Attributed in the *Sacred Harp* to "John G. McCurry & Power" and dated 1852. For a variant of this tune used among the negroes see *White Spirituals*, p. 256. Miss Gilchrist states that the text of this song is No. 51 in the first *English Primitive Methodist Hymn Book*, about 1823.

No. 165

GREAT DAY or WHERE WILL YOU STAND, OSH 386

Pentachordal, cannot be classified (I II 3 IV V — —)

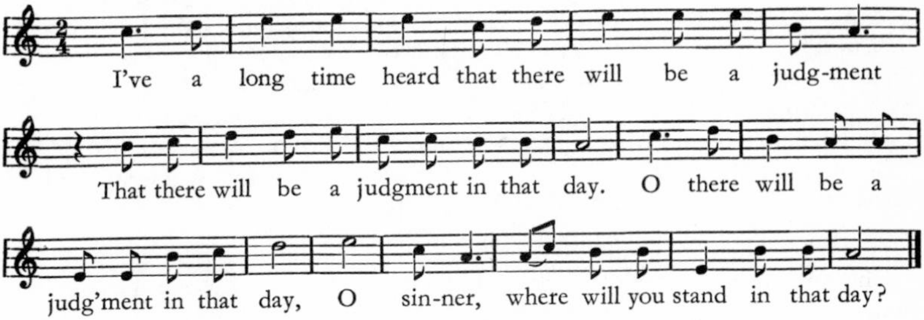
I've a long time heard that there will be a judg-ment
That there will be a judgment in that day. O there will be a
judg'ment in that day, O sin-ner, where will you stand in that day?

I've a long time heard that the moon will be bleeding,
That the moon will be bleeding in that day.

I've a long time heard that the stars will be falling, *etc.*
I've a long time heard that the earth will be burning, *etc.*

This song bears the date 1859 and the composer's name, John P. Rees. But beside the title we read: "As sung by Judge Falkerner of Ala." We may therefore conclude that Rees recorded on that date this older tune from the singing of the Alabama magistrate. Melodic similarities are seen in 'Trooper and the Maid', Sharp, i., 305. A recent negro version from Beaufort, S. C., is in *The Carolina Low-Country*, p. 250.

No. 166

SHOUT ON, PRAY ON or ANTIOCH, OSH 277

Hexatonic, mode 2 b (I — 3 IV V 6 7)

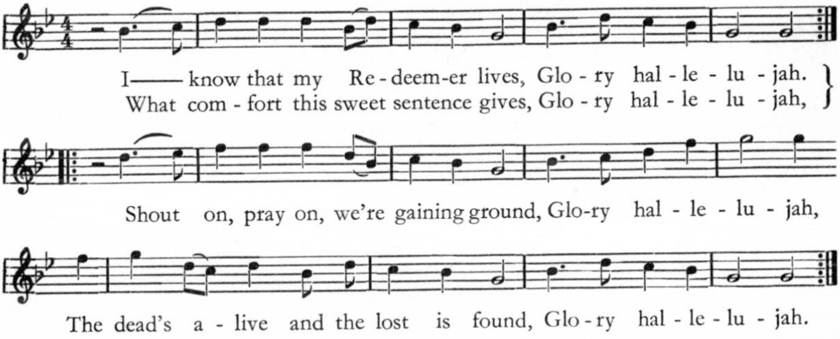
I—— know that my Re-deem-er lives, Glo-ry hal-le-lu-jah.
What com-fort this sweet sentence gives, Glo-ry hal-le-lu-jah,
Shout on, pray on, we're gaining ground, Glo-ry hal-le-lu-jah,
The dead's a-live and the lost is found, Glo-ry hal-le-lu-jah.

There are three more stanzas of this hymn, the core of which is attributed to Daniel Medley "about 1784." The tune first appeared in the *Social Harp*, 1855, where it is attributed to F. C. Wood, a Georgian. A tune and text variant is 'We'll Go On', REV 252. A negro version of this spiritual may be seen in Dett, 195. See also *White Spirituals*, p. 259. 'Antioch' looks like a make-over from 'Columbus' in this collection. The tune is cleverly fitted also to a worldly ballad 'Edward', found in eastern Tennessee; see Sharp, i., 47. It is found also fitted to the worldly ballad 'Cruel Mother' in North Carolina; see Sharp, i., 58. 'Little Musgrave and Lady Barnard', Sharp, i., 162, shows definite influence of 'Antioch'. See also for melodic similarities 'Trooper and the Maid', Sharp, i., 305; and 'Bridle and Saddle', Sharp, i., 305; and 'Bridle and Saddle', Sharp, ii., 329.

No. 167

WE'LL SHOUT AND GIVE HIM GLORY or REVIVAL SONG, OL 254

Hexatonic, mode 3 A (I II III — V VI VII)

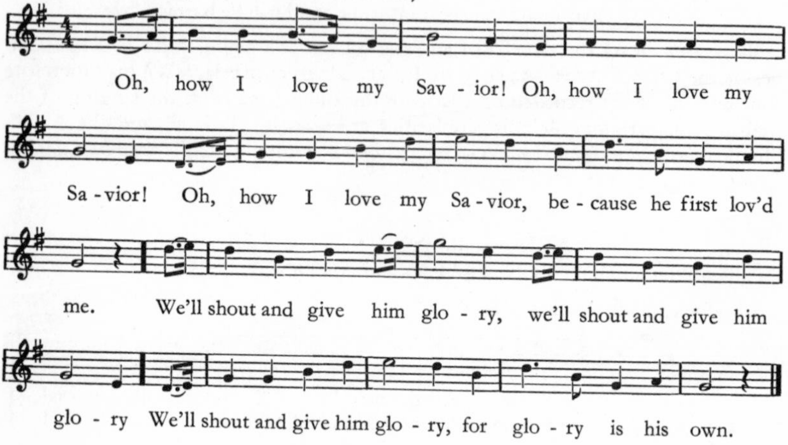
Oh, how I love my Sav - ior! Oh, how I love my
Sa - vior! Oh, how I love my Sa - vior, be - cause he first lov'd
me. We'll shout and give him glo - ry, we'll shout and give him
glo - ry We'll shout and give him glo - ry, for glo - ry is his own.

I feel the work reviving, *etc.*
Reviving in my soul.
Chorus

I'm on my way to Zion, *etc.*
The New Jerusalem.
Chorus

O Christians, will you meet me? *etc.*
On Canaan's happy shore?
Chorus

By the grace of God, I'll meet you, *etc.*
On Canaan's happy shore.
Chorus

O brothers, will you meet me? *etc.*
O sisters, will you meet me? *etc.*
O mourners, will you meet me? *etc.*
O sinners, will you meet me? *etc.*

The *Olive Leaf* editor calls it a "refrain song."

No. 168

SWEET MORNING, OSH 421

Hexatonic, mode 2 A (I II 3 IV V — 7)

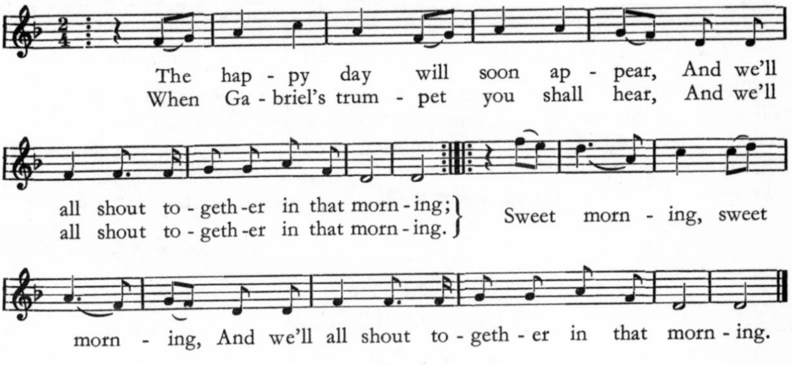
The hap - py day will soon ap - pear, And we'll
When Ga - briel's trum - pet you shall hear, And we'll
all shout to - geth - er in that morn - ing;
all shout to - geth - er in that morn - ing.
Sweet morn - ing, sweet
morn - ing, And we'll all shout to - geth - er in that morn - ing.

Behold the righteous marching home,
And we'll all *etc.*
And all the angels bid them come,
And we'll all *etc.*

Found also in GOS 254. How the post-Civil War negroes sang this song to pieces and then patched it together with fragments of 'Exhilaration', another song in this collection, is made clear by reference to *Slave Songs*, p. 74, No. 97. The tune of 'Trooper and the Maid', Sharp, i., 305, is the same as that of 'Sweet Morning'.

No. 169

GOOD OLD WAY (A), OSH 213

Pentatonic, mode 3 (I II III — V VI —)

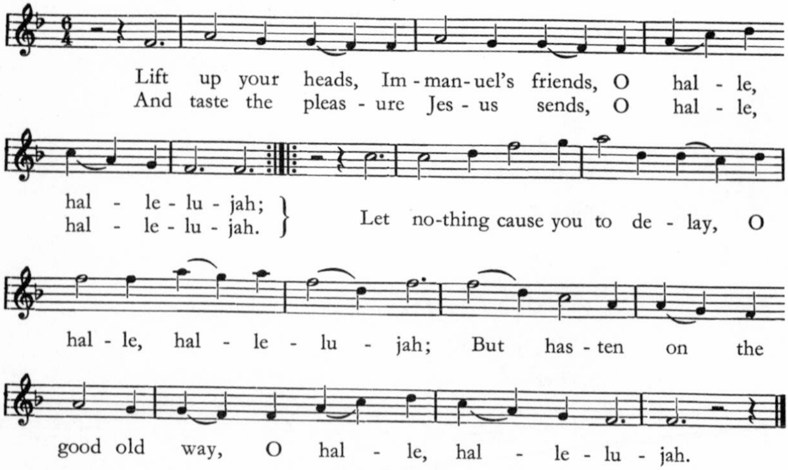
Lift up your heads, Im - man - uel's friends, O hal - le,
And taste the pleas - ure Jes - us sends, O hal - le,
hal - le - lu - jah;
hal - le - lu - jah.
Let no-thing cause you to de - lay, O
hal - le, hal - le - lu - jah; But has - ten on the
good old way, O hal - le, hal - le - lu - jah.

The words of the above song appeared in the *Dover Selection* in the early years of the nineteenth century and in the *Zion Songster*, a spiritual-song collection which appeared in 1832. The first appearance of the tune seems to have been in the *Southern Harmony* of 1835. A related tune in this collection is 'All the Way 'Long It is Jesus'. Further stanzas of the text are given under 'Good Old Way (B)'.

No. 170

ALL THE WAY 'LONG, REV 172

Hexatonic, mode 3 A (I II III — V VI VII)

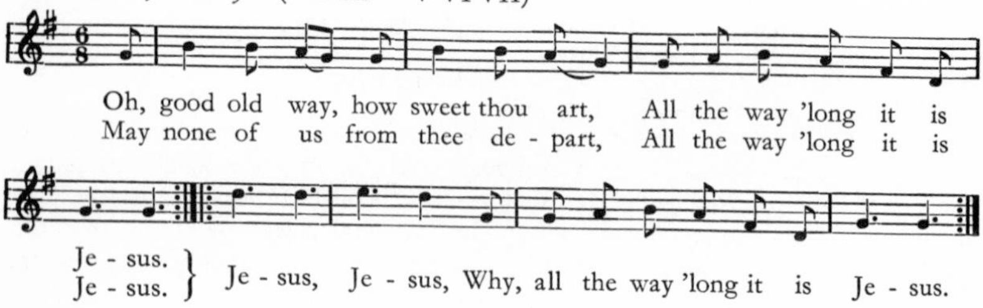
Oh, good old way, how sweet thou art, All the way 'long it is
May none of us from thee de - part, All the way 'long it is
Je - sus.
Je - sus.
Je - sus, Je - sus, Why, all the way 'long it is Je - sus.

But may our actions always say,
We're marching in the good old way.

This note above the rest shall swell,
That Jesus doeth all things well.

Related songs in this collection are 'Good Old Way (A)', 'Good Old Way (B)', and ''Tis a Wonder'.

No. 171

'TIS A WONDER, SOC 44

Hexatonic, mode 3 A (I II III — V VI VII)

O 'tis a glo - rious mys-te - ry, 'Tis a won-der, a won-der, a won-der;
That I should ev - er sav - ed be 'Tis a won-der, a won-der, a won-der.
No heart can think or ful - ly tell, 'Tis a won-der, a won-der; My
God has sav'd my soul from hell, 'Tis a won-der, a won-der, a won-der.

Two further stanzas of the text taken from *Good Old Songs*, No. 511, are:

Great mystery that God should place,
'Tis a wonder *etc.*
His love on any of Adam's race,
'Tis a wonder *etc.*
That I should also share a part,
'Tis a wonder *etc.*
And find a mansion in his heart,
'Tis a wonder *etc.*

Great mystery, I can't tell why
That Christ for sinful worms should die;
Should leave the boundless realms of bliss,
And die for sinners on the cross.

The song is accredited in the *Social Harp* to Henry F. Chandler and dated 1854. A North Carolina variant, recorded in 1916, is in Sharp, ii., 294. A variant in the present collection is 'Look Out', which see for references to related secular tunes. The earliest American recording of this melody known to me is that in Jeremiah Ingalls' *Christian Harmony* of 1805, p. 15. It begins:

> When converts first begin to sing, wonder, wonder, wonder,
> Their happy souls are on the wing, wonder, wonder, wonder.
> Their theme is all redeeming love, glory hallelujah,
> Fain would they be with Christ above, sing glory hallelujah.

No. 172

BOWERS or HAPPY SOULS (B), SOC 82

Pentatonic, mode 3 (I II III — V VI —)

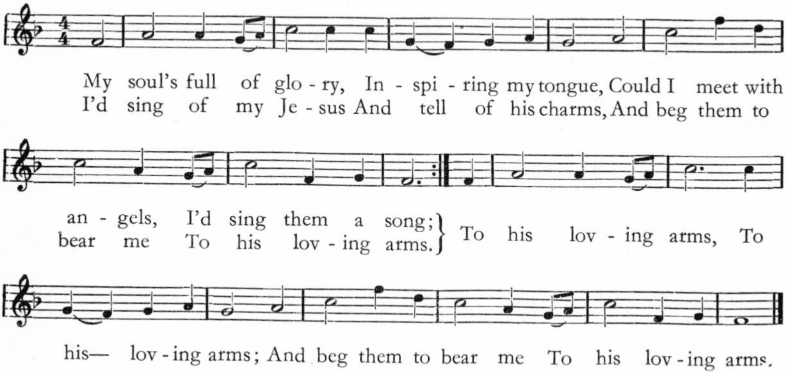
My soul's full of glo - ry, In - spi - ring my tongue, Could I meet with
I'd sing of my Je - sus And tell of his charms, And beg them to
an - gels, I'd sing them a song;
bear me To his lov - ing arms.
To his lov - ing arms, To
his— lov - ing arms; And beg them to bear me To his lov - ing arms.

John G. McCurry places his name as composer at the top of the page where this song is found in the *Social Harp* and dates it 1852. A note at the bottom says: "This tune was arranged as sung by William Bowers, Eagle Grove, Georgia." Eagle Grove is a few miles south of Hartwell. The tune is a clear borrowing from 'Wearing of the Green'. See also 'Our Goodman', Sharp, i., 269, for melodic similarities. Further stanzas of the text are given under 'Glorious Prospect'. In *The Musical Quarterly*, vol. xxii., No. 2, I have called attention to melodic similarities between the above tune (with its variants 'Oh For my Soul's Happy', 'We'll Wait Till Jesus Comes', and 'O When Shall I see Jesus' in this collection) and Stephen Foster's 'Annie My own Love' and 'Hard Times Come Again No More'.

No. 173

HEAVEN'S MY HOME, OSH 119

Hexatonic, mode 3 A (I II III — V VI VII)

Come, all my dear breth-ren and help me to sing, I'm
He died to a - tone for the sins of the world, His
go - ing to Je - sus, he's heaven's great King;
ban-ner is fly - ing his sails are un-furled.
Hea-ven's my home,
heaven's my home; I'm go - ing to Je - sus for heaven's my home.

While here in the valley of conflict I stay,
Oh, give me submission and strength as my day;
In all my afflictions to thee I would come,
Rejoicing in hope of my glorious home.

I long, dearest Lord, in thy beauties to shine,
No more as an exile in sorrow to pine;
And in thy dear image arise from the tomb,
With glorified millions to praise thee at home.

The song is ascribed in the *Original Sacred Harp* to Dr. R. H. Davis and J. S. Terry. This is a re-make of an older tune in four-four time called 'Old Troy' in this collection, and 'Old Troy' in turn is almost identical with, and probably made out of 'Wearing of the Green'.

No. 174

OLD TROY or IN JESUS' BLOOD, SOC 75

Heptatonic ionian, mode 3 A+b (I II III IV V VI VII)

The news of his mer - cy is spread - ing a-broad, And sin-
Their mourning and pray-ing is heard ve - ry loud, And ma-
ners come cry - ing and weep-ing to God.
ny find fa - vor in Je - sus - 'es blood.
In Je - sus - 'es blood, In
Je - sus-'es blood, And ma - ny find fa - vor in Je - sus-'es blood.

For tune relationships see 'Heaven's My Home' and 'Happy Souls (B)' in this collection. John G. McCurry claims the tune in the *Social Harp*. It is taken bodily from 'Wearing of the Green'. A very similar negro spiritual tune is in Dett, p. 42.

No. 175

THERE WILL BE MOURNING or JUDGEMENT SCENES, OL 337

Hexatonic, mode 3 b (I II III IV V VI —)

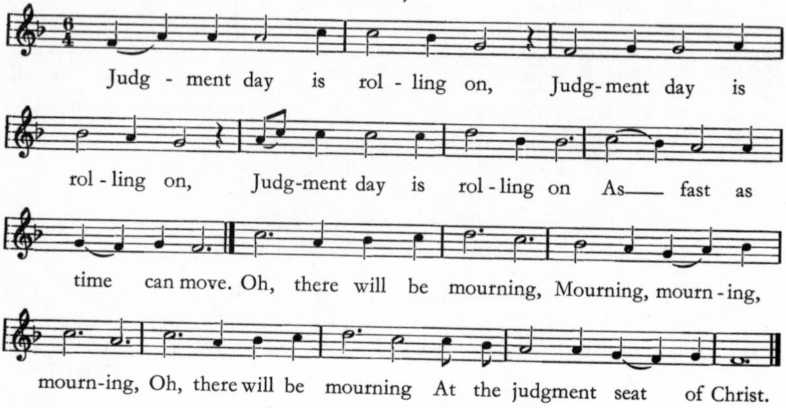
Judg - ment day is rol - ling on, Judg-ment day is
rol - ling on, Judg-ment day is rol - ling on As— fast as
time can move. Oh, there will be mourning, Mourning, mourn - ing,
mourn-ing, Oh, there will be mourning At the judgment seat of Christ.

Wives and husbands there shall part, *etc.*
Shall part to meet no more.
Chorus

Brothers and sisters there shall part, *etc.*
Pastors and people there shall part, *etc.*
Parents and children there shall part, *etc.*

This old air and its words portray, as the *Olive Leaf* author declares, "the gloomy side" of the Last Day. But, he adds consolingly, "Now sing the joyous side, with every verse," thus:

The judgment day is rolling on, *etc.*
And we shall all be there.
Oh, there will be shouting
Shouting, shouting, shouting,
Oh, there will be shouting
At the judgment seat of Christ.

Wives and husbands then shall meet, *etc.*
Shall meet to part no more.
Chorus

and so on also for the "parents and children," and the rest. 'Parting Hymn', in this collection, uses a similar chorus but has a different verse and tune. A negro version is in *Slave Songs*, p. 52.

No. 176

WEEPING PILGRIM or YOU MAY TELL THEM FATHER or I'M A POOR MOURNING PILGRIM, OSH 417

Pentatonic, mode 1 (I II — IV V VI —)

You may tell them, fa - ther, when you see them, I'm a poor mourn-ing
pil-grim, I'm bound for Ca-naan's land. I weep and I mourn, and I
move slowly on, I'm a poor mourning pilgrim, I'm bound for Canaan's land.

The text is probably a parody of 'Rebel Soldier' or 'Poor Stranger', Sharp, ii., 212ff. Especially the refrain verses of the two songs show textual and tonal resemblances. The secular refrain runs:

I am a rebel soldier and far from my home.

The cowboys, too, made use of the 'Rebel Soldier' or 'Mourning Pilgrim' in the song 'Poor Lonesome Cowboy', Sandburg, p. 273, which reads:

I'm a poor lonesome cowboy, and a long way from home.

The spiritual song appeared first in the 1859 edition of the *Sacred Harp*.

No. 177

EXHILARATION or THEN MY TROUBLES WILL BE OVER or I NEVER SHALL FORGET THE DAY, OSH 170

Hexatonic, mode 3 A (I II III — V VI VII)

O may I wor - thy prove to see The saints in
To see the bride, the glitt'ring bride, Close seat - ed
full pros - per - i - ty, Then my troubles will be o - ver.
by my Sa - vior's side, Then my troubles will be o - ver.
I
nev - er shall for - get the day When Je-sus wash'd my sins a - way, And
then my troubles will be o - ver; Will be o - ver, will be
o - ver and re - joic - ing, And then my trou-bles will be o - ver.

I'll praise him while he gives me breath,
I hope to praise him after death.
Then my troubles will be over.
I hope to praise him when I die,
And shout salvation as I fly,
Then my troubles will be over.
Chorus

I soon shall pass the vale of death,
And in his arms resign my breath.
O then my happy soul shall tell,
My Jesus has done all things well.
Chorus

Then shall I see my blessed God,
And praise him in his bright abode.
My theme to all eternity
Shall glory, glory, glory be.
Chorus.

I have no information as to the tune excepting that it appeared in the earliest edition of the *Sacred Harp*, that is, in 1844. The tune and the words of its chorus have served the negroes in the construction of 'Almost Over', SS, No. 97.

No. 178

RESURRECTED or MY FATHER'S GONE or AWAY OVER YONDER or TO WEAR A STARRY CROWN, OSH 524

Pentatonic, mode 3 (I II III — V VI —)

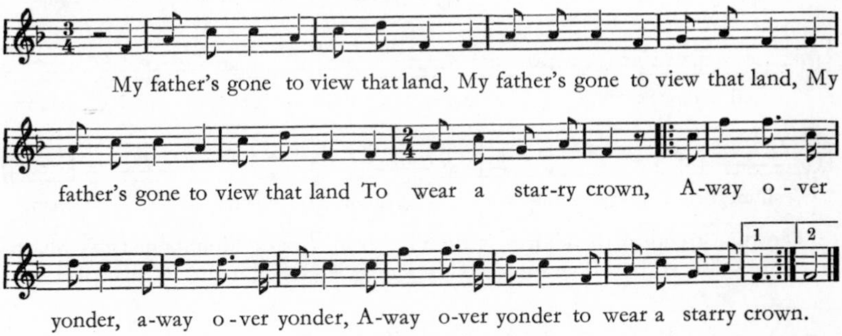
My father's gone to view that land, My father's gone to view that land, My
father's gone to view that land To wear a star-ry crown, A-way o - ver
yonder, a-way o-ver yonder, A-way o-ver yonder to wear a starry crown.

Seaborn M. Denson, widely known fasola country singing-school teacher and musical editor of the 1911 edition of the *Original Sacred Harp*, and author of this song, told me he had heard this song sung in camp meetings around Civil War times in northern Alabama. He recorded it from memory and published it first in the *Union Harp* in 1909. The tune is a member of the 'Roll Jordan' group. See Introduction, page 14, and the song by that name in this collection. Further stanzas read "My mother's gone", "My sister's gone" etc.

The wide spread of this song in the American oral tradition and especially at the time when Mr. Denson heard it in northern Alabama, is indicated by the variant and musically somewhat inferior recording in the *Revivalist*, Albany, New York, 1868. It is there called 'Away over Jordan'. It runs:

My brother's going to wear that crown *etc.*
To wear that starry crown.
    Away over Jordan, with my blessed Jesus,
    Away over Jordan, to wear that starry crown.

My father's gone to wear that crown *etc.*
My mother's gone *etc.*
John Wesley's gone *etc.*
You must live right *etc.*

No. 179

WINGS OF THE MORNING or WESTERN MELODY, BHTBK, p. 213

Pentatonic, mode 3 (I II III — V VI —)

O thou al - might - y Fath - er, Come help me now to praise thy
glo - ry *(These words lacking in my recording)* Oh,
had I the wings of the morn-ing, I'd fly a - way to Ca- naan's
shore; Bright an-gels should con-vey me home To the new Je - ru - sa - lem.

The tune trend of the chorus is found also in 'Rocky Mountain Top', Sharp. ii., 110; and it is the whole tune of 'My Home is Over Jordan' in this collection.

No. 180

WE'LL MARCH AROUND JERUSALEM, REV 358

Heptatonic ionian, mode 3 A+b (I II III IV V VI VII)

O brethren, will you meet me On that de - light-ful shore?
O brethren, will you meet me Where parting is no more?
And we'll
march a - round Je - ru - sa - lem, We'll march a - round Je - ru - sa-
lem, We'll march a-round Je - ru - sa - lem When we ar - rive at home.

Subsequent stanzas use instead of brethren, sister, leader, preacher, young convert, and backslider, with the conclusion:

Yes, bless the Lord, I'll meet you, *etc.*

The above tune, with some alterations, is found as a negro spiritual in Dett, p. 78.

No. 181

RAGAN or I BELONG TO THIS BAND (B), OSH 176

Hexatonic, mode 3 A (I II III — V VI VII)

Fare - well, vain world, I'm go - ing home, I be-
My—— Sav - ior smiles and bids me come, I be-
long to this band, hal - le - lu - jah,
long to this band, hal - le - lu - jah.
Hal - le - lu - jah, hal - le-
lu - jah, I be - long to this band, hal - le - lu - jah.

The above melodic trend will be recognized as that of 'Roll Jordan' and Stephen Foster's 'Susanna'. Compare 'Roll Jordan' in this collection. The chorus — both tune and words — appears also in 'I Belong to This Band (A)'. Further stanzas of the text are given under 'Golden Harp'.

No. 182

DOWN BY THE RIVERSIDE or WE'LL END THIS WAR, REV 68

Hexatonic, mode 3 b (I II III IV V VI —)

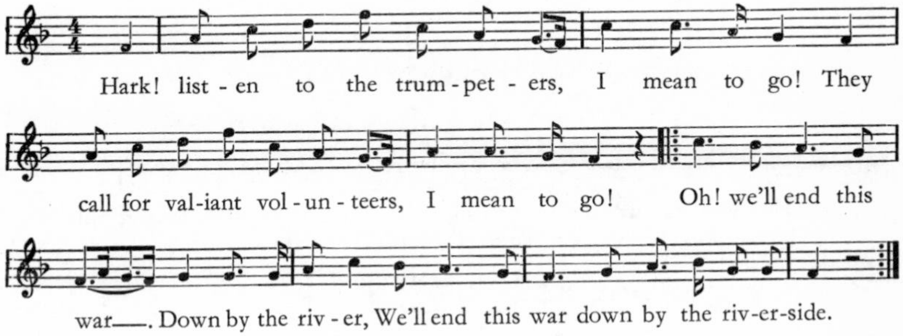
Hark! list - en to the trum - pet - ers, I mean to go! They
call for val-iant vol - un - teers, I mean to go! Oh! we'll end this
war——. Down by the riv - er, We'll end this war down by the riv-er-side.

See Gideon marching out to fight,
I mean to go!
He had no weapon but a light,
I mean to go!
Chorus

He took his pitcher and a lamp,
And stormed with ease the Midian camp.

I've listed during all this war,
Content to have a soldier's fare.

The war is all my soul's delight,
I love the thickest of the fight.

The hottest fight is just begun,
And who will stand and never run?

We want no cowards in our band,
We call for valiant-hearted men.

Fight on, ye conq'ring souls, fight on,
Until the conquest you have won.

I have some friends before me gone,
And I'm resolved to travel on.

Farewell, vain world, I'm going home,
My Savior smiles and bids me come.

I'll tell you what I mean to do,
I mean to go to glory too.

The song bears the name of "Rev. J. K. Tinkham" as its purveyor to the *Revivalist*. A version of the spiritual song, as sung at about the same time (in the 1870's) by the negroes, is in Marsh, No. 85, under the title 'Down by the River'. Another by the same title is in Dett, p. 55; and still another in Dett, p. 74.

No. 183

I'M GOING HOME or I DON'T CARE TO STAY HERE LONG, OSH 282

Pentatonic, mode 3 (I II III — V VI —)

Fare-well, vain world, I'm go - ing home, My Sa - vior smiles and bids me
Sweet an-gels beck-on me a - way To sing God's praise in endless
come, And I don't care to stay here long.
day, And I don't care to stay here long.
Right up yonder, Christians, A-
way up yon - der; O yes, my Lord, For I don't care to stay here long.

Further stanzas of the text are given under 'Golden Harp'. This tune was recorded for the 1850 edition of the *Sacred Harp*, evidently by the Georgian, Leonard P. Breedlove.

No. 184

ROLL JORDAN, OSH 501

Pentatonic, mode 3 (I II III — V VI —)

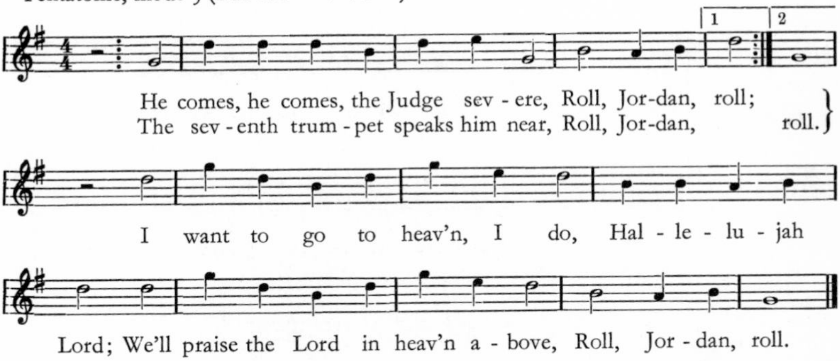
1
2
He comes, he comes, the Judge sev - ere, Roll, Jor-dan, roll;
The sev - enth trum - pet speaks him near, Roll, Jor-dan, roll.
I want to go to heav'n, I do, Hal - le - lu - jah
Lord; We'll praise the Lord in heav'n a - bove, Roll, Jor - dan, roll.

His lightnings flash, his thun-ders roll,
Roll, Jordan, roll;
How welcome to the faithful soul,
Roll, Jordan, roll.

Charles Wesley wrote the text. According to Lightwood, p. 132, it is a parody on a popular secular song which celebrated Admiral Vernon's return to England after taking Portobello in 1739. Its first stanza is:

He comes! He comes! The hero comes!
Sound your trumpets, beat your drums!
From port to port let cannons roar
His welcome to the British shore.

It is found also in SOC, published in 1855. In the Introduction p. 14, I have mentioned the 'Roll Jordan' type of melody; it was named after the above tune. Other melodies of the type in this collection are 'Florence', 'I Belong to this Band (B)', 'Tennessee', 'Jordan', and 'Resurrected'. It is this tune type which influenced Stephen Foster in the making of his 'Susanna Don't You Cry' and 'De Camptown Races'. See in this connection my article in *The Musical Quarterly*, vol. xxii., No. 2. For samples of negro borrowings of 'Roll Jordan' see *White Spirituals*, p. 264; Dett, p. 76; and *Slave Songs*, Nos. 1 and 10.

No. 185

WE'LL ALL PRAISE GOD, REV 381

Hexatonic, mode 3 b (I II III IV V VI —)

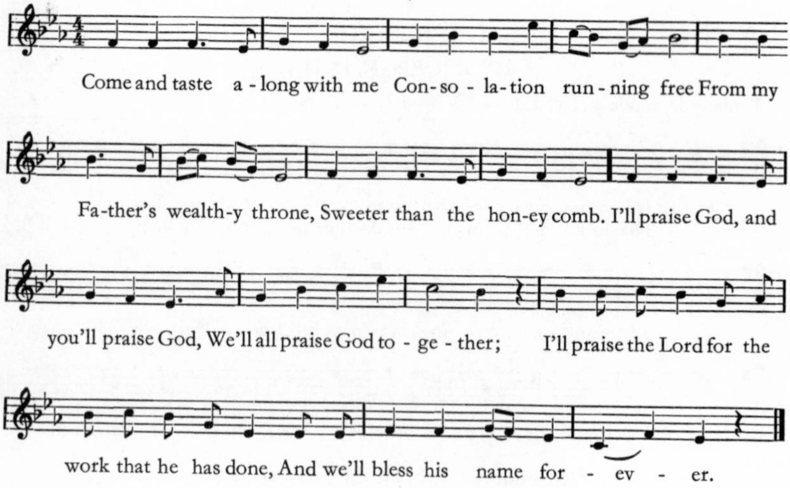
Come and taste a - long with me Con-so - la-tion run - ning free From my
Fa-ther's wealth-y throne, Sweeter than the hon-ey comb. I'll praise God, and
you'll praise God, We'll all praise God to - ge - ther; I'll praise the Lord for the
work that he has done, And we'll bless his name for - ev - er.

Why should Christians feast alone?
Two are better far than one;
The more that comes with free good will
Makes the banquet sweeter still.

Now I go to heaven's door,
Asking for a little more;
Jesus gives a double share,
Calling me his chosen heir.

Goodness, running like a stream
Through the new Jerusalem;
By its constant breaking forth
Sweetens earth and heaven both.

Two more stanzas are in the *Revivalist*. The relationship between this tune and that of Stephen Foster's 'Long-Ago Day' was noted by me in *The Musical Quarterly*, vol. xxii., No. 2.

No. 186

HEAVENLY HOME, SWP 150

Pentatonic, mode 1 (I II — IV V VI —)

O who will join and help me sing, I ne - ver will turn
The praise of Zi - on's conqu'ring King, I ne - ver will turn
back while heaven's in my view.
back while heaven's in my view.
Heaven is my home, my jour-ney
I'll pur - sue, I ne - ver will turn back while hea-ven's in my view.

By faith my journey I'll pursue, I never *etc.*
And bid all earthly things adieu, I never *etc.*

I want my friends to go with me,
I'm bound fair Canaan's land to see.

I want to take them by the hand
And march unto the promised land.

My Jesus dwells on Zion's hill,
And faithful to his promise still.

Then whosoever will, may come,
For Jesus Christ refuseth none.

O what a Captain I have got!
O is not mine a happy lot!

He surely is the sinner's friend,
And one that loves unto the end.

I'm travelling through the wilderness
And seeking for a heavenly rest.

That rest in Jesus Christ is found,
And I will sing it all around.

For fight I must, while here below;
The word of God has taught me so.

Has taught me I shall conqueror be,
In death and through eternity.

My Jesus bids me still press on,
And reaches out to me a crown.

He says to me, be not afraid,
For I can save beyond the grave.

O while I'm singing of his name,
My soul begins to feel the flame.

When he to me his presence gives,
I know that my Redeemer lives.

No. 187

WHEN WE ALL GET TO HEAVEN or RELIGION IS A FORTUNE, OSH 319

Hexatonic, mode 3 b (I II III IV V VI —)

O when shall I see Je - sus And reign with Him a - bove, Shout
And from the flow - ing foun - tain Drink ev - er - last - ing love? Shout
D. C. Re - lig - ion is a for - tune And hea-ven is a home, Shout
glo - ry, hal - le, hal - le - lu - jah;
glo - ry, hal - le, hal - le - lu - jah.
glo - ry, hal - le, hal - le - lu - jah.
When we all get to hea-ven
D. C.
we will shout a - loud and sing, Shout glo - ry hal - le, hal - le - lu - jah.

When shall I be delivered from this vain world of sin,
And with my blessed Jesus drink endless pleasures in?

The text core is generally ascribed to John Leland (1754—1844). See *White Spirituals*, 217ff. Further stanzas are given under 'Faithful Soldier'.

No. 188

BATES or TO HEAR THE TRUMPET SOUND, REV 158

Hexatonic, mode 3 b (I II III IV V VI —)

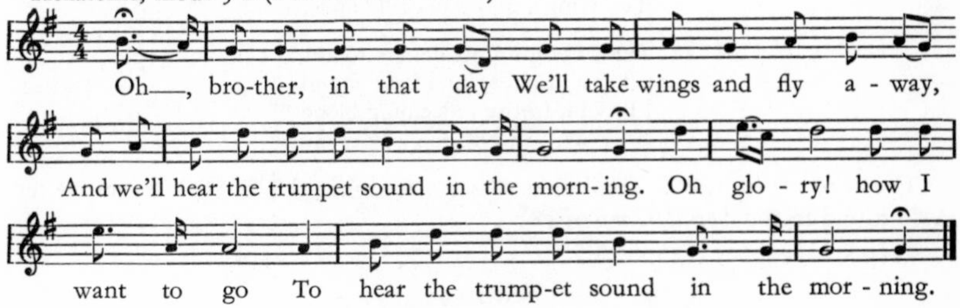
Oh—, bro-ther, in that day We'll take wings and fly a - way,
And we'll hear the trumpet sound in the morn-ing. Oh glo - ry! how I
want to go To hear the trump-et sound in the mor - ning.

Oh, sister, in that day, *etc.*
Oh, preachers, in that day, *etc.*
Oh, leaders, in that day, *etc.*
Oh, converts, in that day, *etc.*

You may bury me in the east,
You may bury me in the west, *etc.*

You may bury me in the north,
You may bury me in the south, *etc.*

A close negro variant of the above spiritual song is in Marsh, p. 136. Both the Marsh song and the present one are rather degenerate descendants, apparently, of 'Morning Trumpet' in this collection. See also *White Spirituals*, p. 254.

No. 189

RIVER OF JORDAN or HAPPY IN THE LORD, OSH 493

Hexatonic, Mode 3 A (I II III — V VI VII)

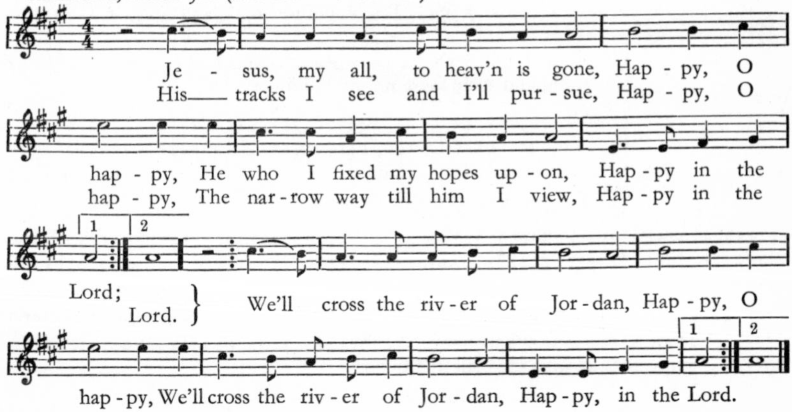
Je - sus, my all, to heav'n is gone, Hap - py, O
His— tracks I see and I'll pur - sue, Hap - py, O
hap - py, He who I fixed my hopes up - on, Hap - py in the
hap - py, The nar - row way till him I view, Hap - py in the
1 2
Lord;
Lord.
We'll cross the riv - er of Jor - dan, Hap - py, O
hap - py, We'll cross the riv - er of Jor - dan, Hap - py, in the Lord.

The way the holy prophets went,
The road that leads from banishment;
I'll go, for all his paths are peace,
The King's highway of holiness.

Then I will tell to sinners round,
What a dear Savior I have found.
I'll point to thy redeeming blood
And say, "Behold the way to God."

The core of the text is attributed to John Cennick, the English hymn writer. Also found in the *Social Harp* of 1855.

No. 190

I'M BOUND FOR THE LAND OF CANAAN or SWEET CANAAN, OSH 87

Pentachordal, cannot be classified (I II III IV V — —)

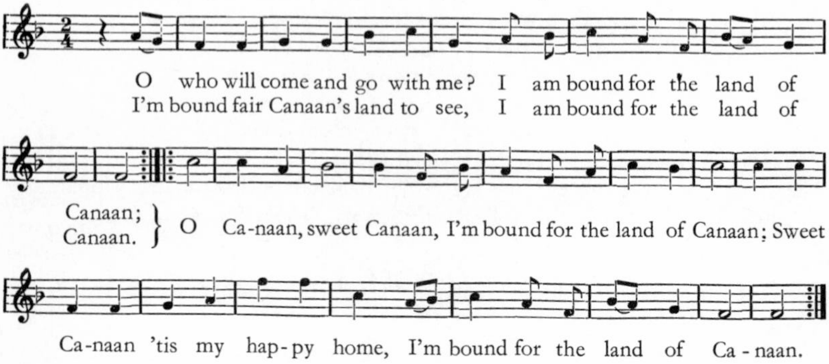
O who will come and go with me? I am bound for the land of Canaan;
I'm bound fair Canaan's land to see, I am bound for the land of Canaan.
O Ca-naan, sweet Canaan, I'm bound for the land of Canaan; Sweet
Ca-naan 'tis my hap-py home, I'm bound for the land of Ca-naan.

I'll join with those who're gone before, I am *etc.*
Where sin and sorrow are no more, I am *etc.*
Chorus

If you get there before I do, I am *etc.*
Look out for me, I'm coming too, I am *etc.*
Chorus

Text is based on a poem by Watts. The stanzas which are associated with the above are numerous, as are also the refrains and choruses. Found also BHTBK (1857), p. 334; and MHTBK (1889), No. 885. In *The Musical Quarterly*, vol. xxii., No. 2, I have shown the relationship between the above tune and Stephen Foster's 'The Glendy Burk' and 'Old Uncle Ned'. See also Dett, p. 188, for a negro song showing some textual and melodic influences.

No. 191

OLD SHIP OF ZION (A), OSH 79

Pentatonic, mode 3 (I II III — V VI —)

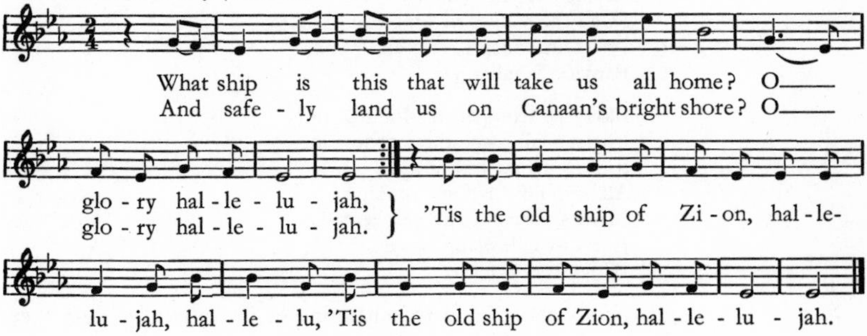
What ship is this that will take us all home? O——
And safe - ly land us on Canaan's bright shore? O——
glo - ry hal - le - lu - jah,
glo - ry hal - le - lu - jah.
'Tis the old ship of Zi - on, hal - le-
lu - jah, hal - le - lu, 'Tis the old ship of Zion, hal - le - lu - jah.

The winds may blow and the billows may foam,
But she is able to land us all home.

She's landed all who've gone before,
And yet she's able to land still more.

If I arrive there before you do,
I'll tell them that you are coming up too.

The text is said to have been written around 1800 by Rev. Samuel Hauser of North Carolina. The tune is called the "North Carolina Version" of the immensely popular song. See *White Spirituals*, 257—258. Closely related to the above tune is 'Sweet Canaan' in this collection.

No. 192

BABYLON IS FALLEN, GOS 613

Heptatonic aeolian, mode 2 A+b (I II 3 IV V 6 7)

Hail the day so long ex - pect-ed, Hail the year of full re-lease;
Zi - on's walls are now e - rect-ed, And her watch-men publish peace.
Through-out Shiloh's wide do - min-ion, Hear the trumpet loud-ly roar. Bab-y-lon is
fall - en, is fall - en, is fall - en, Bab - y - lon is fall - en to rise no more.

All her merchants stand with wonder,
What is this that comes to pass?
Murmuring like the distant thunder,
Crying "O, alas, alas!"
Swell the sound, ye kings and nobles,
Priest and people, rich and poor;
Babylon is fallen *etc.*

Blow the trumpet in Mount Zion!
Christ shall come the second time;
Ruling with a rod of iron,
All who now as foes combine.
Babel's garments we've rejected,
And our fellowship is o'er.
Babylon is fallen *etc.*

Negro borrowings of this chorus and the changing of its tune to a major key are to be seen in Dett, p. 2.

No. 193

MARTIN or WAY OVER IN THE PROMISED LAND, SOC 29

Pentatonic, mode 3 (I II III — V VI —)

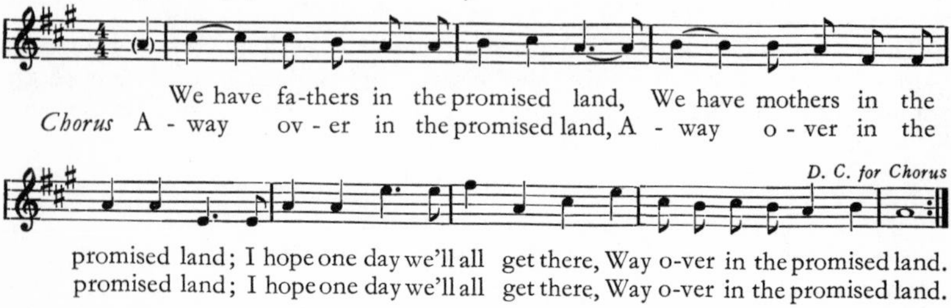
We have fa-thers in the promised land, We have mothers in the
Chorus A - way ov - er in the promised land, A - way o - ver in the
D. C. for Chorus
promised land; I hope one day we'll all get there, Way o-ver in the promised land.
promised land; I hope one day we'll all get there, Way o-ver in the promised land.

John G. McCurry, the compiler of the *Social Harp*, and William C. Davis, both of Georgia, seem to have been the first to record this tune. McCurry dates it 1854. A recently recorded variant of this tune is 'Long White Robe', Richardson, p. 67. Compare for melodic similarities the country dance 'Once I Loved a Maiden Faire' on page 47 of Playford's *The English Dancing Master*.

No. 194

HEBREW CHILDREN, OSH 481

Hexatonic, mode 5 A (I — 3 IV V 6 7)

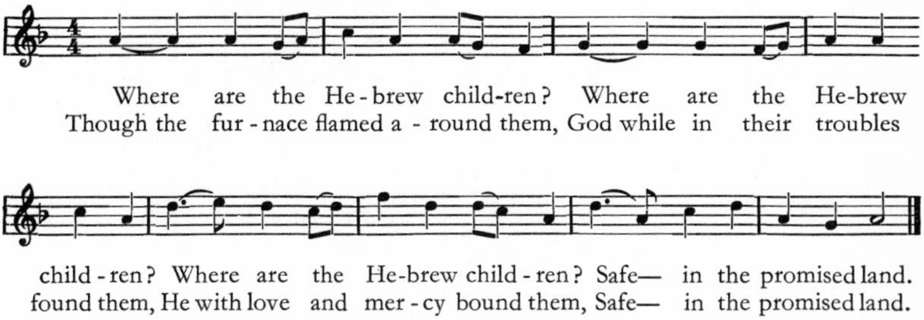
Where are the He-brew child-ren? Where are the He-brew
Though the fur - nace flamed a - round them, God while in their troubles
child - ren? Where are the He-brew child - ren? Safe— in the promised land.
found them, He with love and mer - cy bound them, Safe— in the promised land.

Where are the twelve apostles? *etc.*
They went up through pain and sighing,
Scoffing, scourging, crucifying,
Nobly for their Master dying,
Safe *etc.*

Where are the holy Christians? *etc.*
Those who've washed their robes and made them
White and spotless pure and laid them
Where no earthly stain can fade them,
Safe *etc.*

Of the author, the editor of the OSH says: "Peter Cartwright [the presumptive author of tune and words] was a minister of the gospel, and used this tune in his camp meetings long before it was ever placed in notation. — Peter Cartwright was born in Amherst County, Va., 1785, and died in Sangamond [sic] County, Ill., 1872." The song has been widely sung by the negroes who have added numerous stanzas. See *White Spirituals*, p. 263. A pre-Civil War secular negroid parody on 'Hebrew Children' was published by C. Bradlee & Co., Boston, 1844. Its first stanza is:

O whar is de spot dat we was born on, *(three times)*
Way down in Car'line State.

Mrs. Annabel Morris Buchanan has made an excellent arrangement of a version of 'Hebrew Children' for chorus. It is published by J. Fischer and Brother, New York.

No. 195

COME ALONG AND SHOUT ALONG or HEAVEN BORN SOLDIERS or NEVER GET TIRED, SOC 184

Heptatonic aeolian, mode 2 A+b (I II 3 IV V 6 7)

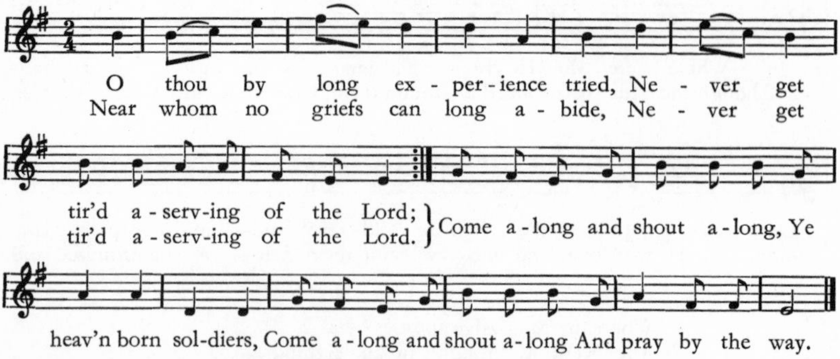

The misfit of words and notes in the first part of the song is quite evident. The compiler of the *Social Harp* credits J. F. Wade with the song and dates it 1854. The popularity of the melodic trend in the above chorus may be realized when we see it in 'Ecstacy' in this collection; in the negro *Slave Songs*, Nos. 78 and 114; in 'William and Polly', Sharp, ii., 141; and 'Rebel Soldier', Sharp, ii., 212—215.

No. 196

TO LAY THIS BODY DOWN or WHITE or I'M A LONG TIME TRAVELING, OSH 288

Hexatonic, mode 1 b (I II — IV V VI 7)

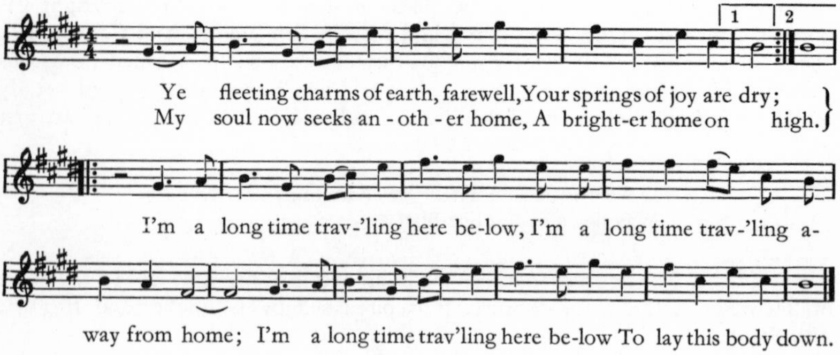

Farewell, my friends, whose tender care
Has long engaged my love;
Your fond embrace I now exchange
For better friends above.

Elder Edmund Dumas of Georgia is supposed to have made the tune. He very likely was the first to record it, that is, for the 1859 edition of the *Sacred Harp*. A variant is 'Converted Thief (A)' in this collection. The negroes have caught the significant part of the chorus in their song 'Lay This Body Down', *Slave Songs*, No. 26. One couplet of this song is

And my soul an' your soul will meet in de day
When we lay dis body down.

No. 197
HAD I WINGS or ECSTACY, OSH 106

Pentatonic, mode 2 (I — 3 IV V — 7)

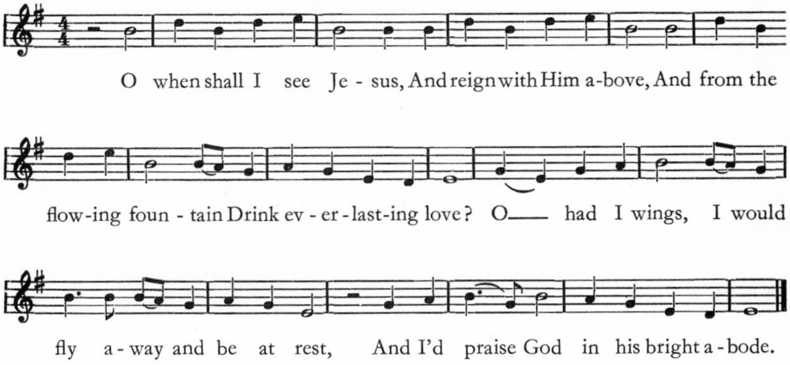
O when shall I see Je - sus, And reign with Him a-bove, And from the
flow-ing foun - tain Drink ev - er - last-ing love? O—— had I wings, I would
fly a - way and be at rest, And I'd praise God in his bright a - bode.

Further stanzas of the John Leland text are given under 'Faithful Soldier'. The tune seems, according to the note in the *Sacred Harp*, to have been first recorded by T. W. Carter of Georgia in the 1840's. The tune of the chorus is essentially the same as in 'Heaven-Born Soldiers'; in the negro tune 'Every Hour in the Day', SS p. 58; the negro tune 'O Daniel', SS p. 94; 'William and Polly', Sharp, ii., 141; 'Rebel Soldier', Sharp, ii., 212—215; and Petrie, Nos. 1191 and 1290.

No. 198

SAVE MIGHTY LORD, OSH 70

Pentatonic, mode 2 (I — 3 IV V — 7)

1
2
Je-sus, my all, to heav'n is gone, Save, might-y Lord;
He whom I fix my hopes up-on, Save, might-y Lord.
O save,

save, mighty Lord, And send con-vert-ing pow-er down, Save, might-y Lord.

Further stanzas of the John Cennick text are given under 'River of Jordan'. The tune is attributed, in the *Social Harp*, p. 99, to J. A. and J. F. Wade.

No. 199

GRACE IS FREE, REV 50

Heptatonic aeolian, minorised, mode 2 A+b (I II 3 IV V 6 7 [VII])

Thy cease-less, un-ex-haus-ted love, Un-mer-it-ed and free,
De-lights our e-vil to re-move, And helps our mis-e-ry.

3
O! hal-le-lu-jah! grace——— is free; There's e-nough for

each there's e-nough for all, There's e-nough for ev-er-more.

Thou waitest to be gracious still;
Thou dost with sinners bear;
That, saved, we may thy goodness feel,
And all thy grace declare.

Thy goodness and thy truth to me,
To every soul abound;
A vast unfathomable sea
Where all our thoughts are drowned.

Its streams the whole creation reach,
So plenteous is the store;
Enough for all, enough for each,
Enough for evermore.

Two more stanzas of text are in the *Revivalist.* The tune is of the type seen in 'The Rejected Lover', Sharp, ii., 96ff.; and a closer variant is 'Come All You Worthy Christians', JFSS, ii., 117.

No. 200

FOR ME THE SAVIOR DIED or ATONEMENT, REV 13

Hexatonic, mode 2 b, with cadentially raised seventh (I — 3 IV V 6 7 [VII])

1
For ev - er here my rest shall be Close to thy bleed-ing side——;
This, all my hope and all my plea, For me the Sa-vior
2
died.
For me the Sa-vior died, For me the Sa - vior died——, This,
all my hope and all my plea, For me the Sa - vior died.

My dying Savior and my God,
Fountain for guilt and sin,
Sprinkle me ever with thy blood,
And cleanse and keep me clean.

Wash me and make me thus thine own,
Wash me and mine thou art;
Wash me, but not my feet alone —
My hands, my head, my heart.

Th'atonement of thy blood apply
Till faith to sight improve;
Till hope in full fruition die,
And all my soul be love.

The tune is related to 'The Greenwood Siding', Cox, p. 522; 'Babe of Bethlehem' in this collection; and 'Come all you Worthy Christians', fourth version, JFSS, ii., 117.

No. 201

HEAVENLY PORT or WE'LL STEM THE STORM, OSH 378

Pentachordal, cannot be classified (I II III IV V — —)

On Jor-dan's storm-y banks I stand And cast a wish-ful eye——
Chorus We'll stem the storm, it won't be long, The heav'nly port is nigh——,

D. C. for Chorus

To Canaan's fair and hap - py land, Where my pos-ses - sions lie.
We'll stem the storm, it won't be long, We'll an - chor by and by.

The words, given more fully under 'Jordan', are Samuel Stenett's. The *Sacred Harp* editors attribute the tune to Elder Edmund Dumas, the Georgia Primitive Baptist preacher, who was at the same time a zealous musician of the fasola variety. A close melodic relative is 'O How I love Jesus', REV 456. It will be seen as akin to 'Merrily we Roll Along'. The tune as adopted by the negroes is found in Dett, p. 189.

No. 202

SAY BROTHERS, REV 173

Heptatonic ionian, mode 3 A + b (I II III IV V VI VII)

Say, brothers, will you meet us? Say, brothers, will you meet us?
Glo - ry, glo - ry hal - le - lu - jah! Glo-ry, glo - ry hal - le - lu - jah!

Say, brothers, will you meet us on Ca-naan's hap - py shore?
Glo - ry, glo - ry hal - le - lu - jah!—— We are march-ing on.

Subsequent stanzas are made by substituting for "brothers" the word "sisters" etc., then come phrases like

By the grace of God we'll meet you, *etc.*
Where parting is no more.

That will be a happy meeting, *etc.*
On Canaan's happy shore.

Jesus lives and reigns forever, *etc.*
On Canaan's happy shore.

Glory, glory hallelujah, *etc.*
Forever, evermore.

This will be recognized as the tune which Julia Ward Howe used for the chorus of her 'Battle Hymn of the Republic'. It is still popular in the above form in negro churches of the South.

No. 203

O BROTHER BE FAITHFUL, REV 433

Hexatonic, mode 3 b (I II III IV V VI —)

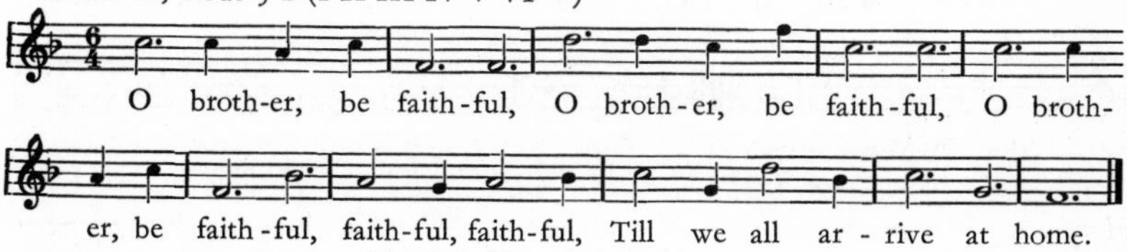
O broth-er, be faith-ful, O broth-er, be faith-ful, O broth-
er, be faith-ful, faith-ful, faith-ful, Till we all ar - rive at home.

Further stanzas are constructed on: O sister, be faithful; There we shall see Jesus; There we shall shout glory; There'll be no more parting; etc.

Miss Gilchrist found the above song in the *Wesleyan Psalmist* (1842); see JFSS, viii., 67. In Flanders and Brown's *Vermont Songs and Ballads* the song (dating from 1831) entitled 'The Gospel Ship' has a chorus text which is identical with the above. A negro version of both tune and words is in *Slave Songs*, No. 71.

No. 204

SOON WE SHALL LAND or AUTAUGA, OSH 322

Heptatonic ionian, mode 3 A+b (I II III IV V VI VII)

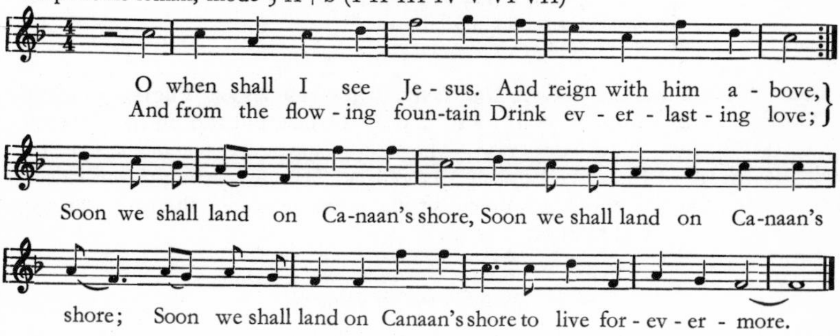
O when shall I see Je - sus. And reign with him a - bove,
And from the flow - ing foun-tain Drink ev - er - last - ing love;
Soon we shall land on Ca-naan's shore, Soon we shall land on Ca-naan's
shore; Soon we shall land on Canaan's shore to live for - ev - er - more.

The text by John Leland is given more fully under 'Faithful Soldier'. The tune reappears with unimportant changes as a negro spiritual in *Slave Songs*, No. 115. The first melodic sentence of the tune is almost identical with the opening of 'The Winter it is Past', Petrie, No. 439.

No. 205

WARRENTON or I AM BOUND FOR THE KINGDOM, GOS 275

Hexatonic, mode 3 A (I II III — V VI VII)

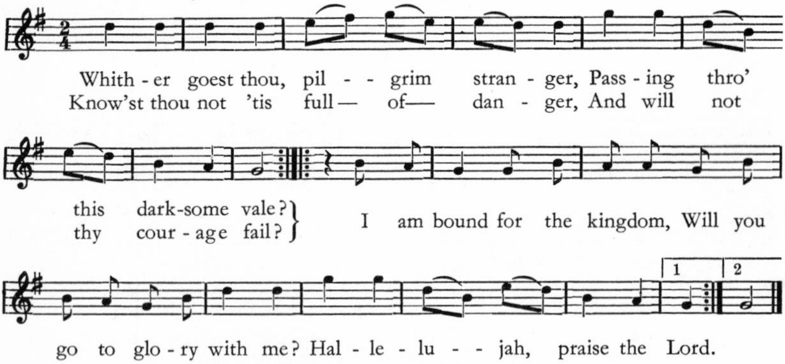
Whith - er goest thou, pil - - grim stran - ger, Pass - ing thro'
Know'st thou not 'tis full— of— dan - ger, And will not
this dark-some vale?
thy cour - age fail?
I am bound for the kingdom, Will you
1
2
go to glo - ry with me? Hal - le - lu - - jah, praise the Lord.

Pilgrim, thou dost justly call me,
Wand'ring o'er this waste so wide;
Yet no harm will e'er befall me,
While I'm blessed with such a Guide.
Chorus

Such a Guide! — no guide attends thee,
Hence for thee my fears arise;
If a guardian pow'r befriend thee,
'Tis unseen by mortal eyes.
Chorus

Four more stanzas are in *Good Old Songs*. It is found also as 'Pilgrim Stranger' in Dadmun's *Melodeon*, Boston, 1861, and as 'Female Pilgrim' in the *Christian Lyre*, 18th edition, New York, 1835. The song is apparently one of the so called dialogue hymns of the early English Methodists. The men sitting on one side of the meeting house, and the women sitting opposite, sang alternate stanzas. Lightwood cites one as follows:

Men: Tell us, O women, we would know
Whither so fast ye move.

Women: We're called to leave the world below,
Are seeking one above.

Chorus: Hallelujah.

See *Hymn Tunes and Their Story*, p. 144.

No. 206

SEND US A BLESSING, SOG 100

Heptatonic ionian, mode 3 A+b (I II III IV V VI VII)

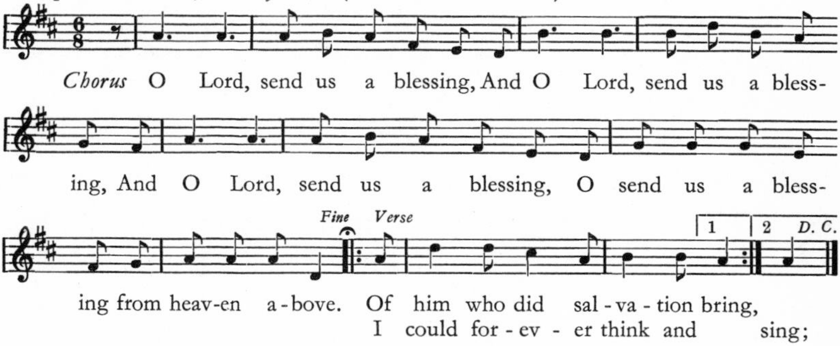
Chorus O Lord, send us a blessing, And O Lord, send us a bless-
ing, And O Lord, send us a blessing, O send us a bless-
Fine Verse
1 2 D. C.
ing from heav-en a-bove. Of him who did sal-va-tion bring,
I could for-ev-er think and sing;

Arise, ye needy, — he'll relieve;
Arise, ye guilty, — he'll forgive.

I ask but grace, and lo, 'tis given;
Ask, and he turns your hell to heaven.

Though sin and sorrow wound my soul,
Jesus, thy balm will make it whole.

Six more stanzas are in *Songs of Grace* under the song 'He was Found Worthy'. This tune is a clear adaptation of 'Johnny's So Long at the Fair.'

No. 207

I WENT DOWN TO THE VALLEY

Pentatonic, mode 1 (I II — IV V VI —)

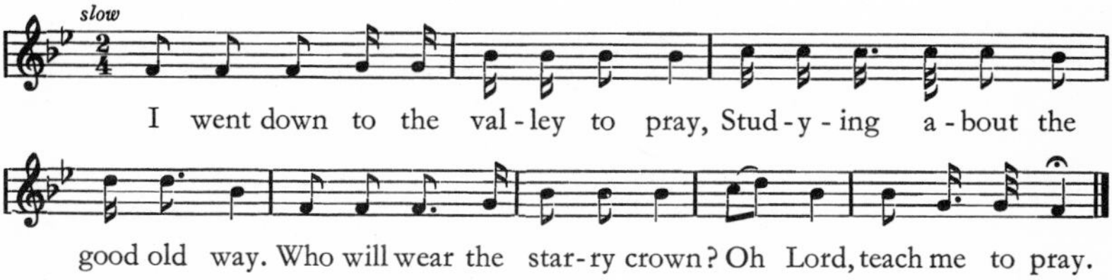
slow
I went down to the val-ley to pray, Stud-y-ing a-bout the
good old way. Who will wear the star-ry crown? Oh Lord, teach me to pray.

Recorded by the author from the singing of Donald Davidson, in Nashville, Tennessee, January 20, 1932. He had heard his father, W. B. Davidson, sing it twenty years before in Fayetteville, Tennessee. Negro versions are in Marsh, p. 156, and *Slave Songs*, No. 104.

No. 208

GIVE ME JESUS, REV 89

Heptatonic ionian, mode 3 A + b (I II III IV V VI VII)

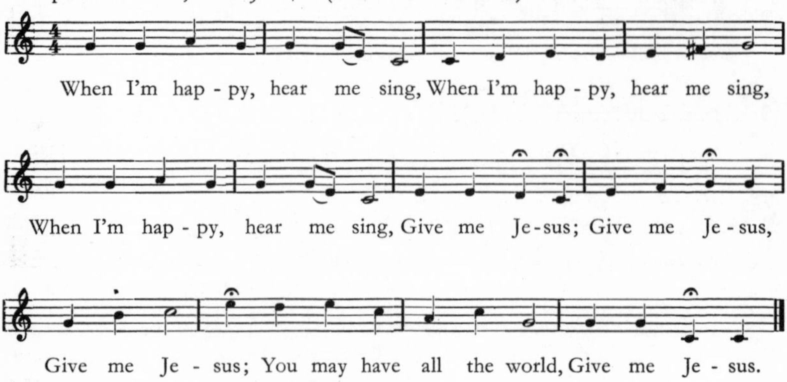
When I'm hap - py, hear me sing, When I'm hap - py, hear me sing,
When I'm hap - py, hear me sing, Give me Je-sus; Give me Je - sus,
Give me Je - sus; You may have all the world, Give me Je - sus.

When in sorrow, hear me pray, *three times*
Give me Jesus, *etc.*

When I'm dying, hear me cry, *three times*
Give me Jesus, *etc.*

When I'm rising, hear me shout, *three times*
Give me Jesus, *etc.*

When in heaven, we will sing, *three times*
Blessed Jesus, *etc.*

By thy grace we are saved, *three times*
Blessed Jesus, *etc.*

The noting of this tune, evidently from oral tradition, will be seen as quite faulty. A close variant of the song was found by Miss Gilchrist in the *Wesleyan Psalmist* and reproduced by her, JFSS, viii., 88. 'Sweet William and Lady Margaret', Davis, p. 570, is similar throughout to this tune. A negro version is in Marsh, p. 140, under the same title. The compilers of *Slave Songs* rejected a song called 'Give Me Jesus' as "spurious", that is, as being of white origin. (See *Slave Songs*, p. vi.)

No. 209

I DON'T EXPECT TO STAY or DONE WITH THE WORLD, OSH 88

Pentatonic, mode 3 (I II III — V VI —)

Je - sus, my all, to heav'n is gone, And I don't ex-pect to
He whom I fix my hopes up - on, And I don't ex-pect to
stay much long - er here;
stay much long - er here.
I am done with the world, and I want to
serve the Lord, And I don't ex - pect to stay much long - er here.

This spiritual with its text core made of the John Cennick words (given more fully under 'River of Jordan') seems to have been first recorded for the earliest edition of the *Sacred Harp*, that is, in the early 1840's. A negro version of the chorus is in Marsh, p. 188.

No. 210

OLD SHIP OF ZION (B) or HAPPY SAILOR, HH 355

Heptatonic ionian, mode 3 A+b (I II III IV V VI VII)

3
Come a - long, come a - long and let us go—— home; O ——
glo - ry hal - le - lu - jah! Our home is o - ver Jor-dan, hal - le-
lu - - jah! Our home is o - ver Jor - dan, Hal - le - lu - jah!

What ship is this that will take us all home?
O glory hallelujah!
'Tis the old ship of Zion *etc.*

Do you think she'll be able to take us all home?
I think she'll be able *etc.*

We have some friends who're gone before;
By and by we'll go and see them.

If you get there before I do,
You may tell them that I'm coming.

What will the Christian do when his lamp burns out?
Go shouting home to heaven.

It is found also in OSH 388. Negro adoptions under the same title are Dett, p. 81, and *Slave Songs*, p. 125. For additional stanzas of the text see 'Old Ship of Zion (A)'. The *Sacred Harp* (1844) version of the text begins:

Come tell me of your ship and what is her name?
Oh, tell me happy sailor.
Come tell me of your captain and what is his fame?
Oh, tell me happy sailor.
She's the old ship of Zion, hallelu, hallelu,
And her captain, Judah's Lion, hallelujah.

An interesting dressing-up of this straightforward folk-text came from Boston in Dadmun's *Melodeon* in 1860, p. 102, where we read:

What vessel are you sailing in?
Pray tell me its name;
Our vessel is the ark of God,
And Christ our Captain's name.

How old the American versions of the 'Ship of Zion' songs are I have not been able to learn. Newman I. White points to versions in the 1820's (*American Negro Folk-Songs*, p. 94).

An early use of the same allegory in religious song is seen in the German folk-song collection of Erk and Böhme, *Deutscher Liederhort*, vol. iii., p. 628f. I find no melodic similarities between the German and the American songs; but the texts show remarkable parallels. To make this clear I shall cite a few of the German stanzas, comparing with them passages taken from various "ship" songs as sung by whites and blacks in America.

From a German manuscript of 1470—1480	*American "ship" songs*
Uf einem stillen wage kumpt uns das schiffelin, es bringt uns riche gabe die heren künigin.	O she runs so level and steady. O see that ship come sailing. Dat ship is heavy loaded. King Jesus is the captain.
Das schiflin das gat stille und bringt uns richen last, der segel ist diu minne, der heilig geist der mast.	O she runs so level and steady. Dat ship is heavy loaded. Behold the sails expanded, Around the towering mast.

A song from the year 1608

Uns kompt ein Schiff gefahren,
Es bringt ein schöne Last,
Darauf viel Engelscharen
Und hat ein großen Mast.

O see that ship come sailing.
Dat ship is heavy loaded.
She's loaded with bright angels.

No. 211

ANGELS HOVERING ROUND, REV 74

Pentatonic, cannot be classified (I II III — V — VII)

There are an - gels hov-'ring round, There are an - gels hov-'ring

round, There are an - - - - gels, an - - - - gels hov - 'ring round.

To carry the tidings home *etc.*
To the new Jerusalem *etc.*
Poor sinners are coming home.
And Jesus bids them come.
Let him that heareth come.
We're on our journey home.

The song is found also in Mason's *Harp of the South*, p. 272, where the composer is given as "Husband". The same tune with minor variations appeared in the 1859 edition of the *Sacred Harp*, p. 425, where it was attributed to J. L. Pickard. Its two one-line verses are:

I am on my journey home *etc.*
To the New Jerusalem *etc.*

No. 212

HOLY WAR, SWP 170

For mode see note below

I've list - ed in the ho - ly war, }
Con - tent to suf - fer sol-dier's fare, }
And we'll all shout for

joy, And we'll give God the glory, And I hope to join the ar-my by and by.

I've fought through many a battle sore,
And I must fight through many more;
And we'll *etc.*

I take my breastplate, sword and shield,
And boldly march into the field.

The banner o'er my head is love,
I draw my rations from above.

The world, the flesh and Satan too
Unite and strive what they can do.

On thee, O Lord, I humbly call,
Uphold me, or my soul must fall.

I've listed and I mean to fight,
Till all my foes are put to flight.

And when the victory I have won,
I'll give the praise to God alone.

Come, fellow-Christians, join with me,
Come, face the foe and never flee.

The heavenly battle is begun,
Come, take the field and win the crown.

With listing orders I have come;
Come rich, come poor, come old or young.

Here's grace's bounty Christ has given,
And glorious crowns laid up in heaven.

But if you will not list and fight,
You'll sink into eternal night.

The tune as it stands is heptatonic dorian. And that is probably a correct notation. The interesting thing is the device employed to legitimize the dorian raised sixth, namely, the device of modulation. The writer of the tune, knowing presumably nothing about the old modes, set his first melodic phrase in *g*-major with a semi-cadence on two of the scale. All went well because the *f*-sharp of *that* key was not represented. But in the second part of the tune the actual *f*-natural appeared; and the only way he saw of handling it was to change the signature to a "natural key chorus" as he specifically calls it. And the final note in the tune agreed with the key which he took to be *a*-minor.

No. 213

O GOD WHAT SHALL I SAY or ALVERSON, REV 181

Hexatonic, mode 5 A (I — 3 IV V 6 7)

When pi - ty prompts me to look round Up - on my fel - low
clay, See men re - ject the gos - pel sound, O God, what
shall I say——? O God, what shall I—— say?

My bowels yearn for dying men,
Doom'd to eternal woe,
Fain would I speak, but 'tis in vain
If God does not speak too.

O sinner, sinner, won't you hear
When in God's name I come?
Upon your peril don't forbear,
Lest hell should be your doom.

One more stanza is in the *Revivalist*. This is a phrygian tune with the second of its scale unused. It reminds one strongly of the melody of 'Gala Water', *Lyric Gems of Scotland*, p. 84.

No. 214

THAT LONESOME VALLEY, Author's recording

Pentatonic, mode 3 (I II III — V VI —)
Slow

You got to go—— that lone-some val - ley—, You got to
go——— there by your - self—. There's no one—— can go there
for you; You got to go there, you got to go there by your - self.

Recorded by the author, February 11, 1933, from the singing of Don West of the Highlander Folk School, Monteagle, Tennessee. Mr. West told me that the two subsequent stanzas began, "You got to lie in that lonesome graveyard" and "Some folks say that John was a Baptist." After each verse the tune is repeated to the words of the first stanza.

The source of this spiritual song is very likely 'In Seaport Town', see Sharp, i., 310, in which there is the recurring phrase:

Till at last they came to a lonesome valley,

and where considerable melodic similarity is to be found. Further traces of this typical folk-tune are in 'Young Beichan', Sharp, i., 79; 'My Mother Bid Me', Sharp, ii., 94, tune D; 'Opossum', Sharp, ii., 353; 'Drivin' Steel', Sandburg, p. 150; the negro song 'You Got to Cross it for Yourself', Sandburg, p. 486; and 'That Lonesome Valley', Grissom, p. 2.

In *The Carolina Low-Country*, pp. 284ff., there are two negro spirituals which lean heavily on 'That Lonesome Valley'. The "lonesome valley" symbolized, among both negroes and whites, also the mourning period which was a necessary forerunner of religious conversion.

No. 215

I'M BOUND TO DIE IN THE ARMY or SERVICE OF THE LORD, OSH 80

Hexatonic, mode 3 b (I II III IV V VI —)

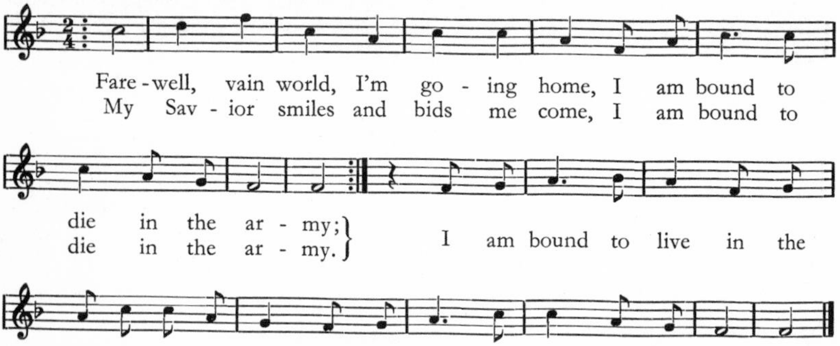
Fare-well, vain world, I'm go - ing home, I am bound to
My Sav - ior smiles and bids me come, I am bound to
die in the ar - my;
die in the ar - my.
I am bound to live in the
service of my Lord, I am bound to die in the ar - my.

Further stanzas of the text are given under 'Golden Harp'. A variant of this tune is 'Promise' in this collection. 'Antioch' in this collection, is also related. The tune 'Service of the Lord' or 'Antioch' seems to have been borrowed by those who sang 'Little Musgrave and Lady Barnard' as it is found in Sharp, i., 162.

Indications that the direction of borrowing was as suggested may be found in the misfit of words to tune in the secular song. See for example where the "ar-my" of the above tune and the "-lu-jah" of 'Antioch' correspond to a mere repetition, "all, all", in the 'Little Musgrave' song. 'Cruel Mother', Sharp, i., 61, tune K, is also closely related to 'Service of the Lord'. For negro adoptions and adaptations see Grissom, p. 60; Marsh, p. 169; *White Spirituals*, pp. 266 and 267; and Dett, p. 120.

No. 216

PROMISE or WITH US TO THE END, SOC 73

Hexatonic, mode 3 b (I II III IV V VI —)

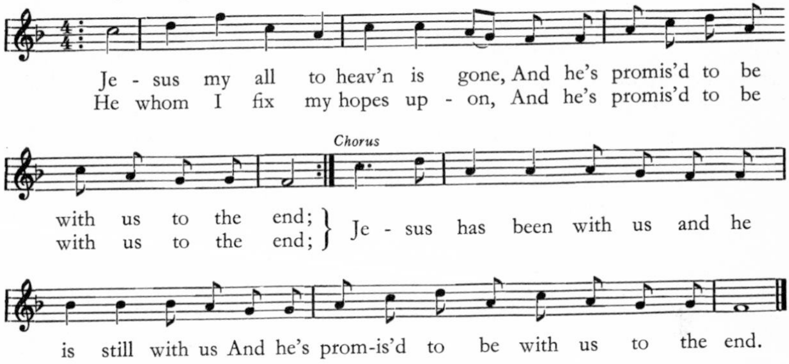

The text is given more fully under 'River of Jordan'. The song is ascribed by the compiler of the *Social Harp* to Henry F. Chandler and dated 1854. The tune has evidently been used for the worldly ballad 'Cruel Mother', see Sharp, i., 61. The chorus reappears in the *Wesleyan Psalmist* (1842) attached to a text which begins:

> Children of God, renounce your fears,
> Jesus says he will be with us to the end.
> Lo, Jesus for your help appears,
> Jesus says he will be with us to the end.
> *Chorus*
> For he has been with us *etc.*

This chorus material, words and tune, is used also in 'He's Promised to be With You' in this collection. See for tune relationships also 'Little Musgrave and Lady Barnard', Sharp, i., 162.

No. 217

NEVER TURN BACK (A), OSH 381

Pentatonic, cannot be classified (I II 3 — V — 7)

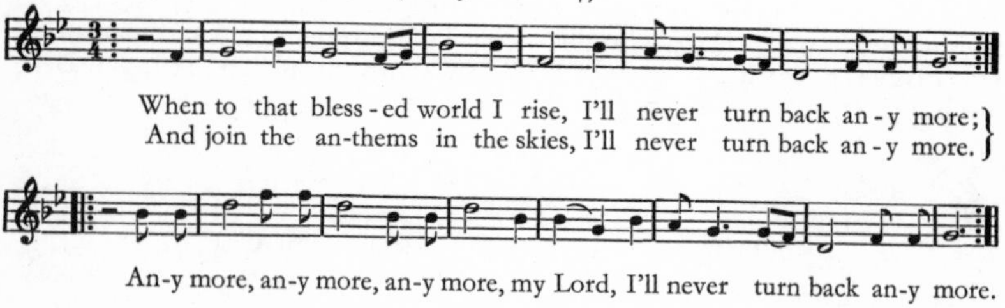
When to that bless-ed world I rise, I'll never turn back an-y more;
And join the an-thems in the skies, I'll never turn back an-y more.
An-y more, an-y more, an-y more, my Lord, I'll never turn back an-y more.

This was a recording from the 1840's. Another, in the *Social Harp* of 1855, p. 52, has the more indigenous reading "I'll never turn back no more." See 'Never Turn Back (B)' in this collection. A negro variant is in Marsh, p. 174. John Powell tells me that Lydia, negro servant in the Powell house in Richmond, Virginia, and a remarkable singer, sings a variant of this tune to the words:

> King cried: "no mo', no mo', my Lord,
> I'll never turn to go back to E-jup Land no mo'."

No. 218

OLD-TIME RELIGION

Pentatonic, mode 3 (I II III — V VI —)

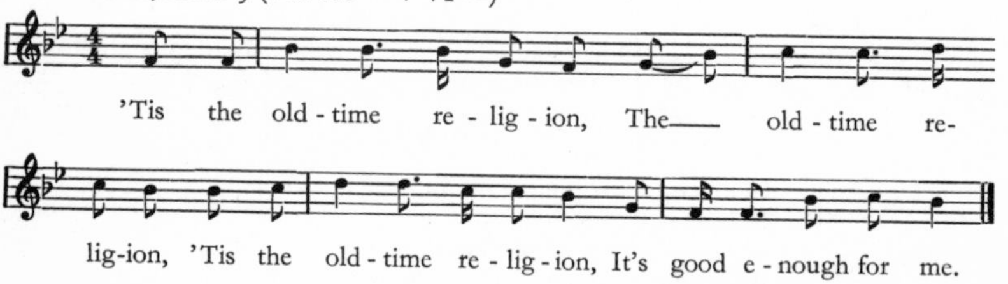
'Tis the old-time re-lig-ion, The— old-time re-
lig-ion, 'Tis the old-time re-lig-ion, It's good e-nough for me.

Subsequent verses have "It was good for Paul and Silas" and for practically everybody. It is the author's recording from memory of hearing it sung at meetings of both negroes and whites. Sharp, ii., 291, has the above tune with a judgment-day text under the title 'Sinner Man', a song which had come from negro sources.

No. 219

TAKE ME HOME or I'M ALONE IN THIS WORLD

Pentatonic, mode 3 (I II III — V VI —)

My fa-ther's gone to glo-ry, I'm a-lone in this world, my
fa-ther's gone to glo-ry, I'm a-lone. My fa-ther's gone to glo-ry,
I'm a-lone in this world; Take me home, dear Sav-ior take me home.

Recorded by the author from the singing of Samuel E. Asbury, September 10, 1932, at Nashville, Tennessee. Mr. Asbury learned it in his boyhood in the 1880's, from hearing it at camp meetings in western North Carolina. Subsequent verses substitute "my mother," "my sister," etc. A negro version of the tune is in *Slave Songs*, p. 18.

No. 220

JESTER or I BELONG TO THIS BAND (A), OSH 531

Pentatonic, mode 3 (I II III — V VI —)

If our fa-thers want to go, Why don't they come a-long? I be-
long to this band, Hal-le-lu-jah. Hal-le-lu-jah, hal-le-
lu-jah, I be-long to this band, hal-le-lu-jah.

The tune was first printed in the *Union Harp* as recorded by S. M. Denson of Alabama. Subsequent verses are made by the use of "mothers", "sisters," etc. That the negroes used this formula is shown in *White Spirituals*, p. 247. The refrain "I Belong to this band, hallelujah" reappears in 'I Belong to This Band (B)' in this collection.

No. 221

LONG-SOUGHT HOME, CHH 159

Hexatonic, mode 3 A (I II III — V VI VII)

Je - ru - sa - lem, my hap - py home, Oh how I long for thee!
When shall my sor-rows have an end, Thy joys when shall I see.

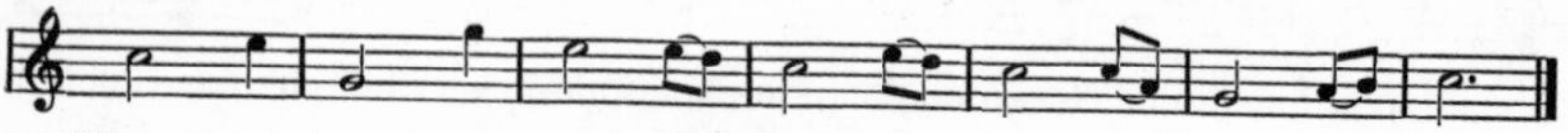

Home, sweet home, my long-sought home, My home in heav'n a - bove.

Thy walls are all of precious stone,
Most glorious to behold;
Thy gates are richly set with pearl,
Thy streets are paved with gold.

Thy garden and thy pleasing green
My study long have been;
Such sparkling light by human sight
Has never yet been seen.

The *Christian Harmony* credits the song to William Bobo, Union, S. C. The words are credited, in the *Primitive Baptist Hymn and Tune Book*, No. 453, to Cowper.

No. 222

BEAUTIFUL HOME SWEET HOME

Pentatonic, mode 3 (I II III — V VI —)

Beauti-ful home, sweet home, Beauti - ful home, sweet home, Beautiful

home, sweet home, Lord, I want to join the angels, beauti-ful home———.

Recorded by the author from the singing of Samuel E. Asbury, September 10, 1932, as he remembered its being sung in the 1880's in camp meetings in western North Carolina. The above is merely the chorus of the song. But it is essentially the same, melodically, as the verse. The text proceeds:

Fathers have a home, sweet home *etc.*
Mothers have a home, sweet home *etc.*
By and by we'll go and see them *etc.*
Won't that be a happy meeting *etc.*

No. 223

COME FRIENDS GO WITH ME, CSH 206

Heptatonic ionian, mode 3 A+b (I II III IV V VI VII)

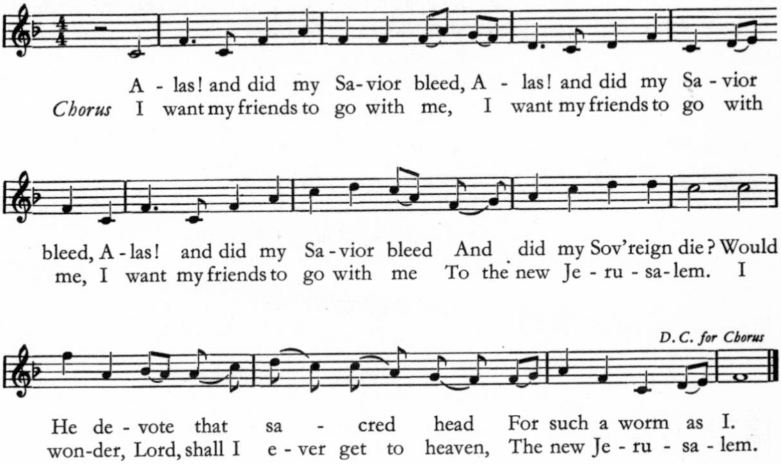
A - las! and did my Sa-vior bleed, A - las! and did my Sa - vior
Chorus I want my friends to go with me, I want my friends to go with
bleed, A - las! and did my Sa - vior bleed And did my Sov'reign die? Would
me, I want my friends to go with me To the new Je - ru - sa-lem. I
D. C. for Chorus
He de - vote that sa - cred head For such a worm as I.
won-der, Lord, shall I e - ver get to heaven, The new Je - ru - sa - lem.

William Hauser included the above tune, with different text, in his *Olive Leaf*. Of the above chorus, "sometimes sung after each verse," he says: "Not worth while to criticise this chorus. Does anybody criticise a camel? No; they take him for his usefulness".

No. 224
I LOVE JESUS, REV 254

Hexatonic, mode 3 A (I II III — V VI VII)

Je - sus, my all, to heav'n has gone, Glo - ry hal - le - lu - jah, He
whom I fix my hopes up - on, Glo- ry hal - le - lu - ja. I love Je - sus,
Chorus
glo - ry hal - le - lu - jah, I love Je - sus, glo - ry hal - le - lu - jah.

Further stanzas of the text are given under 'River of Jordan'. The tune is found in a negro version in Marsh, No. 65. I have, in manuscript, practically the same tune which I recorded from the dulcimer playing of F. S. Russell, Marion, Virginia. He called the tune 'Bonaparte's Retreat'. Compare also the sixteenth century carol tune 'Tempus adest floridum', *The Oxford Book of Carols*, No. 99.

No. 225
HALLELUJAH, OSH 146

Hexatonic, mode 1 b (I II — IV V VI 7)

And let this fee - - ble bo - dy fail—, And
My soul shall quit— this mourn - ful vale— And
let it faint or die;
soar to worlds on high.
And I'll sing hal - - le - lu-
jah, And you'll sing hal - - le - lu - - jah—, And we'll
all sing hal - le - - lu - - jah—, When we ar - rive at home.

This text by Charles Wesley, supplemented by the infectious chorus and sung to this swingful tune, was widely popular in the first part of the nineteenth century. It is given more fully under 'Pleasant Hill'. The song is found, SOH 107 and HH 102.

The tune had qualities which made it widely popular. There is of course no knowing whether the many variant forms which I have found derive from the above tune; but I have given them collectively the name the 'Hallelujah' tune family. Other members of the family in this collection are 'Stephens', 'Pilgrim's Triumph', 'Faithful Soldier', 'Tender Care', 'Heavenly Armor', 'O I'm So Happy', and 'Converted Thief'. Related melodies with secular texts are 'The Reilly Song', Thomas, p. 166; 'Chickens They are Crowing', Sharp, ii., 378; 'Lord Thomas and Fair Eleanor', Sharp, i., 125; 'Virginian Lover', Sharp, ii., 149f.; 'Banks of Sweet Dundee', Sharp, i., 399; 'The Pinery Boy', Shoemaker, p. 262; 'Kilrush Air' Petrie, Nos. 167 and 283; and 'Tweed Side', SMM, p. 9.

No. 226

FEW DAYS, SOC 209

Heptatonic ionian, mode 3 A+b (I II III IV V VI VII)

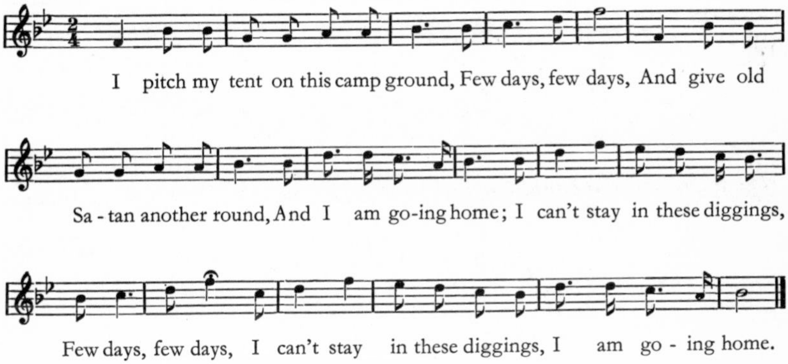
I pitch my tent on this camp ground, Few days, few days, And give old
Sa - tan another round, And I am go-ing home; I can't stay in these diggings,
Few days, few days, I can't stay in these diggings, I am go - ing home.

The compiler of the *Social Harp*, John G. McCurry, claims this song and dates it 1855. A variant of the tune is in Richardson, p. 72. A negro adoption is given in *White Spirituals*, p. 266.

No. 227

PARTING HYMN or JOYFUL or O THAT WILL BE JOYFUL, PB 303

Heptatonic ionian, mode 3 A+b (I II III IV V VI VII)

How pleasant thus to dwell be - low In fel - low - ship of love!
And tho' we part 'tis bliss to know The good shall meet a - bove!
The good shall meet a - bove———, The good shall meet a - bove.
Fine
And tho' we part, 'tis bliss to know The good shall meet a - bove.
And sing the ev - er - last - ing song With those who've gone be - fore.
O that will be joy - ful, joy - ful, joy - ful. O that will be
joy - ful To meet and part no more; To meet and
Dal Segno
part no more———, On Ca - naan's hap - py shore,

James, editor of the 1911 *Original Sacred Harp*, says that 'Joyful' was composed by Rev. Abraham D. Merrell. He was born in New Hampshire 1796 and died in 1878. The first lines of a widely sung parody of this song (or is the above the parody?) are:

The man who has plenty of good peanuts
And giveth his neighbor none,
Shan't have any of my peanuts
When his peanuts are gone.

Miss Gilchrist informs us as to the relatives of tune and words in England. One parody familiar to her was:

John Wesley had a little ghost,
The color of it was white;
It used to swarm up his bed-post
And frighten him at night.

Another, known to Miss Gilchrist, was 'Three Little Kittens', (See JFSS, viii, 86). I also heard this song as a nursery ditty in my early youth in Monson, Maine, in the 1880's. Compare 'Judgment Scenes' in this collection. The tune was used also for the carol 'Joys Seven', *The Oxford Book of Carols*, No. 70.

No. 228

SOMETHING NEW, UHH 35

Pentatonic, mode 3 (I II III — V VI —)

Since man by sin has lost his God, He seeks cre-
a - tion through; And vain - ly strives for sol - id bliss In
try - ing some-thing new —. In try - ing some-thing new, And
vain - ly strives for sol - id bliss In try - ing some-thing new.

The new, possessed like fading flowers,
Soon loses its gay hue;
The bubble now no longer stays,
The soul wants something new.

And could we call all Europe ours,
With India and Peru,
The mind would feel an aching void
And still want something new.

But when we feel a Savior's love,
All good in him we view;
The soul forsakes its vain delights —
In Christ finds all things new.

Also found, SOC 250, GOS 365, SOH 254. A negro adoption and adaptation is cited in *White Spirituals*, p. 249.

No. 229

VICTORIA or ONE MORE RIVER TO CROSS, OSH 290

Hexatonic, mode 3 A (I II III — V VI VII)

A - las! and did my Sav - ior bleed, A - - las! and did
my Sav - ior bleed, A - las! and did my Sav - ior bleed And
did my Sov - reign die? I—— have but one more riv - er to
cross, I—— have but one more ri - ver to cross; I have but
one more ri - ver to cross, And then I'll be at rest.
1
2

The text theme of the chorus is seen in the negro spiritual SS 4:

And I hain't but one more river to cross.

The tune is closely related to 'Gaines', HH 122, this collection; 'Geordie', Sharp, i., 240; 'John of Hazelgreen', Sharp, i., 294; 'False Young Man', (2), Sharp, ii., 52; 'True Lover's Farewell', Sharp, ii., 113 ff. The 'Geordie' text begins with 'As I crossed over London's Bridge'. This may indicate where the revival folk got their suggestion for tune and text of 'One More River to Cross'.

No. 230

NEW INDIAN SONG or WALK AND TALK WITH JESUS, SOC 45

Heptatonic ionian, mode 1 A+B (I II III IV V VI VII)

When I can read my tit - le clear To mansions in the skies,
I'll bid fare-well to ev - 'ry fear And wipe my weeping eyes.
Oh——, walk and talk with Je - sus, Hal - le, hal - le - lu - jah,
Fine
Oh————, there's glo - ry in my soul. Ah, poor sin - ner, you
run from the rock, When the moon goes down in blood, To——
Dal Segno
hide your-self in the moun-tain top, For to hide your-self from God.

Should earth against my soul engage,
And hellish darts be hurled,
Then I can smile at Satan's rage,
And face a frowning world.

Let cares like a wild deluge come,
And storms of sorrow fall;
May I but safely reach my home,
My God, my heaven, my all.

The compiler of the *Social Harp* ascribes this song to J. A. & J. F. Wade and dates it 1854. The words, excepting those of the chorus, are by Watts.

No. 231

SUBSTANTIAL JOYS or I WANT TO GO THERE TOO, SOC 28

Hexatonic, mode 3 b (I II III IV V VI —)

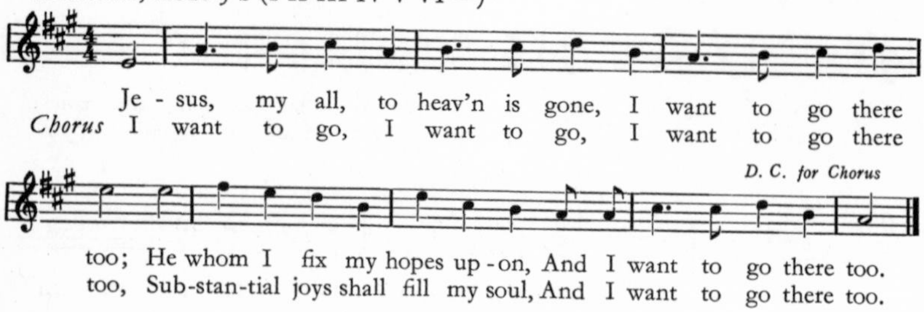

John G. McCurry, compiler of the *Social Harp*, recorded it, according to his note, in 1854. In the 1880's in Monson, Maine, I heard almost precisely the same tune sung to the words:

> Johnny Morgan played the organ,
> His father beat the drum;
> His sister played the tambourine
> And his brother went bum-bum.

The text of the spiritual song is given more completely under 'River of Jordan'. The tune is akin to 'One Man Shall Mow my Meadow' and 'The Knight and the Shepherd's Daughter', in Sharp, *One Hundred English Folksongs*, Nos. 3 and 100.

No. 232

O HE'S TAKEN MY FEET, REV 114

Hexatonic, mode 3 b (I II III IV V VI —)

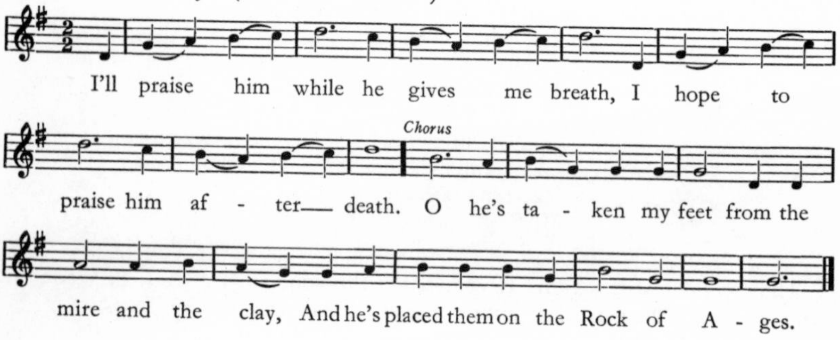

I hope to praise him when I die,
And shout salvation as I fly.
Chorus

And I will tell to sinners round
What a dear Savior I have found.
Chorus

No. 233
MY BIBLE LEADS TO GLORY, REV 385

Hexatonic, 6th missing, cannot be classified, obviously ionian (I II III IV V — VII)

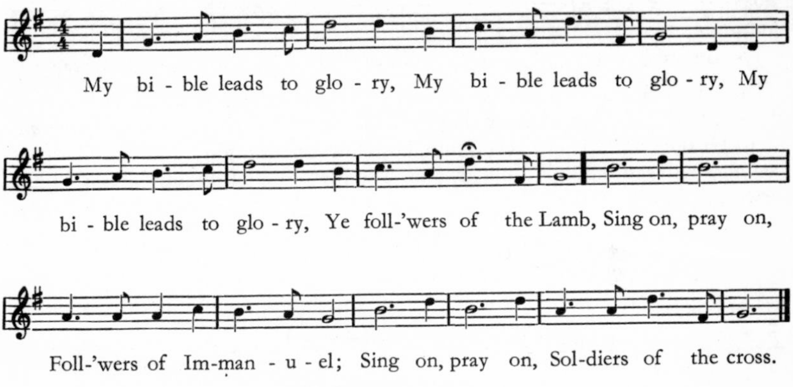
My bi - ble leads to glo - ry, My bi - ble leads to glo - ry, My
bi - ble leads to glo - ry, Ye foll-'wers of the Lamb, Sing on, pray on,
Foll-'wers of Im-man - u - el; Sing on, pray on, Sol-diers of the cross.

Subsequent stanzas are constructed from such sentences as:

Religion makes me happy.
King Jesus is my captain.
I long to see my Savior.
Then farewell, sin and sorrow.
We'll have a shout in glory.
We'll wave our palms forever.

A variant of tune and words is in Richardson, p. 68. The melody is the same as 'Bobbing Around' which was published by Oliver Ditson & Co., Boston, about 1855, as one of a series called *Melodies of the day*.

No. 234

I'M TRAVELING TO MY GRAVE or TRAVELER SOC 37

Pentatonic, mode 1 (I II — IV V VI —)

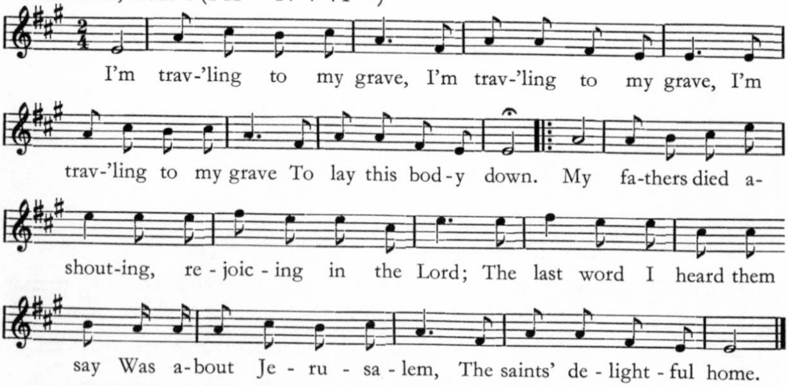
I'm trav-'ling to my grave, I'm trav-'ling to my grave, I'm
trav-'ling to my grave To lay this bod-y down. My fa-thers died a-
shout-ing, re-joic-ing in the Lord; The last word I heard them
say Was a-bout Je-ru-sa-lem, The saints' de-light-ful home.

The song is ascribed in the *Social Harp* to John G. McCurry and Wm. C. Davis and dated 1853. For a variant among the negro spiritual tunes see *White Spirituals*, p. 261. Compare 'I'm a Long Time Traveling' in this collection. Similarity is seen also between the above melody and 'The Merchant's Daughter', second tune, JFSS, i., 160.

No. 235

ON THE OTHER SIDE OF JORDAN, REV 465

Hexatonic, mode 2 A (I II 3 IV V — 7)

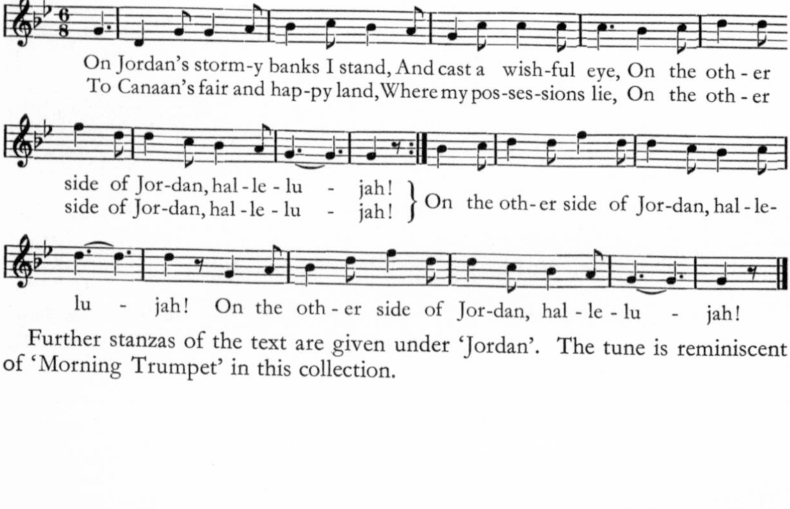
On Jordan's storm-y banks I stand, And cast a wish-ful eye, On the oth-er
To Canaan's fair and hap-py land, Where my pos-ses-sions lie, On the oth-er
side of Jor-dan, hal-le-lu-jah!
side of Jor-dan, hal-le-lu-jah!
On the oth-er side of Jor-dan, hal-le-
lu-jah! On the oth-er side of Jor-dan, hal-le-lu-jah!

Further stanzas of the text are given under 'Jordan'. The tune is reminiscent of 'Morning Trumpet' in this collection.

No. 236

JESUS IS MY FRIEND (B), REV 311

Hexatonic, mode 4 b (I II 3 IV V — 7)

The chorus of the above tune has features similar to 'Jesus Is My Friend (A)', in this collection. The whole tune seems to be a degenerate offspring of 'Davisson's Retirement', in this collection.

No. 237

DERRETT or IT WON'T BE LONG, SOC 108

Hexatonic, mode 4 a (I II — IV V 6 7)

The compiler of the *Social Harp*, John G. McCurry, claims the song and dates it 1847. We know the words as those of John Cennick. Additional stanzas are given under 'River of Jordan'.

No. 238

CARTER or NEVER TURN BACK (B), SOC 52

Hexatonic, mode 2 A (I II 3 IV V — 7)

Je - sus, my all, to heav'n is gone, I'll ne - ver turn back no more;
He whom I fix my hopes up - on, I'll ne - ver turn back no more.

I'll ne-ver turn back no more, my Lord, I'll ne - ver turn back no more.

A variant tune is 'Never Turn Back (A)', this collection. A negro variant is in Marsh, p. 174. Additional stanzas of the text are given under 'River of Jordan'.

No. 239

I WILL ARISE

Pentatonic, mode 2 (I — 3 IV V — 7)

(a)

Come, ye sin - ners, poor and need - y, Weak and wounded, sick and sore,

Je - sus read - y stands to save you, Full of pi - ty, love and pow'r.

Chorus

I will a - rise and go to Je - sus, He will em-brace me in his arms,

In the arms of my dear Sa-vior, O there are ten thousand charms.

Let not conscience make you linger,
Nor of fitness fondly dream;
All the fitness he requireth
Is to feel your need of him.
Chorus

Agonizing in the garden,
Lo, your Master prostrate lies;
On the bloody tree behold him,
Hear him cry before he dies.
Chorus

Lo, th'incarnate God ascended,
Pleads the merit of his blood;
Venture on him, venture wholely,
Let no other trust intrude.
Chorus

I recorded this song from the singing of Donald Davidson, Vanderbilt University, June, 1935. Joseph Hart published this poem in 1759. The refrain text is probably of camp-meeting origin. The tune has been immensely popular for certainly more than a hundred years in the South. Found also SOH 5, HH 217, WP 25, PB 342, OSH 312 (tune with other words), OSH 81 (words with another tune).

The tune is typical of a traditional trend. Many other songs show either close relationship throughout or use single phrases of this melody. The tunes in this collection which are close to the 'I Will Arise' type (mentioned in the Introduction, p. 14) are 'Humble Penitent', and 'Hayden'. Others making use of the second phrase only, marked *a*, are 'Bozrah' and 'New Orleans'. A secular tune in the 'I Will Arise' form is 'The Bird Song', Sharp, ii., 304; and among the secular tunes employing phrase *a* as their tune beginnings are 'Oh Love It is a Killing Thing' and 'When I first Left Old Ireland', Petrie, Nos, 469 and 863; and 'The Cruel Mother', Cox, p. 522. Thomas gives the beginning of a lullaby which doubtlessly belongs to this tune group, see *Devil's Ditties*, p. 17.

No. 240

I WANT A SEAT IN PARADISE or NORTH PORT, OSH 324

Hexatonic, mode 2 A (I II 3 IV V — 7)

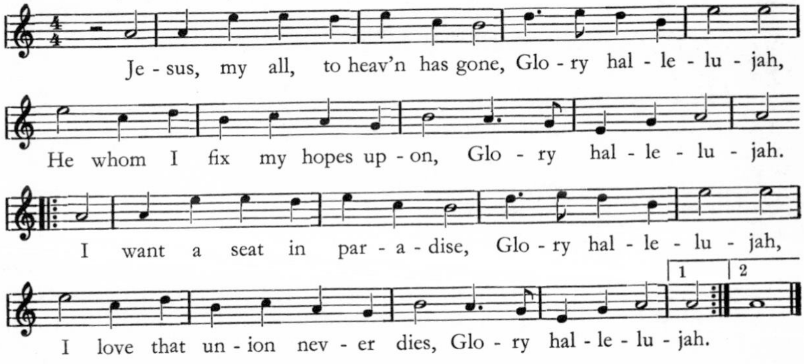
Je - sus, my all, to heav'n has gone, Glo - ry hal - le - lu - jah,
He whom I fix my hopes up - on, Glo - ry hal - le - lu - jah.
I want a seat in par - a - dise, Glo - ry hal - le - lu - jah,
I love that un - ion nev - er dies, Glo - ry hal - le - lu - jah.

The recording of this tune is credited to Dr. R. R. Osborne, a Georgian. The core of the words is by John Cennick, a text which is given more fully under 'River of Jordan'.

The tune is built up easily on the theme of the first two measures which is similar to the beginning of 'Henry Martin', see Rickaby, p. 161, and Sandburg, p. 176. 'Henry Martin' is based on an incident in British marine history which took place in he year 1476. See S. Baring-Gould, *Songs of the West*, song No. 53, and note. Another old relative of the tune seems to be 'There were Three Ravens' which was recorded in 1611 as follows:

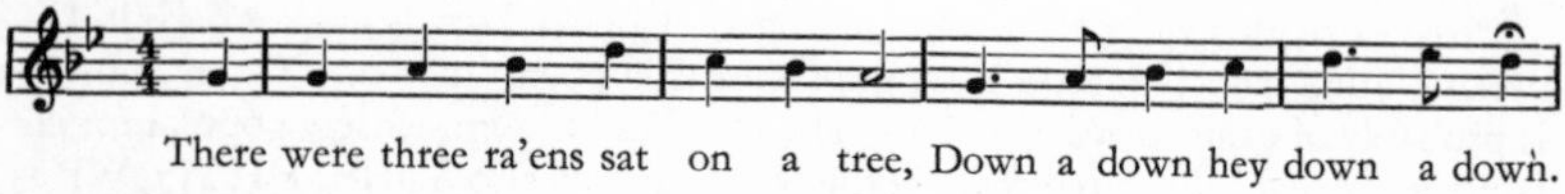
There were three ra'ens sat on a tree, Down a down hey down a down.

See Jackson, *English Melodies from the 13th to the 18th Century*, p. 24. German tunes with practically the same opening phrase and dating from the sixteenth century are in Erk-Böhme, *Deutscher Liederhort*, vol. iii., p. 718.

No. 241
MORNING TRUMPET, OSH 85

Hexatonic, mode 2 A (I II 3 IV V — 7)

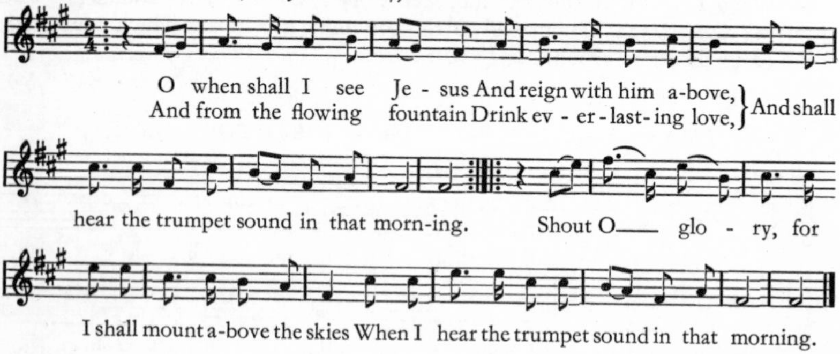
O when shall I see Je - sus And reign with him a-bove,
And from the flowing fountain Drink ev - er - last- ing love,
And shall
hear the trumpet sound in that morn-ing.
Shout O—— glo - ry, for
I shall mount a-bove the skies When I hear the trumpet sound in that morning.

This is one of the best examples of the revival spiritual song. It has the John Leland words of matchless popularity in the southern song region, a refrain in clarion tones, a chorus with rare swing, and a primeval melodic mode.

For a negro version and the black man's story of the song's source see *White Spirituals*, pp. 254—255. Found also SOH (1854) 195, SOC 111, HOC 99. Further stanzas of the text are given under 'Faithful Soldier'. A later and simplified version of 'Morning Trumpet' is 'To Hear the Trumpet Sound' in this collection.

No. 242

GREAT PROVIDER or HE'S PROMISED TO BE WITH YOU, UHP 112

Heptatonic aeolian, mode 2 A+b (I II 3 IV V 6 7)

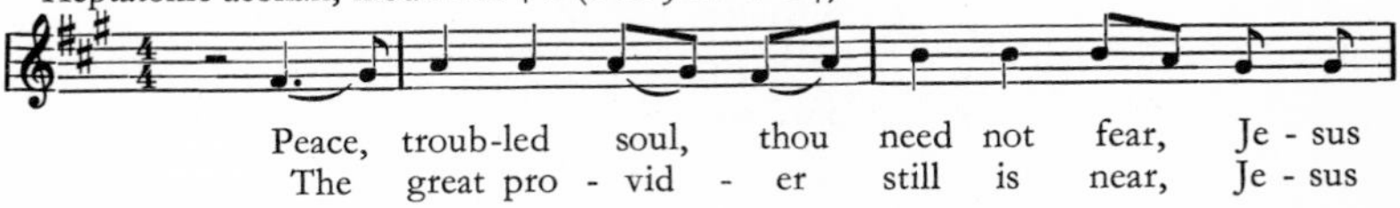
Peace, troub-led soul, thou need not fear, Je - sus
The great pro - vid - er still is near, Je - sus

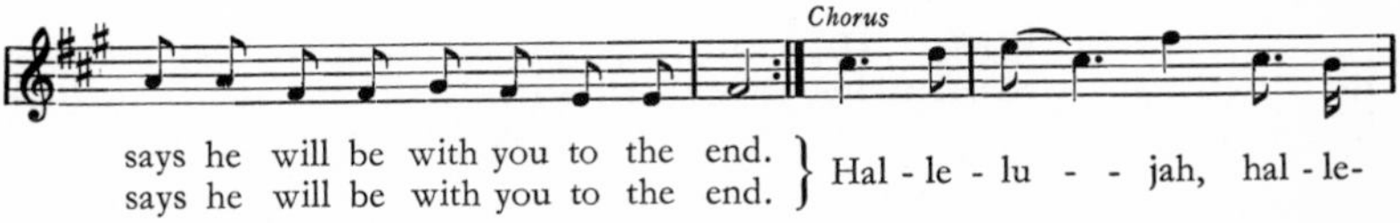
Chorus
says he will be with you to the end.
says he will be with you to the end.
Hal - le - lu - - jah, hal - le-

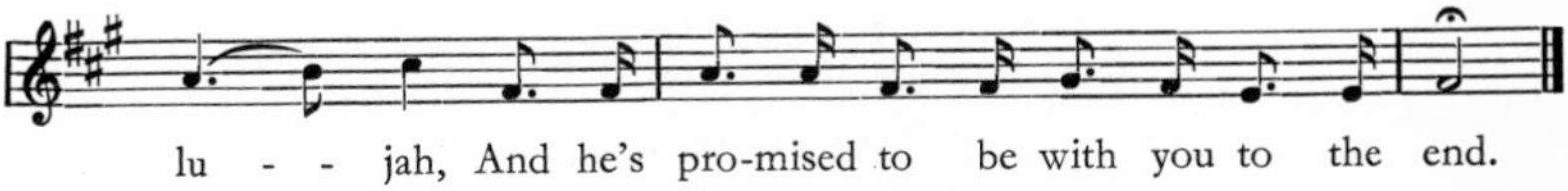
lu - - jah, And he's pro-mised to be with you to the end.

The Lord who built the earth and sky,
In mercy stoops to hear our cry;
His promise all may truly claim,
Ask and receive in Jesus' name.

The tune from the start to the chorus is practically the same as the chorus tune in 'With Us to the End' in this collection. It is claimed by S. M. Denson and dated 1908. Mr. Denson recorded many revival tunes. For data as to his life see *White Spirituals*, p. 107ff. He died 1936. See 'Cruel Mother', Sharp, i., 61, tune K, for melodic similarities.

No. 243

WARFARE, SWP 130

Hexatonic, mode 2 A (I II 3 IV V — 7)

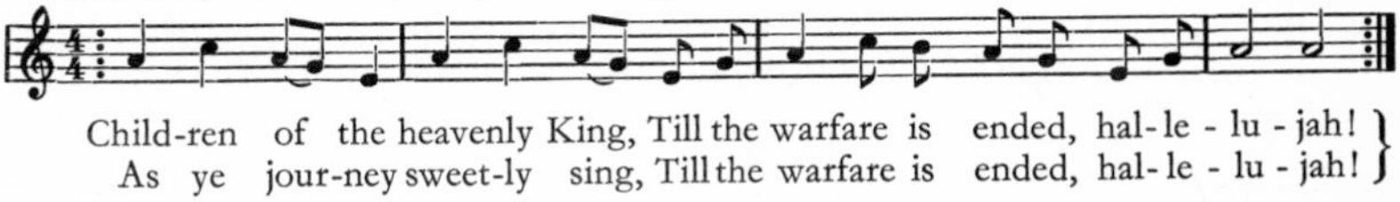
Child-ren of the heavenly King, Till the warfare is ended, hal-le - lu - jah!
As ye jour-ney sweet-ly sing, Till the warfare is ended, hal-le - lu - jah!

Shout glo - ry, child-ren, Till the war-fare is end-ed, hal-le - lu - jah!

Sing your Savior's worthy praise, Till *etc.*
Glorious in his works and ways, Till *etc.*

We are travelling home to God
In the way the fathers trod.

They are happy now, and we
Soon their happiness shall see.

O ye banished seed, be glad!
Christ our advocate is made.

Us to save, our flesh assumes,
Brother to our souls becomes.

Shout, ye little flock, and blest
You on Jesus' throne shall rest.

There your seat is now prepared,
There your kingdom and reward.

Fear not, brethren; joyful stand
On the borders of your land.

Christ, your Father's darling son,
Bids you undismayed go on.

Lord, submissive make us go,
Gladly leaving all below.

Only thou our leader be,
And we still will follow thee.

See 'Till the Warfare is Over', OSH 76, for melodic and textual relationships.

No. 244

GENERAL ROLL CALL, REV 356

Pentatonic, mode 2 with cadentially raised seventh (I — 3 IV V — VII)

If you get there be - fore I do, When the gen - 'ral roll is call'd We'll be there;
Look out for me I'm com - ing too, When the gen - 'ral roll is call'd We'll be there.
We'll be there——, we'll be there——, we'll be there——, When the gen -'ral roll is call'd we'll be there.

We're pressing on to Canaan's land,
We'll join the blood-wash'd pilgrim band.

Then we'll go up the shining way,
And praise the Lord through endless day.

The tune is attributed, in the *Revivalist*, to J. Baker. Two negro spirituals based melodically and textually on this song are in Dett, pp. 121 and 166.

No. 245
SHOUTING PILGRIM, SWP 163

Hexatonic, mode 2 A (I II 3 IV V — 7)

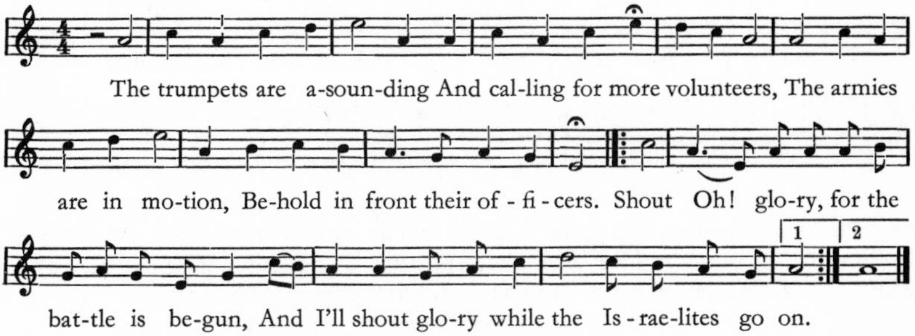
The trumpets are a-soun-ding And cal-ling for more volunteers, The armies
are in mo-tion, Be-hold in front their of - fi - cers. Shout Oh! glo-ry, for the
1
2
bat-tle is be-gun, And I'll shout glo-ry while the Is - rae-lites go on.

I love to live rejoicing, I cannot bear to live lukewarm,
Although there's many blames me for trusting in the Lord alone.
Shout Oh! glory, for I love to praise the Lord,
And I'll shout glory while I hear the gospel word.

I love to live a-shouting, I feel my Savior in my soul,
Sweet heaven drawing nigher, I feel the living waters roll.
Shout Oh! glory, for the glory is begun,
And I'll shout glory while the work is going on.

The time is fast approaching when all religion will be tried,
When Jesus with his jewels will ornament his lovely bride.
Shout Oh! glory, for my soul is full of love,
And I'll shout glory when I meet you all above.

I see the flame arising. — Had I the pinions of a dove,
My soul would then realize the wonders of redeeming love.
Shout Oh! glory, for there's glory in my soul,
And I'll shout glory while I feel the current roll.

The current is a-spreading and sinners coming home to God,
A-weeping and a-mourning, and finding favor in the Lord.
Shout Oh! glory, and my song shall never end,
And I'll shout glory to the sinner's dearest friend.

No. 246

BOUND FOR THE PROMISED LAND, OSH 128

Hexatonic, mode 2 A (I II 3 IV V — 7)

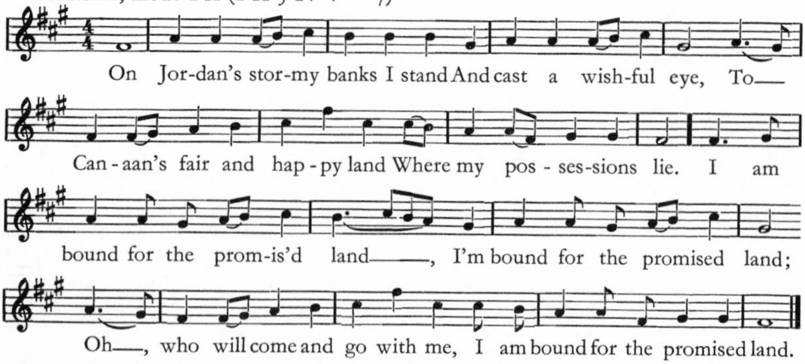
On Jor-dan's stor-my banks I stand And cast a wish-ful eye, To—
Can-aan's fair and hap-py land Where my pos-ses-sions lie. I am
bound for the prom-is'd land——, I'm bound for the promised land;
Oh—, who will come and go with me, I am bound for the promised land.

Further stanzas of the text are given under 'Jordan'. The combination here of the widely sung words of Samuel Stennett and an especially folkish revival phrase has resulted in an enormously well liked spiritual. Found also SOH 51, HH 154, SOC 114, HOC 47, WP 53, GOS 512. Its first appearance in the fasola books seems to have been in the *Southern Harmony* of 1835 where it is attributed to Miss M. Durham. The tune is like 'I'll Go and Enlist for a Sailor', Sharp, *Morris Dances*, Set viii, No. 6.

No. 247

LISBON or I CAN NOT TARRY HERE, SOC 182

Pentatonic, mode 2 (I — 3 IV V — 7)

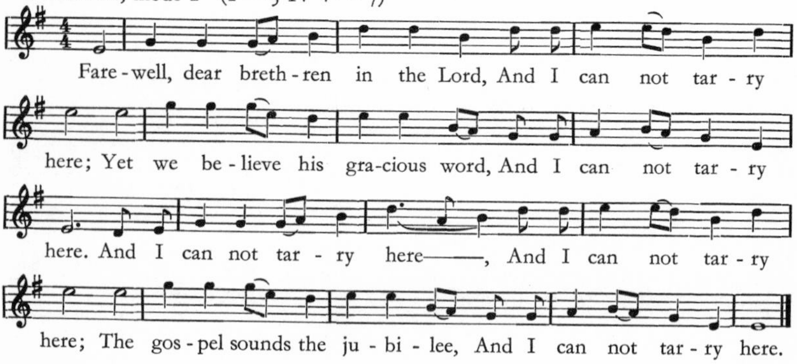
Fare-well, dear breth-ren in the Lord, And I can not tar-ry
here; Yet we be-lieve his gra-cious word, And I can not tar-ry
here. And I can not tar-ry here——, And I can not tar-ry
here; The gos-pel sounds the ju-bi-lee, And I can not tar-ry here.

This song is attributed to Henry F. Chandler and dated 1854. 'The Irish Girl', as sung in Virginia, shows a similar rhythmic trend but is less closely related tonally. See Sharp, ii., 254. Greater melodic resemblance is seen in 'Our Goodman' Sharp, i., 269, tune "D".

No. 248

I WANT TO GO TO GLORY, SWP 168

Hexatonic, cannot be classified (I II 3 IV V 6 —)

Je - sus, my all, to heav'n is gone, I want to go to glo - ry;
He whom I fix my hopes up - on, I want to go to glo - ry. I
want to go, I want to go, I want to go to glo - ry; We've so man-y
tri - als here be - low, They say there are none in glo - ry.

The full text, by Samuel Medley (1738—1799), may be found under 'River of Jordan' in this collection. The *Southern and Western Pocket Harmonist* gives this tune "as sung by Rev. M. L. Little". An old Irish song in Petrie, No. 1164, shows noteworthy similarities. See also 'I Want a Seat in Paradise', in this collection, for further tune relationships.

No. 249

CHRISTIAN RACE, REV 76

Heptatonic dorian, mode 2 A+B (I II 3 IV V VI 7)

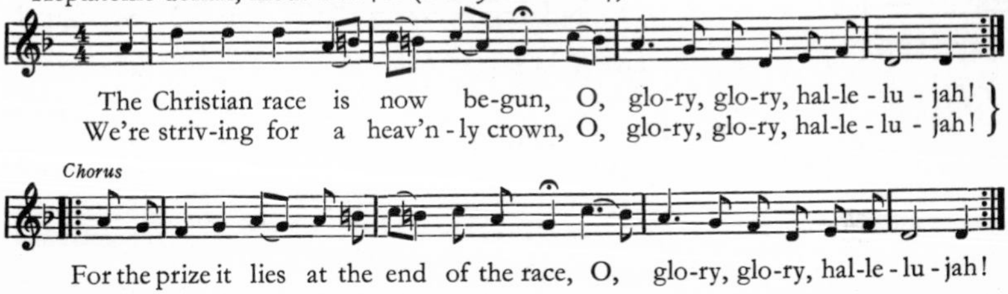
The Christian race is now be-gun, O, glo-ry, glo-ry, hal-le - lu - jah!
We're striv-ing for a heav'n - ly crown, O, glo-ry, glo-ry, hal-le - lu - jah!
Chorus
For the prize it lies at the end of the race, O, glo-ry, glo-ry, hal-le - lu - jah!

We'll run the race and gain the prize,
O, glory *etc.*
Our heav'nly mansion in the skies,
O, glory *etc.*
Chorus
We'll lay aside our every weight,
The way is narrow and straight the gate.

In earnest cry we'll wrestle along;
Then on a kingly throne sit down.

Omnipotence is on our side,
And God himself will be our guide.

Then when the race we've nobly run,
He'll count us worthy of a crown.

The form of the above is "as sung by Rev. G. C. Wells".

No. 250

I YIELD, REV 443

Heptatonic, minor (I II 3 IV V 6 VII)

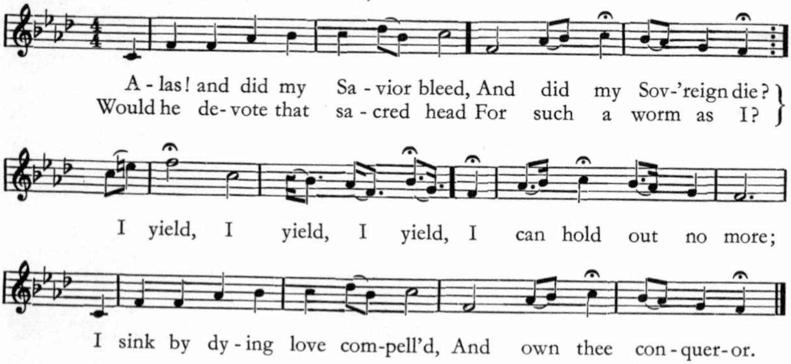
A - las! and did my Sa - vior bleed, And did my Sov-'reign die?
Would he de- vote that sa - cred head For such a worm as I?
I yield, I yield, I yield, I can hold out no more;
I sink by dy - ing love com-pell'd, And own thee con - quer- or.

I suggest the possibility that the editor of the *Revivalist* made his tune over from one which was originally in the dorian mode.

Bibliography

Alderice, Catherine. Manuscript 4-shape-note song book, written in or near Emmittsburg, Maryland, between 1800 and 1830.

Allen, William Francis; Ware, Charles Pickard; and Garrison, Lucy McKim. *Slave Songs of the United States*. C. 1868, reprinted New York, Peter Smith, 1929.

Asbury, Samuel E; and Meyer, Henry E. An article entitled "Old-Time Camp-Meeting Spirituals," *Publications of the Texas Folk-Lore Society*, No. x, Austin, Texas, 1932.

Autobiography of Peter Cartwright, The Backwoods Preacher. Edited by W. P. Strickland. New York, 1857.

Baptist Hymnal, 1902.

Baptist Hymn and Tune Book, 1857.

Baring-Gould, S. *Songs of the West*. London, Methuen, 1890 to 1928.

Barry, Phillips, and others. *British Ballads from Maine*. New Haven, 1929.

Beecher, Henry Ward. *Plymouth Collection*, 1855—1856.

Benson, Louis, F. *The English Hymn*. Philadelphia, The Presbyterian Board of Publication, 1915.

Bible Songs. Edited by M. B. DeWitt, Nashville, 1865.

British Ballads from Maine. (See Barry, Phillips.)

Carolina Low Country. (See Smythe, Augustine T.)

Cartwright, Peter. (See *Autobiography* etc.)

Chandler, Warren A. *Great Revivals and the Great Republic*. Nashville, 1904.

Chappell, William. *Old English Popular Music*. Edited by H. Ellis Wooldridge, London, Chappell, 1893.

Choral-Music. Compiled by Joseph Funk, Harrisonburg, Virginia, 1816.

Christian Harmony or Songster's Companion. Compiled by Jeremiah Ingalls, Exeter, New Hampshire, 1805.

Christian Harmony. Compiled by William Walker, Spartanburg, South Carolina, printed in Philadelphia, 1866.

Christian Lyre. Compiled by Joshua Leavitt, New York, 1830.

Christian Science Hymnal. Boston, 1932.

Church Harmony. Compiled by Henry Smith, Chambersburg, Pennsylvania, printed in Chambersburg, 1834.

Columbian Harmony. Compiled by William Moore, Wilson County, Tennessee, printed in Cincinnati, 1825.

Cox, John Harrington. *Folk-Songs of the South*. Cambridge, Harvard University Press, 1925.

Davis, Arthur Kyle. *Traditional Ballads of Virginia*. Cambridge, Harvard University Press, 1929.

Dett, R. Nathaniel. *Religious Folk-Songs of the Negro*. Hampton, Virginia, Hampton Institute Press, 1927.

Dolph, Edward Arthur. *Sound Off*. New York, Cosmopolitan Book Corporation, 1929.

English Dancing Master, The. By John Playford. Reproduced by Hugh Mellor and Leslie Bridgewater, 1933.

English Folk-Songs for Schools. (See Gould, S. Baring.)

English Musical Repository, The. Edinburgh, 1811.

English Repository, The. Edinburgh, 1811.

Erk, Ludwig C., and Böhme, Franz M. *Deutscher Liederhort*. Three vols., Leipzig, Edition 1925.

Flanders, Helen Hartness; and Brown, George. *Vermont Folk-Songs and Ballads*. Brattleboro, Vermont, Stephen Daye Press, 1932.

Fenner, Thomas P. *Hampton and Its Students*. New York, Putnam's, 1875.
Genuine Church Music. Compiled by Joseph Funk, Mountain Valey, Virginia, printed in Winchester, Virginia, 1832.
Gilchrist, Anne G. (See *Journal of the* [English] *Folk-Song Society.)*
Good Old Songs. Compiled by C. H. Cayce, Thornton, Arkansas, printed in Martin, Tennessee, 1913.
Gray, Roland P. *Songs and Ballads of the Maine Lumberjacks*. Cambridge, Harvard University Press, 1925.
Gould, S. Baring, and Sharp, Cecil J. *English Folk-Songs for Schools*. London, Curwen, no date given.
Greig, Gavin, and Keith, Alexander. *Last Leaves of Traditional Ballads and Ballad Airs*. Aberdeen, 1925.
Grissom, Mary Allen. *The Negro Sings a New Heaven*. Chapel Hill, The University of North Carolina Press, 1930.
Harp of Columbia. Compiled by W. H. and M. L. Swan, Knoxville, Tennessee, printed in Knoxville, 1848.
Harp of the South, The. Compiled by Lowell Mason. Published by Mason Brothers between 1855 and 1869.
Hesperian Harp. Compiled by William Hauser, Wadley, Georgia, printed in Philadelphia, 1848.
Hudson, Arthur Palmer. *Folksongs of Mississippi*. Chapel Hill, University of North Carolina Press, 1936.
Hymns Ancient and Modern. London, Clowes, 1909.
Ingalls, Jeremiah. (See *Christian Harmony or Songster's Companion.)*
Jackson, George Pullen. "Buckwheat Notes." *Musical Quarterly*, xix (1933), No. 4.
— "The Genesis of the Negro Spiritual." *The American Mercury*, xxvi (1932), No. 102.
— "Stephen Foster's Debt to American Folk-Song." *The Musical Quarterly*, vol. xxii, No. 2.
— *White Spirituals in the Southern Uplands*. Chapel Hill, University of North Carolina Press, 1933.
Jackson, Vincent. *English Melodies from the 13th to the 18th Century*. London, Dutton, 1910.
Johnson, Guy B. *Folk Culture on Saint Helena Island*. Chapel Hill, University of North Carolina Press, 1930.
Journal of American Folk-Lore. New York, American Folk-Lore Society.
Journal of the [English] *Folk-Song Society*. London, The Folk-Song Society. Especially vol. viii (1927—1931) pp. 61—95, article by Anne G. Gilchrist, "The Folk Element in Early Revival Hymns and Tunes".
Joyce, P. W. *Irish Music and Song*. Dublin, Gill and Son, new edition, 1901.
Kennedy, David. *Handbook of Scottish Song*. London, Henderson, Rait and Fenton, 1866.
Kentucky Harmony. Compiled by Ananias Davisson, Rockingham County, Virginia, Printed in Harrisonburg, Virginia, ca. 1815. (2d ed., 1817, 4th ed., 1821, and 5th ed., 1826, in Libr. of Congress.) 4th ed., also in McGhee Public Library, Knoxville.
Kirchen-Harmonie. A German supplement to *Church Harmony*, which see.
Knoxville Harmony. Compiled by John B. Jackson, Madisonville, Tennessee, printed in Madisonville and Pumpkintown, 1838.
Krehbiel, Henry E. *Afro-American Folk-Songs*. New York, G. Schirmer, 1914.
Last Leaves. (See Greig, Gavin.)
Lightwood, James Thomas. *Hymn-Tunes and their Story*. London, 1905.
Lyric Gems of Scotland. London, Bayley and Ferguson, no date given.
Marsh, J. B. T. *The Story of the* [Fisk University] *Jubilee Singers*. Boston, 1880.
Melodeon, The. Compiled by J. W. Dadmun, Boston, 1861.
"*Mercer's Cluster*." Popular designation for *The Cluster of Spiritual Songs Divine Hymns and Social Poems*. Compiled by Jesse Mercer, Augusta, Georgia, ca. 1817.
Mersmann, Hans. *Grundlagen einer musikalischen Volksliedforschung*, Leipzig, 1930.
Metcalf, Frank J. *Stories of Hymn Tunes*. New York, Abingdon Press, 1928.

Methodist Hymn Book [of England]. London, 1933.
Methodist Hymnal. Nashville, Tennessee, 1935.
Methodist Hymn and Tune Book. Nashville, Tennessee, 1889.
Missouri Harmony. Compiled by Allen D. Carden, St. Louis, Missouri, printed in Cincinnati, 1820.
Motherwell, William. *Minstrelsy Ancient and Modern.* Paisley's edition, 1873.
Musical Quarterly, The. New York, G. Schirmer.
Newell, William W. *Games and Songs of American Children.* New York, Harper and Brothers, 1911.
New Hymn and Tune Book, The. Nashville, Southern Methodist Publishing House, 1880.
Olive Leaf. Compiled by William Hauser and Benjamin Turner, Wadley, Georgia, printed in Philadelphia, 1878.
Original Sacred Harp. Edited by Joe S. James, Atlanta, Georgia, printed in Atlanta, 1911. It is an enlarged and annotated edition of the 1844 *Sacred Harp*, which see.
Oxford Book of Carols, The. Edited by Percy Dearmer, R. Vaughan Williams and Martin Shaw. London. Oxford University Press, Third Impression, 1931.
Petrie, George. *The Complete Collection of Ancient Irish Music.* Edited by Charles Villiers Stanford, London, Boosey and Co., 1903.
Playford. (See *English Dancing Master, The.)*
Plymouth Collection. Compiled by Henry Ward Beecher, 1855.
Primitive Baptist Hymn and Tune Book. Compiled by John R. Daily, printed in Madisonville, Kentucky, 1902.
Publications of The Texas Folk-Lore Society. (See Asbury, Samuel E.)
Revivalist. Compiled by Joseph Hillman, Troy, New York, 1868; revised and enlarged edition printed in Albany, New York, 1872.
Richardson, Ethel Park. *American Mountain Songs.* Edited and arranged by Sigmund Spaeth, New York, Greenburg, 1927.
Rickaby, Franz. *Ballads and Songs of the Shanty-Boy.* Cambridge, Harvard University Press, 1926.
Sacred Harp. Compiled by B. F. White and E. J. King, Hamilton, Georgia, printed in Philadelphia, 1844. Cf. *Original Sacred Harp.*
Sacred Harp. Edited by W. M. Cooper, Dothan, Alabama, printed in various places, first in Dothan, 1902. It is an enlarged edition of the 1844 *Sacred Harp*, which see.
Sandburg, Carl. *The American Songbag.* New York, Harcourt, Brace and Co., 1927
Scarbrough, Dorothy. *On the Trail of the Negro Folk-Songs.* Cambridge, Harvard University Press, 1925.
Scots Musical Museum. Compiled by James Johnson and Robert Burns, Edinburgh, 1787—1803.
Sharp, Cecil J., and Campbell, Olive Dame. *English Folk Songs From the Southern Appalachians.* New York, Putnam's, 1917.
Sharp, Cecil J. *English Folk Songs from the Southern Appalachians.* Two volumes, edited by Maud Karpeles, London, Oxford University Press, Humphrey Milford, 1932.
— *One Hundred English Folksongs.* Boston, Ditson, 1916.
— *The Morris Book.* Five parts, London, Novello, 1912—1913.
— *English Folk-Song, Some Conclusions.* London, Novello, 1907.
Shoemaker, Henry W. *Mountain Minstrelsy of Pennsylvania.* Third edition, Philadelphia, 1931.
Singer's Companion, The. New York, 1854.
Slave Songs. (See Allen, William Francis.)
Smythe, Augustine T. and others. *The Carolina Low-Country.* New York, Macmillan, 1931.
Smith, Reed. *South Carolina Ballads.* Cambridge, Harvard University Press, 1928.
Social Harp. Compiled by John G. McCurry, Andersonville, Georgia, printed in Philadelphia, 1855.
Social Hymn and Tune Book. Philadelphia, Presbyterian Publication Committee, 1865.
Songs of Grace. Compiled by E. S. Lorenz and I. Baltzell, Dayton, Ohio, United Brethren Publishing House, 1879.

Southern and Western Pocket Harmonist. Compiled by William Walker, Spartanburg, South Carolina, printed in Philadelphia, 1846.

Southern Folklore Quarterly. Gainesville, Florida.

Southern Harmony. Compiled by William Walker, Spartanburg, South Carolina, printed in New Haven, Connecticut, 1835.

Supplement to the Kentucky Harmony. Compiled by Ananias Davisson, Rockingham County. Virginia, printed in Harrisonburg, Virginia, 1820. (In McGhee Public Libr., Knoxville.)

Texas Folk-Lore Society, Publications of. (See Asbury, Samuel E.)

Thomas, Jean. *Devil's Ditties*. Chicago, W. Wilbur Hatfield, 1931.

Tillett, Wilbur, F. *The Hymns and Writers of the Church*. Nashville, Smith and Lamar, 1911.

Timbrel of Zion. Compiled by T. K. Collins, Jr., Philadelphia, 1854.

Union Harmony. Compiled by William Caldwell, Maryville, Tennessee, printed in Maryville, 1837.

Union Harmony. Compiled by George Hendrickson, Mountain Valley, Virginia, printed in Mountain Valley, 1848.

Union Harp and History of Songs. Compiled by Joe S. James, Douglasville, Georgia, printed in Douglasville (?), 1909.

Virginia Harmony. Compiled by James P. Carrell and David S. Clayton, Lebanon, Virginia, printed in Winchester, Virginia, 1831.

Wesleyan Psalmist. Compiled by M. L. Scudder, (place?), 1842.

Western Harmony. Compiled by Allen D. Carden, Samuel J. Rogers, F. Moore, and J. Green, printed in Nashville, 1824.

Western Psalmodist. Compiled by Andrew W. Johnson, Cornersville, Tennessee, printed in Nashville, Tennessee, 1853.

White, Newman I. *American Negro Folk-Songs*. Cambridge, Harvard University Press, 1928.

White Spirituals. (See Jackson, George Pullen.)

Work, John Wesley. *Folk Song of the American Negro*. Nashville, Tennessee, Fisk University Press, 1915.

Wyman, Loraine, and Brockway, Howard. *Lonesome Tunes*. New York, Gray, 1916.

Zion's Harp. Place and year unknown, probably between 1825 and 1840, 312 pages, texts only.

Zion's Harp. 33 pages of tunes, issued as a companion to Nettleton's *Village Hymns*, compiled by N. and S. S. Jocelyn, registered in the District of Connecticut, 1824.

List of Abbreviations of Titles

BHTBK	Baptist Hymn and Tune Book, 1857
BS	Bible Songs (DeWitt)
CH	Church Harmony (Smith)
CHH	Christian Harmony (Walker)
CHI	Christian Harmony (Ingalls)
COH	Columbian Harmony (Moore)
CSH	Sacred Harp, 1902 (Cooper)
DT	Religious Folk-Songs of the Negro (Dett)
GCM	Genuine Church Music (Funk)
GOS	Good Old Songs (Cayce)
HH	Hesperian Harp (Hauser)
HOC	Harp of Columbia (Swan)
JAFL	Journal of American Folk-Lore
JFSS	Journal of the [English] Folk-Song Society
KYH	Kentucky Harmony (Davisson)
KNH	Knoxville Harmony (Jackson)
MHTBK	Methodist Hymn and Tune Book, 1889
MOH	Missouri Harmony (Carden)
OL	Olive Leaf (Hauser)
OSH	Original Sacred Harp (James)
PB	Primitive Baptist Hymn and Tune Book (Daily)
REV	Revivalist (Hillman)
SCB	South Carolina Ballads (Smith)
SH	Sacred Harp, 1844 (White and King)
SKH	Supplement to the Kentucky Harmony (Davisson)
SMM	Scots Musical Museum (Johnson)
SOC	Social Harp (McCurry)
SOG	Songs of Grace (Lorenz and Baltzell)
SOH	Southern Harmony (Walker)
SS	Slave Songs of the United States (Allen, Ware, and Garrison)
SWP	Southern and Western Pocket Harmonist (Walker)
TZ	Timbrel of Zion (Collins)
UH	Union Harmony (Caldwell)
UHH	Union Harmony (Hendrickson)
UHP	Union Harp and History of Songs (James)
VH	Virginia Harmony (Carrell)
WH	Western Harmony (Carden, Rogers, Moore, and Green)
WP	Western Psalmodist (Johnson)
WS	White Spirituals in the Southern Uplands (Jackson)

Index of Songs by Titles

Index of First Lines

(Italicized numbers, used where reference is made to several songs with the same first lines, indicate where the *fuller* text is given.)

CATALOGUE OF DOVER BOOKS

Music

A GENERAL HISTORY OF MUSIC, Charles Burney. A detailed coverage of music from the Greeks up to 1789, with full information on all types of music: sacred and secular, vocal and instrumental, operatic and symphonic. Theory, notation, forms, instruments, innovators, composers, performers, typical and important works, and much more in an easy, entertaining style. Burney covered much of Europe and spoke with hundreds of authorities and composers so that this work is more than a compilation of records . . . it is a living work of careful and first-hand scholarship. Its account of thoroughbass (18th century) Italian music is probably still the best introduction on the subject. A recent NEW YORK TIMES review said, "Surprisingly few of Burney's statements have been invalidated by modern research . . . still of great value." Edited and corrected by Frank Mercer. 35 figures. Indices. 1915pp. 5⅜ x 8. 2 volumes. T36 The Set, Clothbound **$12.50**

A DICTIONARY OF HYMNOLOGY, John Julian. This exhaustive and scholarly work has become known as an invaluable source of hundreds of thousands of important and often difficult to obtain facts on the history and use of hymns in the western world. Everyone interested in hymns will be fascinated by the accounts of famous hymns and hymn writers and amazed by the amount of practical information he will find. More than 30,000 entries on individual hymns, giving authorship, date and circumstances of composition, publication, textual variations, translations, denominational and ritual usage, etc. Biographies of more than 9,000 hymn writers, and essays on important topics such as Christmas carols and children's hymns, and much other unusual and valuable information. A 200 page double-columned index of first lines — the largest in print. Total of 1786 pages in two reinforced clothbound volumes. 6¼ x 9¼. The set, T333 Clothbound **$15.00**

MUSIC IN MEDIEVAL BRITAIN, F. Ll. Harrison. The most thorough, up-to-date, and accurate treatment of the subject ever published, beautifully illustrated. Complete account of institutions and choirs; carols, masses, and motets; liturgy and plainsong; and polyphonic music from the Norman Conquest to the Reformation. Discusses the various schools of music and their reciprocal influences; the origin and development of new ritual forms; development and use of instruments; and new evidence on many problems of the period. Reproductions of scores, over 200 excerpts from medieval melodies. Rules of harmony and dissonance; influence of Continental styles; great composers (Dunstable, Cornysh, Fairfax, etc.); and much more. Register and index of more than 400 musicians. Index of titles. General Index. 225-item bibliography. 6 Appendices. xix + 491pp. 5⅝ x 8¾. T705 Clothbound **$10.00**

THE MUSIC OF SPAIN, Gilbert Chase. Only book in English to give concise, comprehensive account of Iberian music; new Chapter covers music since 1941. Victoria, Albéniz, Cabezón, Pedrell, Turina, hundreds of other composers; popular and folk music; the Gypsies; the guitar; dance, theatre, opera, with only extensive discussion in English of the Zarzuela; virtuosi such as Casals; much more. "Distinguished . . . readable," Saturday Review. 400-item bibliography. Index. 27 photos. 383pp. 5⅜ x 8. T549 Paperbound **$2.00**

ON STUDYING SINGING, Sergius Kagen. An intelligent method of voice-training, which leads you around pitfalls that waste your time, money, and effort. Exposes rigid, mechanical systems, baseless theories, deleterious exercises. "Logical, clear, convincing . . . dead right," Virgil Thomson, N.Y. Herald Tribune. "I recommend this volume highly," Maggie Teyte, Saturday Review. 119pp. 5⅜ x 8. T622 Paperbound **$1.25**

WILLIAM LAWES, M. Lefkowitz. This is the definitive work on Lawes, the versatile, prolific, and highly original "King's musician" of 17th century England. His life is reconstructed from original documents, and nearly every piece he ever wrote is examined and evaluated: his fantasias, pavans, violin "sonatas," lyra viol and bass viol suites, and music for harp and theorbo; and his songs, masques, and theater music to words by Herrick ("Gather Ye Rosebuds"), Jonson, Suckling, Shirley, and others. The author shows the innovations of dissonance, augmented triad, and other Italian influences Lawes helped introduce to England. List of Lawes' complete works and several complete scores by this major precursor of Purcell and the 18th century developments. Index. 5 Appendices. 52 musical excerpts, many never before in print. Bibliography. x + 320pp. 5⅜ x 8. T706 Clothbound **$10.00**

THE FUGUE IN BEETHOVEN'S PIANO MUSIC, J. V. Cockshoot. The first study of a neglected aspect of Beethoven's genius: his ability as a writer of fugues. Analyses of early studies and published works demonstrate his original and powerful contributions to composition. 34 works are examined, with 143 musical excerpts. For all pianists, teachers, students, and music-minded readers with a serious interest in Beethoven. Index. 93-item bibliography. Illustration of original score for "Fugue in C." xv + 212pp. 5⅝ x 8⅜. T704 Clothbound **$6.00**

CATALOGUE OF DOVER BOOKS

JOHANN SEBASTIAN BACH, Philipp Spitta. The complete and unabridged text of the definitive study of Bach. Written some 70 years ago, it is still unsurpassed for its coverage of nearly all aspects of Bach's life and work. There could hardly be a finer non-technical introduction to Bach's music than the detailed, lucid analyses which Spitta provides for hundreds of individual pieces. 26 solid pages are devoted to the B minor mass, for example, and 30 pages to the glorious St. Matthew Passion. This monumental set also includes a major analysis of the music of the 18th century: Buxtehude, Pachelbel, etc. "Unchallenged as the last word on one of the supreme geniuses of music," John Barkham, SATURDAY REVIEW SYNDICATE. Total of 1819pp. 2 volumes. Heavy cloth binding. 5⅜ x 8. T252 The set, Clothbound **$12.50**

THE LIFE OF MOZART, O. Jahn. Probably the largest amount of material on Mozart's life and works ever gathered together in one book! Its 1350 authoritative and readable pages cover every event in his life, and contain a full critique of almost every piece he ever wrote, including sketches and intimate works. There is a full historical-cultural background, and vast research into musical and literary history, sources of librettos, prior treatments of Don Juan legend, etc. This is the complete and unaltered text of the definitive Townsend translation, with foreword by Grove. 5 engraved portraits from Salzburg archives. 4 facsimiles in Mozart's hand. 226 musical examples. 4 Appendixes, including complete list of Mozart's compositions, with Köchel numbers (fragmentary works included). Total of xxviii + 1352pp. Three volume set. 5⅜ x 8. T85 Vol. I Clothbound **$5.00**
T86 Vol. II Clothbound **$5.00**
The set **$10.00**

BEETHOVEN'S QUARTETS, J. de Marliave. The most complete and authoritative study ever written, enjoyable for scholar and layman alike. The 16 quartets and Grand Fugue are all analyzed bar by bar and theme by theme, not over-technically, but concentrating on mood and effects. Complete background material for each composition: influences, first reviews, etc. Preface by Gabriel Fauré. Introduction and notes by J. Escarra. Translated by Hilda Andrews. 321 musical examples. xxiii + 379pp. 5⅜ x 8. T694 Paperbound **$1.85**

STRUCTURAL HEARING: TONAL COHERENCE IN MUSIC, Felix Salzer. Written by a pupil of the late Heinrich Schenker, this is not only the most thorough exposition in English of the Schenker method but also extends the Schenker approach to include modern music, the middle ages, and renaissance music. It explores the phenomenon of tonal organization by means of a detailed analysis and discussion of more than 500 musical pieces. It casts new light for the reader acquainted with harmony upon the understanding of musical compositions, problems of musical coherence, and connection between theory and composition. "Has been the foundation on which all teaching in music theory has been based at this college," Leopold Mannes, President of The Mannes College of Music. 2 volumes. Total of 658pp. 6½ x 9¼. The set, T418 Clothbound **$8.00**

ANTONIO STRADIVARI: HIS LIFE AND WORK (1644-1737), W. Henry Hill, Arthur F. Hill, and Alfred E. Hill. Still the only book that really delves into life and art of the incomparable Italian craftsman, maker of the finest musical instruments in the world today. The authors, expert violin-makers themselves, discuss Stradivari's ancestry, his construction and finishing techniques, distinguished characteristics of many of his instruments and their locations. Included, too, is story of introduction of his instruments into France, England, first revelation of their supreme merit, and information on his labels, number of instruments made, prices, mystery of ingredients of his varnish, tone of pre-1684 Stradivari violin and changes between 1684 and 1690. An extremely interesting, informative account for all music lovers, from craftsman to concert-goer. Republication of original (1902) edition. New introduction by Sydney Beck, Head of Rare Book and Manuscript Collections, Music Division, New York Public Library. Analytical index by Rembert Wurlitzer. Appendixes. 68 illustrations. 30 full-page plates. 4 in color. xxvi + 315pp. 5⅜ x 8½. T425 Paperbound **$2.25**

THREE CLASSICS IN THE AESTHETIC OF MUSIC, Claude Debussy, Ferrucio Busoni, and Charles Ives. Three very different points of view by three top-ranking modern composers. "M. Croche, the Dilettante-Hater" consists of twenty-five brief articles written by Debussy between the years 1901 and 1905, a sparkling collection of personal commentary on a wide range of topics. Busoni's "Toward a New Aesthetic of Music" considers the nature of absolute music in an attempt to suggest answers to the question, What are the aims of music?, and discusses modern systems of tonality and harmony, the concept of unity of keys, etc. Ives's "Essays Before a Sonata," a literary complement to the movements of the author's "Concord, 1845" piano sonata, contains his most mature analysis of his art. Stimulating reading for musicians, music lovers, and philosophers of the arts. iv + 188pp. 5⅜ x 8½. T320 Paperbound **$1.45**

CATALOGUE OF DOVER BOOKS

Say It language phrase books

These handy phrase books (128 to 196 pages each) make grammatical drills unnecessary for an elementary knowledge of a spoken foreign language. Covering most matters of travel and everyday life each volume contains:

Over 1000 phrases and sentences in immediately useful forms — foreign language plus English.

Modern usage designed for Americans. Specific phrases like, "Give me small change," and "Please call a taxi."

Simplified phonetic transcription you will be able to read at sight.

The only completely indexed phrase books on the market.

Covers scores of important situations: — Greetings, restaurants, sightseeing, useful expressions, etc.

These books are prepared by native linguists who are professors at Columbia, N.Y.U., Fordham and other great universities. Use them independently or with any other book or record course. They provide a supplementary living element that most other courses lack. Individual volumes in:

Russian 75¢	**Italian 75¢**	**Spanish 75¢**	**German 75¢**
Hebrew 75¢	**Danish 75¢**	**Japanese 75¢**	**Swedish 75¢**
Dutch 75¢	**Esperanto 75¢**	**Modern Greek 75¢**	**Portuguese 75¢**
Norwegian 75¢	**Polish 75¢**	**French 75¢**	**Yiddish 75¢**
Turkish 75¢		**English for German-speaking people 75¢**	
English for Italian-speaking people 75¢		**English for Spanish-speaking people 75¢**	

Large clear type. 128-196 pages each. 3½ x 5¼. Sturdy paper binding.

Listen and Learn language records

LISTEN & LEARN is the only language record course designed especially to meet your travel and everyday needs. It is available in separate sets for FRENCH, SPANISH, GERMAN, JAPANESE, RUSSIAN, MODERN GREEK, PORTUGUESE, ITALIAN and HEBREW, and each set contains three 33⅓ rpm long-playing records—1½ hours of recorded speech by eminent native speakers who are professors at Columbia, New York University, Queens College.

Check the following special features found only in LISTEN & LEARN:

- **Dual-language recording. 812 selected phrases and sentences,** over 3200 words, spoken first in English, then in their foreign language equivalents. A suitable pause follows each foreign phrase, allowing you time to repeat the expression. You learn by unconscious assimilation.
- **128 to 206-page manual** contains everything on the records, plus a simple phonetic pronunciation guide.
- **Indexed for convenience. The only set on the market** that is completely indexed. No more puzzling over where to find the phrase you need. Just look in the rear of the manual.
- **Practical.** No time wasted on material you can find in any grammar. LISTEN & LEARN covers central core material with phrase approach. Ideal for the person with limited learning time.
- **Living, modern expressions,** not found in other courses. Hygienic products, modern equipment, shopping—expressions used every day, like "nylon" and "air-conditioned."
- **Limited objective.** Everything you learn, no matter where you stop, is immediately useful. You have to finish other courses, wade through grammar and vocabulary drill, before they help you.
- **High-fidelity recording.** LISTEN & LEARN records equal in clarity and surface-silence any record on the market costing up to $6.

"Excellent . . . the spoken records . . . impress me as being among the very best on the market," **Prof. Mario Pei,** Dept. of Romance Languages, Columbia University. "Inexpensive and well-done . . . it would make an ideal present," CHICAGO SUNDAY TRIBUNE. "More genuinely helpful than anything of its kind which I have previously encountered," **Sidney Clark,** well-known author of "ALL THE BEST" travel books.

UNCONDITIONAL GUARANTEE. Try LISTEN & LEARN, then return it within 10 days for full refund if you are not satisfied.

Each set contains three twelve-inch 33⅓ records, manual, and album.

SPANISH	the set **$5.95**	GERMAN	the set **$5.95**
FRENCH	the set **$5.95**	ITALIAN	the set **$5.95**
RUSSIAN	the set **$5.95**	JAPANESE	the set **$5.95**
PORTUGUESE	the set **$5.95**	MODERN GREEK	the set **$5.95**
MODERN HEBREW	the set **$5.95**		

Trubner Colloquial Manuals

These unusual books are members of the famous Trubner series of colloquial manuals. They have been written to provide adults with a sound colloquial knowledge of a foreign language, and are suited for either class use or self-study. Each book is a complete course in itself, with progressive, easy to follow lessons. Phonetics, grammar, and syntax are covered, while hundreds of phrases and idioms, reading texts, exercises, and vocabulary are included. These books are unusual in being neither skimpy nor overdetailed in grammatical matters, and in presenting up-to-date, colloquial, and practical phrase material. Bilingual presentation is stressed, to make thorough self-study easier for the reader.

COLLOQUIAL HINDUSTANI, A. H. Harley, formerly Nizam's Reader in Urdu, U. of London. 30 pages on phonetics and scripts (devanagari & Arabic-Persian) are followed by 29 lessons, including material on English and Arabic-Persian influences. Key to all exercises. Vocabulary. 5 x 7½. 147pp. Clothbound **$1.75**

COLLOQUIAL PERSIAN, L. P. Elwell-Sutton. Best introduction to modern Persian, with 90 page grammatical section followed by conversations, 35-page vocabulary. 139pp. Clothbound **$1.75**

COLLOQUIAL ARABIC, DeLacy O'Leary. Foremost Islamic scholar covers language of Egypt, Syria, Palestine, & Northern Arabia. Extremely clear coverage of complex Arabic verbs & noun plurals; also cultural aspects of language. Vocabulary. xviii + 192pp. 5 x 7½. Clothbound **$2.50**

COLLOQUIAL GERMAN, P. F. Doring. Intensive thorough coverage of grammar in easily-followed form. Excellent for brush-up, with hundreds of colloquial phrases. 34 pages of bilingual texts. 224pp. 5 x 7½. Clothbound **$1.75**

COLLOQUIAL SPANISH, W. R. Patterson. Castilian grammar and colloquial language, loaded with bilingual phrases and colloquialisms. Excellent for review or self-study. 164pp. 5 x 7½. Clothbound **$1.75**

COLLOQUIAL FRENCH, W. R. Patterson. 16th revision of this extremely popular manual. Grammar explained with model clarity, and hundreds of useful expressions and phrases; exercises, reading texts, etc. Appendixes of new and useful words and phrases. 223pp. 5 x 7½. Clothbound **$1.75**

COLLOQUIAL CZECH, J. Schwarz, former headmaster of Lingua Institute, Prague. Full easily followed coverage of grammar, hundreds of immediately useable phrases, texts. Perhaps the best Czech grammar in print. "An absolutely successful textbook," JOURNAL OF CZECHO-SLOVAK FORCES IN GREAT BRITAIN. 252pp. 5 x 7½. Clothbound **$3.00**

COLLOQUIAL RUMANIAN, G. Nandris, Professor of University of London. Extremely thorough coverage of phonetics, grammar, syntax; also included 70-page reader, and 70-page vocabulary. Probably the best grammar for this increasingly important language. 340pp. 5 x 7½. Clothbound **$2.50**

COLLOQUIAL ITALIAN, A. L. Hayward. Excellent self-study course in grammar, vocabulary, idioms, and reading. Easy progressive lessons will give a good working knowledge of Italian in the shortest possible time. 5 x 7½. Clothbound **$1.75**

COLLOQUIAL TURKISH, Yusuf Mardin. Very clear, thorough introduction to leading cultural and economic language of Near East. Begins with pronunciation and statement of vowel harmony, then 36 lessons present grammar, graded vocabulary, useful phrases, dialogues, reading, exercises. Key to exercises at rear. Turkish-English vocabulary. All in Roman alphabet. x + 288pp. 4¾ x 7¼. Clothbound **$4.00**

DUTCH-ENGLISH AND ENGLISH-DUTCH DICTIONARY, F. G. Renier. For travel, literary, scientific or business Dutch, you will find this the most convenient, practical and comprehensive dictionary on the market. More than 60,000 entries, shades of meaning, colloquialisms, idioms, compounds and technical terms. Dutch and English strong and irregular verbs. This is the only dictionary in its size and price range that indicates the gender of nouns. New orthography. xvii + 571pp. 5½ x 6¼. T224 Clothbound **$2.75**

LEARN DUTCH, F. G. Renier. This book is the most satisfactory and most easily used grammar of modern Dutch. The student is gradually led from simple lessons in pronunciation, through translation from and into Dutch, and finally to a mastery of spoken and written Dutch. Grammatical principles are clearly explained while a useful, practical vocabulary is introduced in easy exercises and readings. It is used and recommended by the Fulbright Committee in the Netherlands. Phonetic appendices. Over 1200 exercises; Dutch-English, English-Dutch vocabularies. 181pp. 4¼ x 7¼. T441 Clothbound **$2.25**

Literature, History of Literature

ARISTOTLE'S THEORY OF POETRY AND THE FINE ARTS, edited by S. H. Butcher. The celebrated Butcher translation of this great classic faced, page by page, with the complete Greek text. A 300 page introduction discussing Aristotle's ideas and their influence in the history of thought and literature, and covering art and nature, imitation as an aesthetic form, poetic truth, art and morality, tragedy, comedy, and similar topics. Modern Aristotelian criticism discussed by John Gassner. lxxvi + 421pp. 5⅜ x 8. T42 Paperbound **$2.00**

INTRODUCTIONS TO ENGLISH LITERATURE, edited by B. Dobrée. Goes far beyond ordinary histories, ranging from the 7th century up to 1914 (to the 1940's in some cases.) The first half of each volume is a specific detailed study of historical and economic background of the period and a general survey of poetry and prose, including trends of thought, influences, etc. The second and larger half is devoted to a detailed study of more than 5000 poets, novelists, dramatists; also economists, historians, biographers, religious writers, philosophers, travellers, and scientists of literary stature, with dates, lists of major works and their dates, keypoint critical bibliography, and evaluating comments. The most compendious bibliographic and literary aid within its price range.

Vol. I. THE BEGINNINGS OF ENGLISH LITERATURE TO SKELTON, (1509), W. L. Renwick, H. Orton. 450pp. 5⅛ x 7⅞. T75 Clothbound **$4.50**

Vol. II. THE ENGLISH RENAISSANCE, 1510-1688, V. de Sola Pinto. 381pp. 5⅛ x 7⅞. T76 Clothbound **$4.50**

Vol. III. AUGUSTANS AND ROMANTICS, 1689-1830, H. Dyson, J. Butt. 320pp. 5⅛ x 7⅞. T77 Clothbound **$4.50**

Vol. IV. THE VICTORIANS AND AFTER, 1830-1940's, E. Batho, B. Dobrée. 360pp. 5⅛ x 7⅞. T78 Clothbound **$4.50**

EPIC AND ROMANCE, W. P. Ker. Written by one of the foremost authorities on medieval literature, this is the standard survey of medieval epic and romance. It covers Teutonic epics, Icelandic sagas, Beowulf, French chansons de geste, the Roman de Troie, and many other important works of literature. It is an excellent account for a body of literature whose beauty and value has only recently come to be recognized. Index. xxiv + 398pp. 5⅜ x 8. T355 Paperbound **$2.00**

THE POPULAR BALLAD, F. B. Gummere. Most useful factual introduction; fund of descriptive material; quotes, cites over 260 ballads. Examines, from folkloristic view, structure; choral, ritual elements; meter, diction, fusion; effects of tradition, editors; almost every other aspect of border, riddle, kinship, sea, ribald, supernatural, etc., ballads. Bibliography. 2 indexes. 374pp. 5⅜ x 8. T548 Paperbound **$1.65**

MASTERS OF THE DRAMA, John Gassner. The most comprehensive history of the drama in print, covering drama in every important tradition from the Greeks to the Near East, China, Japan, Medieval Europe, England, Russia, Italy, Spain, Germany, and dozens of other drama producing nations. This unsurpassed reading and reference work encompasses more than 800 dramatists and over 2000 plays, with biographical material, plot summaries, theatre history, etc. "Has no competitors in its field," THEATRE ARTS. "Best of its kind in English," NEW REPUBLIC. Exhaustive 35 page bibliography. 77 photographs and drawings. Deluxe edition with reinforced cloth binding, headbands, stained top. xxii + 890pp. 5⅜ x 8. T100 Clothbound **$6.95**

THE DEVELOPMENT OF DRAMATIC ART, D. C. Stuart. The basic work on the growth of Western drama from primitive beginnings to Eugene O'Neill, covering over 2500 years. Not a mere listing or survey, but a thorough analysis of changes, origins of style, and influences in each period; dramatic conventions, social pressures, choice of material, plot devices, stock situations, etc.; secular and religious works of all nations and epochs. "Generous and thoroughly documented researches," Outlook. "Solid studies of influences and playwrights and periods," London Times. Index. Bibliography. xi + 679pp. 5⅜ x 8. T693 Paperbound **$2.75**

A SOURCE BOOK IN THEATRICAL HISTORY (SOURCES OF THEATRICAL HISTORY), A. M. Nagler. Over 2000 years of actors, directors, designers, critics, and spectators speak for themselves in this potpourri of writings selected from the great and formative periods of western drama. On-the-spot descriptions of masks, costumes, makeup, rehearsals, special effects, acting methods, backstage squabbles, theatres, etc. Contemporary glimpses of Molière rehearsing his company, an exhortation to a Roman audience to buy refreshments and keep quiet, Goethe's rules for actors, Belasco telling of $6500 he spent building a river, Restoration actors being told to avoid "lewd, obscene, or indecent postures," and much more. Each selection has an introduction by Prof. Nagler. This extraordinary, lively collection is ideal as a source of otherwise difficult to obtain material, as well as a fine book for browsing. Over 80 illustrations. 10 diagrams. xxiii + 611pp. 5⅜ x 8. T515 Paperbound **$2.75**

CATALOGUE OF DOVER BOOKS

WORLD DRAMA, B. H. Clark. The dramatic creativity of a score of ages and eras — all in two handy compact volumes. Over 1/3 of this material is unavailable in any other current edition! 46 plays from Ancient Greece, Rome, Medieval Europe, France, Germany, Italy, England, Russia, Scandinavia, India, China, Japan, etc. — including classic authors like Aeschylus, Sophocles, Euripides, Aristophanes, Plautus, Marlowe, Jonson, Farquhar, Goldsmith, Cervantes, Molière, Dumas, Goethe, Schiller, Ibsen, and many others. This creative collection avoids hackneyed material and includes only completely first-rate works which are relatively little known or difficult to obtain. "The most comprehensive collection of important plays from all literature available in English," SAT. REV. OF LITERATURE. Introduction. Reading lists. 2 volumes. 1364pp. 5⅜ x 8. Vol. 1, T57 Paperbound **$2.25**
Vol. 2, T59 Paperbound **$2.25**

MASTERPIECES OF THE RUSSIAN DRAMA, edited with introduction by G. R. Noyes. This only comprehensive anthology of Russian drama ever published in English offers complete texts, in 1st-rate modern translations, of 12 plays covering 200 years. Vol. 1: "The Young Hopeful," Fonvisin; "Wit Works Woe," Griboyedov; "The Inspector General," Gogol; "A Month in the Country," Turgenev; "The Poor Bride," Ostrovsky; "A Bitter Fate," Pisemsky. Vol. 2: "The Death of Ivan the Terrible," Alexey Tolstoy "The Power of Darkness," Lev Tolstoy; "The Lower Depths," Gorky; "The Cherry Orchard," Chekhov; "Professor Storitsyn," Andreyev; "Mystery Bouffe," Mayakovsky. Bibliography. Total of 902pp. 5⅜ x 8.
Vol. 1 T647 Paperbound **$2.00**
Vol. 2 T648 Paperbound **$2.00**

EUGENE O'NEILL: THE MAN AND HIS PLAYS, B. H. Clark. Introduction to O'Neill's life and work. Clark analyzes each play from the early THE WEB to the recently produced MOON FOR THE MISBEGOTTEN and THE ICEMAN COMETH revealing the environmental and dramatic influences necessary for a complete understanding of these important works. Bibliography. Appendices. Index. ix + 182pp. 5⅜ x 8. T379 Paperbound **$1.25**

THE HEART OF THOREAU'S JOURNALS, edited by O. Shepard. The best general selection from Thoreau's voluminous (and rare) journals. This intimate record of thoughts and observations reveals the full Thoreau and his intellectual development more accurately than any of his published works: self-conflict between the scientific observer and the poet, reflections on transcendental philosophy, involvement in the tragedies of neighbors and national causes, etc. New preface, notes, introductions. xii + 228pp. 5⅜ x 8. T741 Paperbound **$1.45**

H. D. THOREAU: A WRITER'S JOURNAL, edited by L. Stapleton. A unique new selection from the Journals concentrating on Thoreau's growth as a conscious literary artist, the ideals and purposes of his art. Most of the material has never before appeared outside of the complete 14-volume edition. Contains vital insights on Thoreau's projected book on Concord, thoughts on the nature of men and government, indignation with slavery, sources of inspiration, goals in life. Index. xxxiii + 234pp. 5⅜ x 8. T678 Paperbound **$1.55**

THE HEART OF EMERSON'S JOURNALS, edited by **Bliss Perry.** Best of these revealing Journals, originally 10 volumes, presented in a one volume edition. Talks with Channing, Hawthorne, Thoreau, and Bronson Alcott; impressions of Webster, Everett, John Brown, and Lincoln; records of moments of sudden understanding, vision, and solitary ecstasy. "The essays do not reveal the power of Emerson's mind . . . as do these hasty and informal writings," N.Y. Times. Preface by Bliss Perry. Index. xiii + 357pp. 5⅜ x 8. T477 Paperbound **$1.85**

FOUNDERS OF THE MIDDLE AGES, E. K. Rand. This is the best non-technical discussion of the transformation of Latin pagan culture into medieval civilization. Covering such figures as Tertullian, Gregory, Jerome, Boethius, Augustine, the Neoplatonists, and many other literary men, educators, classicists, and humanists, this book is a storehouse of information presented clearly and simply for the intelligent non-specialist. "Thoughtful, beautifully written," AMERICAN HISTORICAL REVIEW. "Extraordinarily accurate," Richard McKeon, THE NATION. ix + 365pp. 5⅜ x 8. T369 Paperbound **$1.85**

PLAY-MAKING: A MANUAL OF CRAFTSMANSHIP, William Archer. With an extensive, new introduction by John Gassner, Yale Univ. The permanently essential requirements of solid play construction are set down in clear, practical language: theme, exposition, foreshadowing, tension, obligatory scene, peripety, dialogue, character, psychology, other topics. This book has been one of the most influential elements in the modern theatre, and almost everything said on the subject since is contained explicitly or implicitly within its covers. Bibliography. Index. xlii + 277pp. 5⅜ x 8. T651 Paperbound **$1.75**

HAMBURG DRAMATURGY, G. E. Lessing. One of the most brilliant of German playwrights of the eighteenth-century age of criticism analyzes the complex of theory and tradition that constitutes the world of theater. These 104 essays on aesthetic theory helped demolish the regime of French classicism, opening the door to psychological and social realism, romanticism. Subjects include the original functions of tragedy; drama as the rational world; the meaning of pity and fear, pity and fear as means for purgation and other Aristotelian concepts; genius and creative force; interdependence of poet's language and actor's interpretation; truth and authenticity; etc. A basic and enlightening study for anyone interested in aesthetics and ideas, from the philosopher to the theatergoer. Introduction by Prof. Victor Lange. xxii + 265pp. 4½ x 6⅜. T32 Paperbound **$1.45**

Philosophy, Religion

GUIDE TO PHILOSOPHY, C. E. M. Joad. A modern classic which examines many crucial problems which man has pondered through the ages: Does free will exist? Is there plan in the universe? How do we know and validate our knowledge? Such opposed solutions as subjective idealism and realism, chance and teleology, vitalism and logical positivism, are evaluated and the contributions of the great philosophers from the Greeks to moderns like Russell, Whitehead, and others, are considered in the context of each problem. "The finest introduction," BOSTON TRANSCRIPT. Index. Classified bibliography. 592pp. 5⅜ x 8.
T297 Paperbound **$2.00**

HISTORY OF ANCIENT PHILOSOPHY, W. Windelband. One of the clearest, most accurate comprehensive surveys of Greek and Roman philosophy. Discusses ancient philosophy in general, intellectual life in Greece in the 7th and 6th centuries B.C., Thales, Anaximander, Anaximenes, Heraclitus, the Eleatics, Empedocles, Anaxagoras, Leucippus, the Pythagoreans, the Sophists, Socrates, Democritus (20 pages), Plato (50 pages), Aristotle (70 pages), the Peripatetics, Stoics, Epicureans, Sceptics, Neo-platonists, Christian Apologists, etc. 2nd German edition translated by H. E. Cushman. xv + 393pp. 5⅜ x 8. T357 Paperbound **$1.85**

ILLUSTRATIONS OF THE HISTORY OF MEDIEVAL THOUGHT AND LEARNING, R. L. Poole. Basic analysis of the thought and lives of the leading philosophers and ecclesiastics from the 8th to the 14th century—Abailard, Ockham, Wycliffe, Marsiglio of Padua, and many other great thinkers who carried the torch of Western culture and learning through the "Dark Ages": political, religious, and metaphysical views. Long a standard work for scholars and one of the best introductions to medieval thought for beginners. Index. 10 Appendices. xiii + 327pp. 5⅜ x 8. T674 Paperbound **$1.85**

PHILOSOPHY AND CIVILIZATION IN THE MIDDLE AGES, M. de Wulf. This semi-popular survey covers aspects of medieval intellectual life such as religion, philosophy, science, the arts, etc. It also covers feudalism vs. Catholicism, rise of the universities, mendicant orders, monastic centers, and similar topics. Unabridged. Bibliography. Index. viii + 320pp. 5⅜ x 8.
T284 Paperbound **$1.85**

AN INTRODUCTION TO SCHOLASTIC PHILOSOPHY, Prof. M. de Wulf. Formerly entitled SCHOLASTICISM OLD AND NEW, this volume examines the central scholastic tradition from St. Anselm, Albertus Magnus, Thomas Aquinas, up to Suarez in the 17th century. The relation of scholasticism to ancient and medieval philosophy and science in general is clear and easily followed. The second part of the book considers the modern revival of scholasticism, the Louvain position, relations with Kantianism and Positivism. Unabridged. xvi + 271pp. 5⅜ x 8.
T296 Clothbound **$3.50**
T283 Paperbound **$1.75**

A HISTORY OF MODERN PHILOSOPHY, H. Höffding. An exceptionally clear and detailed coverage of western philosophy from the Renaissance to the end of the 19th century. Major and minor men such as Pomponazzi, Bodin, Boehme, Telesius, Bruno, Copernicus, da Vinci, Kepler, Galileo, Bacon, Descartes, Hobbes, Spinoza, Leibniz, Wolff, Locke, Newton, Berkeley, Hume, Erasmus, Montesquieu, Voltaire, Diderot, Rousseau, Lessing, Kant, Herder, Fichte, Schelling, Hegel, Schopenhauer, Comte, Mill, Darwin, Spencer, Hartmann, Lange, and many others, are discussed in terms of theory of knowledge, logic, cosmology, and psychology. Index. 2 volumes, total of 1159pp. 5⅜ x 8. T117 Vol. 1, Paperbound **$2.00**
T118 Vol. 2, Paperbound **$2.00**

ARISTOTLE, A. E. Taylor. A brilliant, searching non-technical account of Aristotle and his thought written by a foremost Platonist. It covers the life and works of Aristotle; classification of the sciences; logic; first philosophy; matter and form; causes; motion and eternity; God; physics; metaphysics; and similar topics. Bibliography. New Index compiled for this edition. 128pp. 5⅜ x 8. T280 Paperbound **$1.00**

THE SYSTEM OF THOMAS AQUINAS, M. de Wulf. Leading Neo-Thomist, one of founders of University of Louvain, gives concise exposition to central doctrines of Aquinas, as a means toward determining his value to modern philosophy, religion. Formerly "Medieval Philosophy Illustrated from the System of Thomas Aquinas." Trans. by E. Messenger. Introduction. 151pp. 5⅜ x 8. T568 Paperbound **$1.25**

LEIBNIZ, H. W. Carr. Most stimulating middle-level coverage of basic philosophical thought of Leibniz. Easily understood discussion, analysis of major works: "Theodicy," "Principles of Nature and Grace," "Monadology"; Leibniz's influence; intellectual growth; correspondence; disputes with Bayle, Malebranche, Newton; importance of his thought today, with reinterpretation in modern terminology. "Power and mastery," London Times. Bibliography. Index. 226pp. 5⅜ x 8. T624 Paperbound **$1.35**

THE SENSE OF BEAUTY, G. Santayana. A revelation of the beauty of language as well as an important philosophic treatise, this work studies the "why, when, and how beauty appears, what conditions an object must fulfill to be beautiful, what elements of our nature make us sensible of beauty, and what the relation is between the constitution of the object and the excitement of our susceptibility." "It is doubtful if a better treatment of the subject has since been published," PEABODY JOURNAL. Index. ix + 275pp. 5⅜ x 8.
T238 Paperbound **$1.00**

PROBLEMS OF ETHICS, Moritz Schlick. The renowned leader of the "Vienna Circle" applies the logical positivist approach to a wide variety of ethical problems: the source and means of attaining knowledge, the formal and material characteristics of the good, moral norms and principles, absolute vs. relative values, free will and responsibility, comparative importance of pleasure and suffering as ethical values, etc. Disarmingly simple and straightforward despite complexity of subject. First English translation, authorized by author before his death, of a thirty-year old classic. Translated and with an introduction by David Rynin. Index. Foreword by Prof. George P. Adams. xxi + 209pp. 5⅜ x 8. T946 Paperbound **$1.45**

AN INTRODUCTION TO EXISTENTIALISM, Robert G. Olson. A new and indispensable guide to one of the major thought systems of our century, the movement that is central to the thinking of some of the most creative figures of the past hundred years. Stresses Heidegger and Sartre, with careful and objective examination of the existentialist position, values—freedom of choice, individual dignity, personal love, creative effort—and answers to the eternal questions of the human condition. Scholarly, unbiased, analytic, unlike most studies of this difficult subject, Prof. Olson's book is aimed at the student of philosophy as well as at the reader with no formal training who is looking for an absorbing, accessible, and thorough introduction to the basic texts. Index. xv + 221pp. 5⅜ x 8½. T55 Paperbound **$1.45**

SYMBOLIC LOGIC, C. I. Lewis and C. H. Langford. Since first publication in 1932, this has been among most frequently cited works on symbolic logic. Still one of the best introductions both for beginners and for mathematicians, philosophers. First part covers basic topics which easily lend themselves to beginning study. Second part is rigorous, thorough development of logistic method, examination of some of most difficult and abstract aspects of symbolic logic, including modal logic, logical paradoxes, many-valued logic, with Prof. Lewis' own contributions. 2nd revised (corrected) edition. 3 appendixes, one new to this edition. 524pp. 5⅜ x 8. S170 Paperbound **$2.00**

WHITEHEAD'S PHILOSOPHY OF CIVILIZATION, A. H. Johnson. A leading authority on Alfred North Whitehead synthesizes the great philosopher's thought on civilization, scattered throughout various writings, into unified whole. Analysis of Whitehead's general definition of civilization, his reflections on history and influences on its development, his religion, including his analysis of Christianity, concept of solitariness as first requirement of personal religion, and so on. Other chapters cover views on minority groups, society, civil liberties, education. Also critical comments on Whitehead's philosophy. Written with general reader in mind. A perceptive introduction to important area of the thought of a leading philosopher of our century. Revised index and bibliography. xii + 211pp. 5⅜ x 8½.
T996 Paperbound **$1.50**

WHITEHEAD'S THEORY OF REALITY, A. H. Johnson. Introductory outline of Whitehead's theory of actual entities, the heart of his philosophy of reality, followed by his views on nature of God, philosophy of mind, theory of value (truth, beauty, goodness and their opposites), analyses of other philosophers, attitude toward science. A perspicacious lucid introduction by author of dissertation on Whitehead, written under the subject's supervision at Harvard. Good basic view for beginning students of philosophy and for those who are simply interested in important contemporary ideas. Revised index and bibliography. xiii + 267pp. 5⅜ x 8½.
T989 Paperbound **$1.50**

MIND AND THE WORLD-ORDER, C. I. Lewis. Building upon the work of Peirce, James, and Dewey, Professor Lewis outlines a theory of knowledge in terms of "conceptual pragmatism." Dividing truth into abstract mathematical certainty and empirical truth, the author demonstrates that the traditional understanding of the a priori must be abandoned. Detailed analyses of philosophy, metaphysics, method, the "given" in experience, knowledge of objects, nature of the a priori, experience and order, and many others. Appendices. xiv + 446pp. 5⅜ x 8. T359 Paperbound $2.25

SCEPTICISM AND ANIMAL FAITH, G. Santayana. To eliminate difficulties in the traditional theory of knowledge, Santayana distinguishes between the independent existence of objects and the essence our mind attributes to them. Scepticism is thereby established as a form of belief, and animal faith is shown to be a necessary condition of knowledge. Belief, classical idealism, intuition, memory, symbols, literary psychology, and much more, discussed with unusual clarity and depth. Index. xii + 314pp. 5⅜ x 8. T235 Clothbound **$3.50**
T236 Paperbound **$1.50**

LANGUAGE AND MYTH, E. Cassirer. Analyzing the non-rational thought processes which go to make up culture, Cassirer demonstrates that beneath both language and myth there lies a dominant unconscious "grammar" of experience whose categories and canons are not those of logical thought. His analyses of seemingly diverse phenomena such as Indian metaphysics, the Melanesian "mana," the Naturphilosophie of Schelling, modern poetry, etc., are profound without being pedantic. Introduction and translation by Susanne Langer. Index. x + 103pp. 5⅜ x 8. T51 Paperbound **$1.25**

Americana

THE EYES OF DISCOVERY, J. Bakeless. A vivid reconstruction of how unspoiled America appeared to the first white men. Authentic and enlightening accounts of Hudson's landing in New York, Coronado's trek through the Southwest; scores of explorers, settlers, trappers, soldiers. America's pristine flora, fauna, and Indians in every region and state in fresh and unusual new aspects. "A fascinating view of what the land was like before the first highway went through," Time. 68 contemporary illustrations, 39 newly added in this edition. Index. Bibliography. x + 500pp. 5⅜ x 8. T761 Paperbound **$2.00**

AUDUBON AND HIS JOURNALS, J. J. Audubon. A collection of fascinating accounts of Europe and America in the early 1800's through Audubon's own eyes. Includes the Missouri River Journals —an eventful trip through America's untouched heartland, the Labrador Journals, the European Journals, the famous "Episodes", and other rare Audubon material, including the descriptive chapters from the original letterpress edition of the "Ornithological Studies", omitted in all later editions. Indispensable for ornithologists, naturalists, and all lovers of Americana and adventure. 70-page biography by Audubon's granddaughter. 38 illustrations. Index. Total of 1106pp. 5⅜ x 8.
T675 Vol I Paperbound **$2.25**
T676 Vol II Paperbound **$2.25**
The set **$4.50**

TRAVELS OF WILLIAM BARTRAM, edited by Mark Van Doren. The first inexpensive illustrated edition of one of the 18th century's most delightful books is an excellent source of first-hand material on American geography, anthropology, and natural history. Many descriptions of early Indian tribes are our only source of information on them prior to the infiltration of the white man. "The mind of a scientist with the soul of a poet," John Livingston Lowes. 13 original illustrations and maps. Edited with an introduction by Mark Van Doren. 448pp. 5⅜ x 8.
T13 Paperbound **$2.00**

GARRETS AND PRETENDERS: A HISTORY OF BOHEMIANISM IN AMERICA, A. Parry. The colorful and fantastic history of American Bohemianism from Poe to Kerouac. This is the only complete record of hoboes, cranks, starving poets, and suicides. Here are Pfaff, Whitman, Crane, Bierce, Pound, and many others. New chapters by the author and by H. T. Moore bring this thorough and well-documented history down to the Beatniks. "An excellent account," N. Y. Times. Scores of cartoons, drawings, and caricatures. Bibliography. Index. xxviii + 421pp. 5⅝ x 8⅜. T708 Paperbound **$1.95**

THE EXPLORATION OF THE COLORADO RIVER AND ITS CANYONS, J. W. Powell. The thrilling first-hand account of the expedition that filled in the last white space on the map of the United States. Rapids, famine, hostile Indians, and mutiny are among the perils encountered as the unknown Colorado Valley reveals its secrets. This is the only uncut version of Major Powell's classic of exploration that has been printed in the last 60 years. Includes later reflections and subsequent expedition. 250 illustrations, new map. 400pp. 5⅝ x 8⅜.
T94 Paperbound **$2.00**

THE JOURNAL OF HENRY D. THOREAU, Edited by Bradford Torrey and Francis H. Allen. Henry Thoreau is not only one of the most important figures in American literature and social thought; his voluminous journals (from which his books emerged as selections and crystallizations) constitute both the longest, most sensitive record of personal internal development and a most penetrating description of a historical moment in American culture. This present set, which was first issued in fourteen volumes, contains Thoreau's entire journals from 1837 to 1862, with the exception of the lost years which were found only recently. We are reissuing it, complete and unabridged, with a new introduction by Walter Harding, Secretary of the Thoreau Society. Fourteen volumes reissued in two volumes. Foreword by Henry Seidel Canby. Total of 1888pp. 8⅜ x 12¼. T312-3 Two volume set, Clothbound **$20.00**

GAMES AND SONGS OF AMERICAN CHILDREN, collected by William Wells Newell. A remarkable collection of 190 games with songs that accompany many of them; cross references to show similarities, differences among them; variations; musical notation for 38 songs. Textual discussions show relations with folk-drama and other aspects of folk tradition. Grouped into categories for ready comparative study: Love-games, histories, playing at work, human life, bird and beast, mythology, guessing-games, etc. New introduction covers relations of songs and dances to timeless heritage of folklore, biographical sketch of Newell, other pertinent data. A good source of inspiration for those in charge of groups of children and a valuable reference for anthropologists, sociologists, psychiatrists. Introduction by Carl Withers. New indexes of first lines, games. 5⅜ x 8½. xii + 242pp. T354 Paperbound **$1.65**

CATALOGUE OF DOVER BOOKS

GARDNER'S PHOTOGRAPHIC SKETCH BOOK OF THE CIVIL WAR, Alexander Gardner. The first published collection of Civil War photographs, by one of the two or three most famous photographers of the era, outstandingly reproduced from the original positives. Scenes of crucial battles: Appomattox, Manassas, Mechanicsville, Bull Run, Yorktown, Fredericksburg, etc. Gettysburg immediately after retirement of forces. Battle ruins at Richmond, Petersburg, Gaines'Mill. Prisons, arsenals, a slave pen, fortifications, headquarters, pontoon bridges, soldiers, a field hospital. A unique glimpse into the realities of one of the bloodiest wars in history, with an introductory text to each picture by Gardner himself. Until this edition, there were only five known copies in libraries, and fewer in private hands, one of which sold at auction in 1952 for $425. Introduction by E. F. Bleiler. 100 full page 7 x 10 photographs (original size). 224pp. 8½ x 10¾. T476 Clothbound **$6.00**

A BIBLIOGRAPHY OF NORTH AMERICAN FOLKLORE AND FOLKSONG, Charles Haywood, Ph.D. The only book that brings together bibliographic information on so wide a range of folklore material. Lists practically everything published about American folksongs, ballads, dances, folk beliefs and practices, popular music, tales, similar material—more than 35,000 titles of books, articles, periodicals, monographs, music publications, phonograph records. Each entry complete with author, title, date and place of publication, arranger and performer of particular examples of folk music, many with Dr. Haywood's valuable criticism, evaluation. Volume I, "The American People," is complete listing of general and regional studies, titles of tales and songs of Negro and non-English speaking groups and where to find them, Occupational Bibliography including sections listing sources of information, folk material on cowboys, riverboat men, 49ers, American characters like Mike Fink, Frankie and Johnnie, John Henry, many more. Volume II, "The American Indian," tells where to find information on dances, myths, songs, ritual of more than 250 tribes in U.S., Canada. A monumental product of 10 years' labor, carefully classified for easy use. "All students of this subject . . . will find themselves in debt to Professor Haywood," Stith Thompson, in American Anthropologist. ". . . a most useful and excellent work," Duncan Emrich, Chief Folklore Section, Library of Congress, in "Notes." Corrected, enlarged republication of 1951 edition. New Preface. New index of composers, arrangers, performers. General index of more than 15,000 items. Two volumes. Total of 1301pp. 6⅛ x 9¼. T797-798 Clothbound **$12.50**

INCIDENTS OF TRAVEL IN YUCATAN, John L. Stephens. One of first white men to penetrate interior of Yucatan tells the thrilling story of his discoveries of 44 cities, remains of once-powerful Maya civilization. Compelling text combines narrative power with historical significance as it takes you through heat, dust, storms of Yucatan; native festivals with brutal bull fights; great ruined temples atop man-made mounds. Countless idols, sculptures, tombs, examples of Mayan taste for rich ornamentation, from gateways to personal trinkets, accurately illustrated, discussed in text. Will appeal to those interested in ancient civilizations, and those who like stories of exploration, discovery, adventure. Republication of last (1843) edition. 124 illustrations by English artist, F. Catherwood. Appendix on Mayan architecture, chronology. Two volume set. Total of xxviii + 927pp.
Vol I T926 Paperbound **$2.00**
Vol II T927 Paperbound **$2.00**
The set **$4.00**

A GENIUS IN THE FAMILY, Hiram Percy Maxim. Sir Hiram Stevens Maxim was known to the public as the inventive genius who created the Maxim gun, automatic sprinkler, and a heavier-than-air plane that got off the ground in 1894. Here, his son reminisces—this is by no means a formal biography—about the exciting and often downright scandalous private life of his brilliant, eccentric father. A warm and winning portrait of a prankish, mischievous, impious personality, a genuine character. The style is fresh and direct, the effect is unadulterated pleasure. "A book of charm and lasting humor . . . belongs on the 'must read' list of all fathers," New York Times. "A truly gorgeous affair," New Statesman and Nation. 17 illustrations, 16 specially for this edition. viii + 108pp. 5⅜ x 8½.
T948 Paperbound **$1.00**

HORSELESS CARRIAGE DAYS, Hiram P. Maxim. The best account of an important technological revolution by one of its leading figures. The delightful and rewarding story of the author's experiments with the exact combustibility of gasoline, stopping and starting mechanisms, carriage design, and engines. Captures remarkably well the flavor of an age of scoffers and rival inventors not above sabotage; of noisy, uncontrollable gasoline vehicles and incredible mobile steam kettles. ". . . historic information and light humor are combined to furnish highly entertaining reading," New York Times. 56 photographs, 12 specially for this edition. xi + 175pp. 5⅜ x 8½. T964 Paperbound **$1.35**

BODY, BOOTS AND BRITCHES: FOLKTALES, BALLADS AND SPEECH FROM COUNTRY NEW YORK, Harold W. Thompson. A unique collection, discussion of songs, stories, anecdotes, proverbs handed down orally from Scotch-Irish grandfathers, German nurse-maids, Negro workmen, gathered from all over Upper New York State. Tall tales by and about lumbermen and pirates, canalers and injun-fighters, tragic and comic ballads, scores of sayings and proverbs all tied together by an informative, delightful narrative by former president of New York Historical Society. ". . . a sparkling homespun tapestry that every lover of Americana will want to have around the house," Carl Carmer, New York Times. Republication of 1939 edition. 20 line-drawings. Index. Appendix (Sources of material, bibliography). 530pp. 5⅜ x 8½. T411 Paperbound **$2.00**

New Books

101 PATCHWORK PATTERNS, Ruby Short McKim. With no more ability than the fundamentals of ordinary sewing, you will learn to make over 100 beautiful quilts: flowers, rainbows, Irish chains, fish and bird designs, leaf designs, unusual geometric patterns, many others. Cutting designs carefully diagrammed and described, suggestions for materials, yardage estimates, step-by-step instructions, plus entertaining stories of origins of quilt names, other folklore. Revised 1962. 101 full-sized patterns. 140 illustrations. Index. 128pp. 7⅞ x 10¾.
T773 Paperbound **$1.85**

ESSENTIAL GRAMMAR SERIES
By concentrating on the essential core of material that constitutes the semantically most important forms and areas of a language and by stressing explanation (often bringing parallel English forms into the discussion) rather than rote memory, this new series of grammar books is among the handiest language aids ever devised. Designed by linguists and teachers for adults with limited learning objectives and learning time, these books omit nothing important, yet they teach more usable language material and do it more quickly and permanently than any other self-study material. Clear and rigidly economical, they concentrate upon immediately usable language material, logically organized so that related material is always presented together. Any reader of typical capability can use them to refresh his grasp of language, to supplement self-study language records or conventional grammars used in schools, or to begin language study on his own. Now available:

ESSENTIAL GERMAN GRAMMAR, Dr. Guy Stern & E. F. Bleiler. Index. Glossary of terms. 128pp. 4½ x 6⅜.
T422 Paperbound **75¢**

ESSENTIAL FRENCH GRAMMAR, Dr. Seymour Resnick. Index. Cognate list. Glossary. 159pp. 4½ x 6⅜.
T419 Paperbound **75¢**

ESSENTIAL ITALIAN GRAMMAR, Dr. Olga Ragusa. Index. Glossary. 111pp. 4½ x 6⅜.
T779 Paperbound **75¢**

ESSENTIAL SPANISH GRAMMAR, Dr. Seymour Resnick. Index. 50-page cognate list. Glossary. 138pp. 4½ x 6⅜.
T780 Paperbound **75¢**

PHILOSOPHIES OF MUSIC HISTORY: A Study of General Histories of Music, 1600-1960, Warren D. Allen. Unquestionably one of the most significant documents yet to appear in musicology, this thorough survey covers the entire field of historical research in music. An influential masterpiece of scholarship, it includes early music histories; theories on the ethos of music; lexicons, dictionaries and encyclopedias of music; musical historiography through the centuries; philosophies of music history; scores of related topics. Copiously documented. New preface brings work up to 1960. Index. 317-item bibliography. 9 illustrations; 3 full-page plates. 5⅜ x 8½. xxxiv + 382pp.
T282 Paperbound **$2.00**

MR. DOOLEY ON IVRYTHING AND IVRYBODY, Finley Peter Dunne. The largest collection in print of hilarious utterances by the irrepressible Irishman of Archey Street, one of the most vital characters in American fiction. Gathered from the half dozen books that appeared during the height of Mr. Dooley's popularity, these 102 pieces are all unaltered and uncut, and they are all remarkably fresh and pertinent even today. Selected and edited by Robert Hutchinson. 5⅜ x 8½. xii + 244p.
T626 Paperbound **$1.00**

TREATISE ON PHYSIOLOGICAL OPTICS, Hermann von Helmholtz. Despite new investigations, this important work will probably remain preeminent. Contains everything known about physiological optics up to 1925, covering scores of topics under the general headings of dioptrics of the eye, sensations of vision, and perecptions of vision. Von Helmholtz's voluminous data are all included, as are extensive supplementary matter incorporated into the third German edition, new material prepared for 1925 English edition, and copious textual annotations by J. P. C. Southall. The most exhaustive treatise ever prepared on the subject, it has behind it a list of contributors that will never again be duplicated. Translated and edited by J. P. C. Southall. Bibliography. Indexes. 312 illustrations. 3 volumes bound as 2. Total of 1749pp. 5⅜ x 8.
S15-16 Two volume set, Clothbound **$15.00**

THE ARTISTIC ANATOMY OF TREES, Rex Vicat Cole. Even the novice with but an elementary knowledge of drawing and none of the structure of trees can learn to draw, paint trees from this systematic, lucid instruction book. Copiously illustrated with the author's own sketches, diagrams, and 50 paintings from the early Renaissance to today, it covers composition; structure of twigs, boughs, buds, branch systems; outline forms of major species; how leaf is set on twig; flowers and fruit and their arrangement; etc. 500 illustrations. Bibliography. Indexes. 347pp. 5⅜ x 8.
T1016 Clothbound **$4.50**

HOW PLANTS GET THEIR NAMES, L. H. Bailey. In this basic introduction to botanical nomenclature, a famed expert on plants and plant life reveals the confusion that can result from misleading common names of plants and points out the fun and advantage of using a sound, scientific approach. Covers every aspect of the subject, including an historical survey beginning before Linnaeus systematized nomenclature, the literal meaning of scores of Latin names, their English equivalents, etc. Enthusiastically written and easy to follow, this handbook for gardeners, amateur horticulturalists, and beginning botany students is knowledgeable, accurate and useful. 11 illustrations. Lists of Latin, English botanical names. 192pp. 5⅜ x 8½. T796 Paperbound **$1.15**

PIERRE CURIE, Marie Curie. Nobel Prize winner creates a memorable portrait of her equally famous husband in a fine scientific biography. Recounting his childhood, his haphazard education, and his experimental research (with his brother) in the physics of crystals, Mme. Curie brings to life the strong, determined personality of a great scientist at work and discusses, in clear, straightforward terms, her husband's and her own work with radium and radioactivity. A great book about two very great founders of modern science. Includes Mme. Curie's autobiographical notes. Translated by Charlotte and Vernon Kellogg. viii + 120pp. 5⅜ x 8½. T199 Paperbound **$1.00**

STYLES IN PAINTING: A Comparative Study, Paul Zucker. Professor of Art History at Cooper Union presents an important work of art-understanding that will guide you to a fuller, deeper appreciation of masterpieces of art and at the same time add to your understanding of how they fit into the evolution of style from the earliest times to this century. Discusses general principles of historical method and aesthetics, history of styles, then illustrates with more than 230 great paintings organized by subject matter so you can see at a glance how styles have changed through the centuries. 236 beautiful halftones. xiv + 338pp. 5⅝ x 8½. T760 Paperbound **$2.00**

NEW VARIORUM EDITION OF SHAKESPEARE
One of the monumental feats of Shakespeare scholarship is the famous New Variorum edition, containing full texts of the plays together with an entire reference library worth of historical and critical information: all the variant readings that appear in the quartos and folios; annotations by leading scholars from the earliest days of Shakespeare criticism to the date of publication; essays on meaning, background, productions by Johnson, Addison, Fielding, Lessing, Hazlitt, Coleridge, Ulrici, Swinburne, and other major Shakespeare critics; original sources of Shakespeare's inspiration. For the first time, this definitive edition of Shakespeare's plays, each printed in a separate volume, will be available in inexpensive editions to scholars, to teachers and students, and to every lover of Shakespeare and fine literature. Now ready:

KING LEAR, edited by Horace Howard Furness. Bibliography. List of editions collated in notes. viii + 503pp. 5⅜ x 8½. T1000 Paperbound **$2.25**

MACBETH, edited by Horace Howard Furness Jr. Bibliography. List of editions collated in notes. xvi + 562pp. 5⅜ x 8½. T1001 Paperbound **$2.25**

ROMEO AND JULIET, edited by Horace Howard Furness. Bibliography. List of editions collated in notes. xxvi + 480pp. 5⅜ x 8½. T1002 Paperbound **$2.25**

OTTHELLO, edited by Horace Howard Furness. Bibliography. List of editions collated in notes. x + 471pp. 5⅜ x 8½. T1003 Paperbound **$2.25**

HAMLET, edited by Horace Howard Furness. Bibliography. List of editions collated in notes. Total of 926pp. 5⅜ x 8½. T1004-1005 Two volume set, Paperbound **$4.50**

THE GARDENER'S YEAR, Karel Capek. The author of this refreshingly funny book is probably best known in U. S. as the author of "R. U. R.," a biting satire on the machine age. Here, his satiric genius finds expression in a wholly different vein: a warm, witty chronicle of the joys and trials of the amateur gardener as he watches over his plants, his soil and the weather from January to December. 59 drawings by Joseph Capek add an important second dimension to the fun. "Mr. Capek writes with sympathy, understanding and humor," NEW YORK TIMES. "Will delight the amateur gardener, and indeed everyone else," SATURDAY REVIEW. Translated by M. and R. Weatherall. 59 illustrations. 159pp. 4½ x 6½. T1014 Paperbound **$1.00**

THE ADVANCE OF THE FUNGI, E. C. Large. The dramatic story of the battle against fungi, from the year the potato blight hit Europe (1845) to 1940, and of men who fought and won it: Pasteur, Anton de Bary, Tulasne, Berkeley, Woronin, Jensen, many others. Combines remarkable grasp of facts and their significance with skill to write dramatic, exciting prose. "Philosophically witty, fundamentally thoughtful, always mature," NEW YORK HERALD TRIBUNE. "Highly entertaining, intelligent, penetrating," NEW YORKER. Bibliography. 64 illustrations. 6 full-page plates. 488pp. 5⅜ x 8½. T437 Paperbound **$2.25**

THE PAINTER'S METHODS AND MATERIALS, A. P. Laurie. Adviser to the British Royal Academy discusses the ills that paint is heir to and the methods most likely to counteract them. Examining 48 masterpieces by Fra Lippo Lippi, Millais, Boucher, Rembrandt, Romney, Van Eyck, Velazquez, Michaelangelo, Botticelli, Frans Hals, Turner, and others, he tries to discover how special and unique effects were achieved. Not conjectural information, but certain and authoritative. Beautiful, sharp reproductions, plus textual illustrations of apparatus and the results of experiments with pigments and media. 63 illustrations and diagrams. Index. 250pp. 5⅜ x 8. T1019 Clothbound **$3.75**

CATALOGUE OF DOVER BOOKS

CHANCE, LUCK AND STATISTICS, H. C. Levinson. The theory of chance, or probability, and the science of statistics presented in simple, non-technical language. Covers fundamentals by analyzing games of chance, then applies those fundamentals to immigration and birth rates, operations research, stock speculation, insurance rates, advertising, and other fields. Excellent course supplement and a delightful introduction for non-mathematicians. Formerly "The Science of Chance." Index. xiv + 356pp. 5⅜ x 8. T1007 Paperbound **$1.75**

THROUGH THE ALIMENTARY CANAL WITH GUN AND CAMERA: A Fascinating Trip to the Interior, George S. Chappell. An intrepid explorer, better known as a major American humorist, accompanied by imaginary camera-man and botanist, conducts this unforgettably hilarious journey to the human interior. Wildly imaginative, his account satirizes academic pomposity, parodies cliché-ridden travel literature, and cleverly uses facts of physiology for comic purposes. All the original line drawings by Otto Soglow are included to add to the merriment. Preface by Robert Benchley. 17 illustrations. xii + 116pp. 5⅜ x 8½. T376 Paperbound **$1.00**

TALKS TO TEACHERS ON PSYCHOLOGY and to Students on Some of Life's Ideals, William James. America's greatest psychologist invests these lectures with immense personal charm, invaluable insights, and superb literary style. 15 Harvard lectures, 3 lectures delivered to students in New England touch upon psychology and the teaching of art, stream of consciousness, the child as a behaving organism, education and behavior, association of ideas, the gospel of relaxation, what makes life significant, and other related topics. Interesting, and still vital pedagogy. x + 146pp. 5⅜ x 8½. T261 Paperbound **$1.00**

A WHIMSEY ANTHOLOGY, collected by Carolyn Wells. Delightful verse on the lighter side: logical whimsies, poems shaped like decanters and flagons, lipograms and acrostics, alliterative verse, enigmas and charades, anagrams, linguistic and dialectic verse, tongue twisters, limericks, travesties, and just about very other kind of whimsical poetry ever written. Works by Edward Lear, Gelett Burgess, Poe, Lewis Carroll, Henley, Robert Herrick, Christina Rossetti, scores of other poets will entertain and amuse you for hours. Index. xiv + 221pp. 5⅜ x 8½. T1020 Paperbound **$1.25**

LANDSCAPE PAINTING, R. O. Dunlop. A distinguished modern artist is a perfect guide to the aspiring landscape painter. This practical book imparts to even the uninitiated valuable methods and techniques. Useful advice is interwoven throughout a fascinating illustrated history of landscape painting, from Ma Yüan to Picasso. 60 half-tone reproductions of works by Giotto, Giovanni Bellini, Piero della Francesca, Tintoretto, Giorgione, Raphael, Van Ruisdael, Poussin, Gainsborough, Monet, Cezanne, Seurat, Picasso, many others. Total of 71 illustrations, 4 in color. Index. 192pp. 7⅜ x 10. T1018 Clothbound **$6.00**

PRACTICAL LANDSCAPE PAINTING, Adrian Stokes. A complete course in landscape painting that trains the senses to perceive as well as the hand to apply the principles underlying the pictorial aspect of nature. Author fully explains tools, value and nature of various colors, and instructs beginners in clear, simple terms how to apply them. Places strong emphasis on drawing and composition, foundations often neglected in painting texts. Includes pictorial-textual survey of the art from Ancient China to the present, with helpful critical comments and numerous diagrams illustrating every stage. 93 illustrations. Index. 256pp. 5⅜ x 8. T1017 Clothbound **$3.75**

PELLUCIDAR, THREE NOVELS: AT THE EARTH'S CORE, PELLUCIDAR, TANAR OF PELLUCIDAR, Edgar Rice Burroughs. The first three novels of adventure in the thrill-filled world within the hollow interior of the earth. David Innes's mechanical mole drills through the outer crust and precipitates him into an astonishing world. Among Burroughs's most popular work. Illustrations by J. Allan St. John. 5⅜ x 8½. T1051 Paperbound **$2.00**
T1050 Clothbound **$3.75**

JOE MILLER'S JESTS OR, THE WITS VADE-MECUM. Facsimile of the first edition of famous 18th century collection of repartees, bons mots, puns and jokes, the father of the humor anthology. A first-hand look at the taste of fashionable London in the Age of Pope. 247 entertaining anecdotes, many involving well-known personages such as Colley Cibber, Sir Thomas More, Rabelais, rich in humor, historic interest. New introduction contains biographical information on Joe Miller, fascinating history of his enduring collection, bibliographical information on collections of comic material. Introduction by Robert Hutchinson. 96pp. 5⅜ x 8½. Paperbound **$1.00**

THE HUMOROUS WORLD OF JEROME K. JEROME. Complete essays and extensive passages from nine out-of-print books ("Three Men on Wheels," "Novel Notes," "Told After Supper," "Sketches in Lavender, Blue and Green," "American Wives and Others," 4 more) by a highly original humorist, author of the novel "Three Men in a Boat." Human nature is JKJ's subject: the problems of husbands, of wives, of tourists, of the human animal trapped in the drawing room. His sympathetic acceptance of the shortcomings of his race and his ability to see humor in almost any situation make this a treasure for those who know his work and a pleasant surprise for those who don't. Edited and with an introduction by Robert Hutchinson. xii + 260pp. 5⅜ x 8½. T58 Paperbound **$1.00**